"Susan Ambrose and Laura Wankel make a compelling case for change in higher ed, laying out a strategy for college and university leaders to break down their legacy structures and invent something new. This book is necessary reading for every professor, administrator, and trustee who cares about what the future holds for one of our most treasured assets."

Jeffrey J. Selingo
New York Times bestselling author and special advisor,
Arizona State University

"Rapidly changing demographics and technological advance demand innovation in higher education that integrates, rather than polarizes, skills acquisition and intellectual engagement. Ambrose and Wankel deftly shift our focus from the university to the learner and a complex system of stakeholders, where collaboration, flexibility, and creativity are essential for our nation to thrive. This carefully researched analysis offers both challenge and hope with reasoned guidance for transformative leadership."

Susan Rundell Singer, Ph.D.
Provost and Vice President for Academic Affairs, Rollins College

"*Higher Education's Road to Relevance: Navigating Complexity* should be on every higher education administrator's reading list. Ambrose and Wankel highlight a myriad of ways in which our current system of offering degrees is vulnerable to shifts in technologies, political will, demographics, and new competitors. Rather than merely point out these vulnerabilities, they offer examples of innovation that could be adapted and adopted to mitigate or even leverage these changes for greater student success and institutional health. It is a refreshing look at where we are today in American higher education and should ignite serious strategic conversations on every college campus."

Tom Green, Ph.D.
Associate Executive Director
Consulting and SEM
AACRAO

"This is a must-read for faculty, staff and key stakeholders working to help colleges and universities advance their mission in very turbulent times. The authors make a compelling case for the transformational period in which colleges and universities operate and suggest a range of important conversations that should be occurring on every campus. We are in a period of rapid change with substantial "headwinds" in higher education and this book frames these critical issues and the need for new thinking and innovation going forward."

Kevin Kruger, PhD.
President
NASPA
Student Affairs Administrators
In Higher Education

"This book is an illuminating synthesis of the dynamics within and around higher education. Its gift is its focus on harnessing these shifts to seize the opportunity to become higher *learning* rather than higher *education*."

Philomena Mantella, PhD.
President
Grand Valley State University

It is a pleasure to read a book about higher education that is both urgent and optimistic. *Higher Education's Road to Relevance* presents a compact treatment of a big landscape, connecting the contexts demanding change to the research and strategies needed to respond. Their thesis is not only that transformation is necessary, but that we have the evidentiary base, and a huge range of models and practices, to justify the optimism.

Randy Bass
Vice Provost for Education
Professor of English
Director, Red House / Baker Trust for Transformational Learning
Georgetown University

Higher Education's Road to Relevance

Navigating Complexity

Susan A. Ambrose
Laura A. Wankel

A Wiley Brand

Published by Jossey-Bass
A Wiley Brand
111 River St, Hoboken, NJ 07030
www.josseybass.com

Jossey-Bass books and products are available through most bookstores. To contact Jossey-Bass directly call our Customer Care Department within the U.S. at 800-956-7739, outside the U.S. at 317-572-3986, or fax 317-572-4002.

Wiley also publishes its books in a variety of electronic formats and by print-on-demand. For more information about Wiley products, visit www.wiley.com.

Library of Congress Cataloging-in-Publication Data

Names: Ambrose, Susan A., 1958- author. | Wankel, Laura A., author.
Title: Higher education's road to relevance : navigating complexity / Susan A. Ambrose, Laura A. Wankel.
Description: First edition. | Hoboken, NJ : Jossey-Bass, [2020] | Includes bibliographical references and index.
Identifiers: LCCN 2019041162 (print) | LCCN 2019041163 (ebook) | ISBN 9781119568384 (hardback) | ISBN 9781119568391 (adobe pdf) | ISBN 9781119568407 (epub)
Subjects: LCSH: Education, Higher—Aims and objectives. | Educational change. | Educational technology.
Classification: LCC LB2322.2 .A534 2020 (print) | LCC LB2322.2 (ebook) | DDC 378.01—dc23
LC record available at https://lccn.loc.gov/2019041162LC ebook record available at https://lccn.loc.gov/2019041163

Cover Design: Wiley
Cover Image: © hardik pethani /Getty Images

Printed in the United States of America
HB Printing

V10015625_111419

CONTENTS

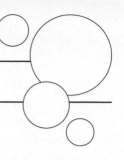

Contents

ACKNOWLEDGMENTS

We are enormously grateful that we both ended up at Northeastern University at the same time, where we began an important professional and personal relationship that impacted and enriched not only our lives but the lives of our students and colleagues, through the holistic and collaborative approach we took to our work. We arrived at Northeastern at a time when the university was experiencing a tremendous amount of substantive change under the transformative leadership of Joseph Aoun, and we are appreciative of the many opportunities we had to engage with members of the Northeastern community to both create new and transform old practices, programs, services, curricula, co-curricula, approaches to teaching and learning, and student engagement strategies. So, we are thankful that we were persuaded by our respective bosses, Steve Director (Susan) and Philly Mantella (Laura), to leave universities we loved to become part of the Northeastern community. We are also thankful to colleagues who helped us to continually clarify our visions and turn them into realities: Kate Ziemer, Cigdem Talgar, Anthony Rini, Mary Loeffelholz, Bruce Ronkin, Marina Macomber, Jane Brown, Jason Campbell Foster, Mary English, Janna Ferguson, and Jen Lehman.

We are also indebted to colleagues and friends who took the time to read our manuscript and provide thoughtful and insightful feedback that left an indelible mark on the finished product. These included Sr. Paula Marie Buley, Bob DiFillippi, Tom Green, Marina Pantazidou, Amelia Parnell, Hilary Schuldt, and Linda Vansupa.

Naturally, this work would not have been possible without the love, support, and patience of our family and closest friends. We want to thank and express our gratitude to Susan's husband Ed, sons Josh and Jake, daughter-in-law Sinem, and future daughter-in-law Julie, and granddaughter Mara, and Laura's children Bret and Katie and son-in-law Barry for all they did to support us through this project.

Finally, we would never have embarked on this journey if we didn't feel privileged to have spent our careers in higher education, serving as best we could the students to whom we were entrusted. It was always all about them! Because we will forever feel a passion for and commitment to educate the future citizens of the world, we spent two years of our lives writing this book. We hope it sparks discussion and debate about what comes next for higher education. We believe in the potential for the evolution of American higher education and are optimistic about our work as educators in the future.

ABOUT THE AUTHORS

Susan A. Ambrose is the Senior Vice Chancellor for Educational Innovation at Northeastern University. She is an internationally recognized expert in translating learning science research to practice in the design of curricula, courses, and other educational experiences for both undergraduate and graduate students. She received her doctorate in American History at Carnegie Mellon University (CMU) and was both a faculty member and an administrator at CMU for 26 years. She has coauthored four books and published numerous peer-reviewed articles and chapters in edited volumes. Her most recent book, *How Learning Works: 7 Research-Based Principles for Smart Teaching*, has been translated into Spanish, Arabic, Japanese, Chinese, Korean, and Italian. She has consulted and conducted workshops and seminars for faculty and administrators around the world, from Colombia, Chile, and Mexico to Singapore, Hong Kong, South Korea, and Taiwan. She has received funding for her work from the National Science Foundation, U.S. Department of Education, Alfred P. Sloan Foundation, Lilly Endowment, Carnegie Corporation of New York, Helmsley Charitable Trust, Alcoa Foundation, Eden Hall Foundation, and the Davis Foundation, among others.

Laura A. Wankel is the Senior Advisor for Strategic Initiatives to the Senior Vice Chancellor for Educational Innovation at Northeastern University, where she earlier served as Vice President for Student Affairs. Previously, she was at Seton Hall University for 17 years as Vice President for Student Affairs, Vice Chancellor for Student Affairs, and Vice President for Student Affairs & Enrollment Services. She has been an active member in NASPA Student Affairs Administrators in Higher Education, at both the regional and national levels, holding a number of leadership positions, including Regional Vice President, Executive Committee, and Chair of the NASPA Board. Dr. Wankel has also been on the editorial boards for the *NASPA Journal* and the *Journal of Student Affairs Research and Practice*. She was honored by the NASPA Foundation and named a Pillar of the Profession in 2015. She received her doctorate in higher education administration from Teachers College, Columbia University. She has been the editor of several educational publications and the author of chapters in edited volumes, book reviews, and articles. She has served in a consulting capacity to number of education-related projects and has served on the board of directors of the Association of Student Affairs at Catholic Colleges and Universities (ASACCU). She has presented on issues in higher education nationally as well as internationally.

Introduction

This is a pivotal moment in higher education. Small colleges are closing or merging with other institutions. For-profit educational entities are experiencing a resurgence under the current administration. Academic departments are being eliminated. Student debt is higher than ever. Forty percent of those who enter college do not finish. Alternatives to college are cropping up across the country. Technology continues to be both a blessing and a curse. Sexual harassment and abuse on campus make headlines daily. Integrity in admissions and other university processes and policies are called into question. Colleges are routinely accused of being too "left-leaning" politically, and free speech issues abound. Employers claim graduates are underprepared. The list goes on and on.

As a result, higher education is in the news daily; some of it is accurate, some less so, some exaggerated, and some in the proverbial "the sky is falling" mode. Our current situation is reported in the popular press, educational dailies, disciplinary publications, and books. However, many of these sources focus on individual social, economic, or political aspects of higher education, such as debt load, the call for alternative credentials, the increasing need for support services (like mental health counseling, student populations with food and/or housing insecurity), the continual rise of technology and its impact, and decreases in state funding.

How can faculty, administrators, and staff both consume and then make sense of all of this information as they continue to evolve education and their institutions? How can they view the challenges just described as opportunities for creative and innovative problem-solving when so much negativity and fear-mongering abounds?

This book attempts to respond to those questions by providing a broad view of the confluence of factors that define this moment in time and their impact on how colleges and universities will need to continue to evolve (chapter 1); the array of skills, perspectives, and competencies that our diverse learners will need to possess in order to live fulfilling lives with successful careers (chapter 2); the various ways institutions might meet the goals they define for themselves based on current realities and future predictions (chapter 3); and an approach that could help institutions move toward action as they embrace disruption and an innovative mindset (chapter 4).

We opted to present a broad brush stroke of the challenges in chapter 1 so that our colleagues can see the big picture and decide for themselves where they might need to explore further as they consider their institution's unique context. Also, while recognizing the convergence of social, economic, and political issues that have landed us where we are today, we do not analyze the cultural forces behind the challenges presented. We leave that to others.

As higher education administrators who believe in the power of education and respect the rich history of our sector for what it has accomplished since the birth of this nation, we, too, wonder what comes next. The confluence of factors seems to indicate that this time in history is different from other times when crises in higher education loomed large, such as post–World War II and the 1960s. However, we engage with our work and this text full of optimism and excitement because the opportunities for creative change are endless. Furthermore, we are confident that universities are full of smart, imaginative, inventive, and resourceful people who have the ability to think outside the box to address the myriad challenging issues. We hope readers enter this text with the same mindset and view chapter 1 as an opportunity to gain a full understanding of the challenges in order to think about possibilities as they read the rest of the chapters. In other words, do not despair that the situation is hopeless—it is not! There is the proverbial light at the end of the tunnel—and it is not an oncoming train. Keep reading, as many great minds are already at work exploring various creative ways to address the challenges we all face.

Higher education must reimagine its role in order to address the changing nature of the world and of work. Not every institution will make the same decisions, nor should they, given that one of the strengths of American higher education has always been its capacity to serve an ever-changing diverse set of needs and learners (e.g., minority-serving institutions, women's colleges, technical schools, community colleges) to achieve a variety of individual, local, and societal goals. Because these interests and needs continue to evolve, along with the nation's and the world's needs, some of us must realign our visions and missions. We see this new imperative as one that demands that we actively take control of our own destiny and navigate the complexity, or others will potentially do it for us.

We do not want to experience the same fate as Kodak or the railroad industry. They both viewed their work too narrowly and relied on their past success when the world around them was changing. Kodak viewed themselves as being in the film business as opposed to the storytelling business and missed the boat on digital imaging, and the railroads viewed themselves as being in the railroad business rather than the transportation business, ignoring the changing needs of travelers (Dan, 2012). Higher education must view itself as being in the learning business, across the life span of learners who have different needs at different points in time. In doing so, we will ensure our relevance in providing both a public and private good that contributes to our collective social, cultural, and economic well-being.

REFERENCES

Dan, A. (2012, January 23). Kodak failed by asking the wrong marketing question. Retrieved from Forbes: https://www.forbes.com/sites/avidan/2012/01/23/kodak-failed-by-asking-the-wrong-marketing-question/#12abc8f53d47

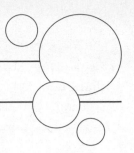

CHAPTER 1

Exploring Challenges and Opportunities: Setting the Context for Change

In this chapter, we describe the confluence of three major factors that have led American higher education to where we are today and that impact our future. These factors are

Growing Public Concern around:
- Return on Investment
- Persistence and Graduation Rates
- Lack of Access
- College Readiness
- Perceived Skills Gap
- Misalignment with Workforce Needs and Public Interest
- Political and Social Context
- Fierce Competition and Confusion in the Marketplace

Radically Changing Employment Landscape, including:
- Accelerating Pace of Change
- Automation
- Globalization
- Changing Nature of Organizations
- The Rise of the Gig Economy
- Increasingly Diverse Workplaces
- Employer View of the Future

5

Expanding Learner Base and Changing Learner Needs that involve:
· Traditional Learners
· Post-traditional Learners

INTRODUCTION

We begin this book by establishing the need for change in higher education, because without a clear understanding of the problem (and the desired end goal/state), it is hard to strategize about pathways to get us there. We are attempting to present a coherent and logical argument based on data, and we believe our colleagues in various roles and different types of colleges and universities will be ready to engage in thinking through how their respective institutions should respond.

It is no secret that the world around us is changing rapidly. No matter your age, socioeconomic status, race, ethnic background, or educational attainment, every day brings something new—for example, an "invention" (app, product, service, etc.), political strife, medical breakthroughs, natural disasters, regional conflicts, economic shifts, and scientific discoveries. All of these changes provide context to the work we do in higher education. While we do not believe that "the sky is falling," given the vast changes in the world—demographically, economically, socially, and politically—we believe that higher education *does* need to (a) evolve in some areas (e.g., think beyond degrees, semesters, and credit hours), (b) shift our focus to be more inclusive (e.g., expand our potential learner base), (c) transform how we deliver, measure, and credential learning (e.g., adopt competency-based education, focus transcripts on knowledge and skills instead of courses, consider the role of adaptive learning platforms), and (d) leave behind some vestiges of ages past (e.g., lectures). We must find new ways to be as flexible, agile, and adaptable as the graduates we send out into the world will need to be.

If we are to remain relevant and add value to our learners' lives, it is essential that we more fully understand the forces and shifts in the world around us—globally, nationally, locally, and institutionally—because that world will both impact and be impacted by our evolution and transformation. It is also important to be able to see that world not only from our own perspective, but also from the perspective of those we "serve"—for example, parents, learners, employers, legislators, and K–12 educators. And we should remember that the public often does not distinguish among institutions the way we do (such as public/private, nonprofit/for profit, residential/commuter, two-year/four-year, technical/liberal arts, urban/suburban), but rather views postsecondary education as one monolithic entity. This means that even if some of the criticisms levied on higher education do not ring true for your institution, department, or courses, we are all tainted and impacted by them.

This chapter identifies and briefly discusses some of the major concerns about, critiques of, and changing forces that affect our industry, as well as the conditions in the world around us that set the stage for thinking about new paradigms that are needed to maintain relevance in the future. After all, "as academics, we have a moral and professional responsibility to help shape the public narrative about learning and education in the United States" (Sullivan, P., 2017, pp. 68–71). If we do not, others will! In fact, some have already asserted that we are close to losing control of our own narrative—to legislators, the media, employers—and must begin to define a compelling and positive future rather than assume the role of victim by allowing others to create it for us (Seymour, 2016). It is in this spirit that we approach our work, and we are hopeful that we will further stimulate the conversation and challenge the status quo with engaging new pathways of possibilities that will transform our educational ecosystems and learning potential commensurate with our emerging new world context.

GROWING PUBLIC CONCERN

Long-held beliefs have supported the notion that higher education provides critical social and economic mobility and a ticket to achieving the American Dream. Consequently, some might argue that access to quality postsecondary education is a critical element to ensuring the vitality and sustainability of our society. Although postsecondary education is not solely a "public good" in the economic sense of the term (i.e., a good that cannot be restricted to only those who pay for it, and consumption by one does not prevent consumption by others), one could certainly make the case that it is a "good" that serves the public interest. Postsecondary education and related research in the United States is a story of continual expansion and integration with our society's needs to develop the talent, skills, technology, and capacity to serve a growing nation. As such, higher education has also been the beneficiary of considerable funding from the public sector, either directly in state- and locally supported institutions or indirectly through federal and state financial aid programs supporting students. In light of the intersection of the perceived need to have access to quality education in order to achieve success and the growing costs to operate these institutions, the public's scrutiny of the academy has reached a new level. The scrutiny has led to growing skepticism in many corners and has fueled public concern on a range of issues.

Return on Investment (ROI). Although we believe that ROI is more than simply attaining a good job, we recognize that job attainment is one publicly embraced measure of postsecondary education's ROI. That said, much of the narrative on higher education focuses on the value higher education provides to individuals given the cost and debt load graduates carry, which impacts their lives in a variety of ways. For example, "a college education is now the second-largest expense an individual is likely to make in a lifetime—right after purchasing a home" (Dickler, 2016, para. 1). However, that characterization understates the negative impact of student debt for many recent graduates because student loan borrowers are not buying homes as they used to given they are not able to save for a down payment (Bauman, 2018; Lew, 2015). According to the National Association of Realtors and American Student Assistance, "student loan debt is delaying homeownership for millennials by an estimated seven years" (Lerner, 2017, para 2). In fact, homeownership for people younger than 35 has declined from 41 percent in 1982 to 35 percent in 2017 (Kitroeff, 2018). The student debt situation is becoming so mainstream that employers and states are looking at new ways to creatively leverage the student debt situation to attract and retain employees. The state of Maine, for example, which has about a third of their workforce either retired or rapidly approaching retirement, recently announced a student loan forgiveness program designed to attract recent graduates to live and work in the state (Sreenivasan, 2018). Some companies have also started to integrate student debt assistance into their employee recruitment and benefits offerings and strategy. In 2015, Fidelity Investments was among the first companies to launch such an effort by paying $10,000 over a five-year period toward student debt for full-time employees. Aetna followed suit in 2017 and also expanded similar benefits for part-time employees. Additionally, Fidelity has been contracted by Hewlett Packard, along with at least 25 other companies, to help them develop similar programs for their employees (Pandey, 2018).

For some college graduates, the situation is even worse; according to U.S. census data reported by the Pew Research

Center, "today's young adults are significantly more likely to be at home for an extended stay compared with previous generations of young adults who lived with their parents" (Fry, 2017, para 1). They put the number of 25-to-35-year-old millennials living at home, as of 2016, at 15 percent, compared to Gen Xers at 10 percent when they were the same age, 8 percent of early baby boomers, and 8 percent of the Silent Generation (Fry, 2017). So, the trend is upward. The median length of time at their parents' home is currently 3 years, which is an increase of 6 months from data collected for 2005–2013 (Fry, 2017). So again, the trend is upward. The term "boomerang generation" may not fit the majority of college graduates currently, but if we continue on this trajectory, it very well could.

Of course, it is not college tuition and subsequent debt alone that accounts for millennials returning home after graduation, but clearly it is one of at least three factors, along with job market realities and housing prices, according to Bleemer, Brown, Lee, and van der Klaauw (2017). These researchers, using data from a variety of sources, conclude that, between 2004 and 2015, there was an 11.4 percent increase in 25-year-olds living with parents and a 12.8 percent decrease in those living with roommates (Bleemer et al., 2017).

What exactly are the numbers we are talking about when we invoke the phrase "debt load"? The Bill & Melinda Gates Foundation reports that 7 in 10 seniors from public and nonprofit colleges have student loans with an average debt of $30,100 (Bill and Melinda Gates Foundation, n.d.), which equates to an average monthly student loan payment for borrowers aged 20–30 of $351 (Student Loan Hero, 2017). According to a 2018 Department of Education report, for those who graduated in 2007–2008, their loan payments accounted for about 12 percent of their monthly salary in 2012 (Cataldi, Woo, & Staklis, 2017). What makes this situation worse is that one-third of student borrowers never even complete college (Bauman, 2018).

10

According to the Federal Reserve Bank of New York, student loan debt had reached $1.53 trillion by the second quarter of 2018 (Singletary, 2018), making it the second largest category of consumer debt after home mortgages. This represents approximately 10.5 percent of U.S. consumer debt. In fact, "Americans spend about $30,000 per student a year—nearly twice as much as the average developed country" (Ripley, 2018, para. 4). Further, the delinquency in payment rates of college-related loans exceeded 10 percent during the fourth quarter of 2017 (Sankar, 2018).

For those who go on to earn an advanced degree, the situation is even more dire. For example, those earning an MBA incur debt of $42,000; Master of Education, $50,879; Master of Science, $50,400; Master of Arts, $58,539; law degree, $140,616; and a medicine and health sciences degree, $161,772 (Bauman, 2018). And the number of graduates pursuing advanced degrees is not small. According to Cataldi, Woo, and Staklis, 44 percent of 2007–2008 bachelor's degree graduates enrolled in another degree program within 4 years of graduating, with 62 percent pursuing a master's degree (2017, p. 2).

Perhaps even more alarming is the number of people over the age of 60 who are experiencing crushing debt related to either their own educational investments or The Direct Parent PLUS Loans for their children. There have been a growing number of bankruptcies and senior citizens reporting that they are living on credit cards and/or working much longer than they anticipated as a result of student loan debt of one kind or another. In fact, according to the Government Accountability Office, in fiscal year 2015 more than 40,000 people age 65 or older had Social Security payments, tax refunds, or other federal payments garnished as a result of defaulting on a parent or student loan. On average, it has been reported that the amount of total debt related to student loans for people above the age of 60 grew 161 percent from 2010 to 2017, representing approximately $86 billion (Andriotis, 2019).

While debt by itself presents some challenges, it is also widely understood that the degree earning premium—that is, the gap in earnings between high school diploma holders and college degrees—has stalled with virtually no change in the gap between 2010 and 2015 (Valletta, 2016). Data from the Georgetown University Center on Education and the Workforce indicate that lifetime earnings for a person with a baccalaureate degree versus an associate degree is $2.3 million as opposed to $1.7 million (Greeley, 2018). Labor analytics firm Burning Glass, in a report completed in 2014, observed a phenomenon they termed "up-credentialing," which essentially was the significant growth in positions that now required a bachelor's degree that previously did not. In one example, 65 percent of postings for an executive secretary/administrative type position required a baccalaureate degree whereas only 19 percent of those currently employed in the role possessed the baccalaureate degree (Burning Glass Technologies, 2014). Plainly stated, the increasing number of employment opportunities requiring the baccalaureate credential as the ticket for entry (while the earning premium gap shrinks and the cost for the credential spirals) creates what some see as an untenable conundrum. This particular combination of forces sets the stage for considerable anxiety and distress within the public domain as individuals consider the pathways to success available to them.

What sometimes adds fuel to the fire around the cost of higher education is the amenities offered on many campuses (some call it the "amenities arms race" (Koch, 2018; Newlon, 2014; Swartz, 2014), including, for example, lazy rivers (e.g., Universities of Alabama, Iowa, and Missouri and Louisiana State University, the latter financed by student fees), climbing walls (e.g., Penn State, Notre Dame, Cornell, University of Colorado Denver, and Stanford), and first-run movie theaters and hot tubs (e.g., High Point University). Obviously, colleges and universities are using this strategy to increase enrollment in a competitive market, often at the expense of students whose tuition dollars were funding the amenities. The good news is that spending on these types of "lavish campus frills" is slowing, due in part to rising tuition and student debt (Selingo, 2017a, para. 5).

Investment in these kinds of amenities is only part of the story. Increasingly, postsecondary institutions have had to invest in services such as transportation, childcare, food pantries, financial and mental health counseling, and emergency loan programs, among other services, to fill the gap for students when other societal structures fail to provide necessary support (Cowen & Seifter, 2018; Smith, 2018). Food insecurity has become a growing concern across the nation's colleges and universities (Phillips, McDaniel, & Croft, 2018). It was reported in April 2018 that more than 570 campus food pantries nationwide are registered with the College & University Food Bank Alliance. In California, a bill was recently passed allocating $7.5 million to fight campus hunger and to facilitate students' connection to other public support programs. The State University of New York mandated that all 64 of its campuses provide a food pantry for their students (Esch, 2018). Individual institutions like Amarillo College have created centers to centralize efforts to address students' needs, creating "a one-stop shop for students to access emergency aid and social services and find resources for their childcare needs . . . also has a free food pantry and clothing bank" (Smith, 2018, para. 7). Unfortunately, at most colleges and universities, these important support services are funded by tuition dollars and student fees.

Furthermore, tuition dollars must also cover unfunded mandates from the federal government to colleges and universities to "undertake and document various activities in their policymaking, planning, and reporting" in order to ensure safe campuses (National Center on Safe and Supportive Learning Environments, n.d., para. 2). These mandates, which number more than 200, include such laws and policies as the Americans with Disabilities

Act, the Drug-Free Schools and Communities Act (DFSCA), the Clery Act, Title IX of the Education Amendments of 1972, the Violence Against Women Act, the Higher Education Opportunity Act, the Family Educational Rights and Privacy Act (FERPA), Federal Policy for the Protection of Human Subjects Regulations, (the "Common Rule"), and the Student Exchange and Visitor Information System (SEVIS), among others (Higher Education Compliance Alliance, n.d.). While many of these requirements are reasonable and important, they are also expensive. For example, Virginia Commonwealth University, in response to a request from Congress, estimated that they spend "$13 million annually to comply with more than 200 federal regulations," while the University of Virginia estimated their costs at $20 million per year (S. Martin, 2017).

For all of these reasons, tuition will continue to increase—as will student debt—unless we change the higher education model. If we do not intervene, the expectation that the ROI for a college degree is a launching pad for young peoples' careers and lives will not be realized.

Persistence and Graduation Rates. Hand in hand with the concern over rising tuition and debt is the disappointing picture of graduation rates. According to the National Student Clearinghouse, 31 million people in the United States have some college credits and no degree (Shapiro et al., 2014). Furthermore, "children from families earning more than $90,000 have a 1-in-2 chance of getting a bachelor's degree by 24. That falls to a 1 in 17 chance for families earning under $35,000" (Selingo, 2018). The U.S. Department of Education reports that "three years after first enrolling, comparatively more first-generation students who began postsecondary education in 2003–04, had left postsecondary education without earning a postsecondary credential (33 percent) than had their continuing-generation peers whose parents attended some college (26 percent) and whose parents earned a bachelor's degree (14 percent)" (Cataldi, Bennett, & Chen, 2018, p. 4). And to top it off, "the 6-year graduation rate for first-time, full-time undergraduate students who began seeking a bachelor's degree at a 4-year degree-granting institution in fall 2010 was 60 percent" (National Center for Education Statistics, n.d., para. 1).

Add to this group the continued lagging educational attainment of underrepresented minorities, including low-income, first-generation Latino and black students. For example, compared to white adults, the "gap in bachelor's degree attainment has doubled, from 9 to 20 percent for Hispanic residents since 1974 and from 6 to 13 percent for Black residents since 1964" (Office of Planning, Evaluation and Policy Development, 2016, p. 1). First-generation college students still lag behind those students whose parents are degree holders. The U.S. Department of Education indicates that "among 2002 high school sophomores, 46 percent of students who had a parent with a bachelor's degree and 59 percent who had a parent with a master's degree or higher had obtained a bachelor's degree or higher by 2012, compared to 17 percent of students who had parents with no postsecondary education experience" (Redford & Hoyer, 2017, p. 1). In fact, the proportion of first-generation students has been declining, from 37 percent in 1999–2000 to 33 percent in 2011–2012 (Cataldi, Bennett, & Chen, 2018, p. 1). These data on access are especially discouraging given the myriad programs and investment (at the national, state, and institutional levels) over the past decade that have focused on the attraction and persistence of underrepresented minorities.

The situation is even worse for black and Latino adults holding a bachelor's or an associate's degree. In a 2018 study, the Education Trust (n.d.) found that, compared with 47.1 percent of white adults, just 30.8 percent of black adults and 22 percent of Latino adults earned some form of college degree. Loan delinquency is also a serious problem and is reported to be considerably higher across all constituencies and institutional types

15

among those students who do not complete their program of study (Sankar, 2018). Higher education is failing many of our young people!

Having just cited those discouraging numbers, like others we are skeptical that they provide the whole story. Considerable frustration exists with the graduation data collection methods that historically focused on the traditionally aged student population, which represents a shrinking percentage of the total number of students enrolled in postsecondary education. In fact, in 2016, some 55 percent of students receiving a bachelor's degree and more than 60 percent of students at community colleges attended part-time. In an attempt to create a more complete picture of what is happening in student persistence and completion, a number of changes and initiatives are under way. The Bill & Melinda Gates Foundation and Carnegie Corporation have supported six higher education associations that represent the vast majority of higher education institutions across the nation in an effort to create a more comprehensive view and set of metrics to collect data that include transfer and post-traditional students. The Student Achievement Measure (SAM) is a collaboration of higher education institutions who are voluntarily participating in a project designed to collect data on the many pathways that students take to complete a course of study (Engle, 2016). The National Student Clearinghouse Research Center is also interested in collecting accurate data and has recently begun reporting on pathways students follow across institutions to earn their degrees (Shapiro et al., 2018).

The Department of Education is also trying to address the serious shortcomings in data reporting and announced a number of changes in the fall of 2017. Some of the new data will provide a better picture of part-time enrollments, regardless of whether or not the student was a first-time enrollee or started in a semester other than the fall. The availability of these new data, although still constrained since student-level tracking remains off limits, will provide more information on more students in more programs (Lederman, 2017).

Increasing accuracy of the data, however, will not address the larger issue that higher education is not supporting millions of students who begin and never finish, impacting their employment opportunities and long-term financial well-being.

Lack of Access. We previously mentioned that one-third of student borrowers never complete college—which translates to some 31 million people in the United States with some college credits and no credential (Shapiro et al., 2014). We know the impact that will have on their economic well-being if they do not remedy this situation; one 2017 study indicates that a college graduate's median lifetime earnings are twice as much as a high school graduate (Schanzenback, Bauer, & Breitwieser, 2017). Furthermore, many of these individuals are now adults with jobs and families, and little extra time or income to support furthering their education.

The discussions regarding access should not only be examined through the lens of racial, ethnic, socioeconomic, or first-generation status. Geographic considerations might also present barriers for some, especially post-traditional students, who represent the largest growing segment enrolled in postsecondary programs. Frequently, post-traditional students are also managing households, family, and work responsibilities while trying to juggle pursuit of an education. Proximity to available education can have a major impact on access, so much so that the American Council on Education commissioned a study to better understand the impact of geography on access. The study determined that there are several "education deserts" across the nation that impact rural students disproportionately (Hillman & Wiechman, 2016, p. 6). A similar study, conducted by the Chronicle of Higher Education, suggests that 11.2 million, or 3.5 percent, of the adult population reside in "educational deserts" (Myers, 2018, para. 7). Several universities have recognized the potential opportunity in recruiting in these areas and have launched targeted efforts to recruit students; however, most of these efforts appear to be primarily focused on traditionally aged individuals (Pappano, 2017).

College Readiness. Even for many who have access, readiness is an issue (ACT, 2013), especially for those high school students who come from low-performing schools. This reality not only keeps some high school graduates out of college, but can also negatively impact their academic achievement and persistence to graduation if they choose to attend. The numbers of students who are required to take at least some remedial coursework upon entry to postsecondary education is significant. According to a report prepared by the National Center for Education Statistics (NCES), 68 percent of those students entering 2-year institutions and nearly 40 percent entering 4-year institutions were required to participate in remedial education. These data are alarming and should raise concern at multiple levels. Remedial coursework often creates additional barriers to persistence and completion by slowing advancement to graduation since they often do not count toward graduation requirements, frequently causing students to exhaust their financial aid eligibility prior to degree completion (Long, 2014). There is some indication that this may be changing, as the California State University System has decided to "replace remedial classes with credit-bearing courses that span two semesters with support classes offered in tandem as a way to help more students at its 23 campuses graduate faster, and with fewer costs" (Black, 2018, para. 1).

In addition to the enormous cost associated with offering developmental courses, we also need to consider the enormous cost of K–12 education that is potentially falling short of preparing students for success. Unfortunately, high-stakes testing is still a reality in secondary education. And given that the results impact school funding, teachers often find themselves compromising their values and standards to ensure results. Many of these teachers lament "teaching to the test," by which they mean teaching discrete pieces of knowledge and skills that align with test questions, as opposed to focusing learning on developing knowledge and a set of key skills, practicing them to the point where they can be combined fluently and used with a fair degree of automaticity, and knowing when and where to apply them appropriately (Ambrose, Bridges, Dipietro, Lovett, & Norman, 2010). Craig Jerald provides concrete examples of this as he distinguishes between "curriculum teaching" and "item-teaching":

> For example, if students will be tested on fractions, curriculum teachers will cover a range of knowledge and skills related to fractions so students understand what fractions are, know how to manipulate them mathematically, understand how to use them to solve more complex problems, and are able to communicate with and about them. Item teachers narrow their instruction, organizing their teaching around clones of the particular questions most likely to be found on the test—and thus teach only the bits of knowledge students are most likely to encounter on exams. For example, item teachers might drill students on a small set of vocabulary words expected to be assessed rather than employing instructional strategies that help students develop the kind of rich and broad vocabulary that best contributes to strong reading comprehension. (Jerald, 2006, p. 2)

In other words, item-teaching enables students to directly "map" question types on high-stakes exams—such as standardized state exams—to problems they have done on practice tests. This type of educational experience limits students' ability, for

19

example, to understand principles underlying solutions to problems, reason their way through a problem, and/or transfer what they have learned to new contexts—the critical thinking and problem-solving skills that college professors expect high school graduates to possess. So, cost, in both of these cases (higher and secondary education), can be measured not only in dollars and time, but also in educator stress and student motivation and confidence, resulting in students unprepared for college.

There is also a question about the nature and amount of reading and writing that high school students currently engage in that impacts college readiness. ACT reported in 2006 that "barely half of all high school graduates possess college-level reading skills," and we are not confident that the situation has changed (ACT, 2006). This statistic is alarming given research that clearly shows that "'deep' reading and reading for pleasure may be the most important things you can do to prepare for college" (P. Sullivan, 2016, para. 6), because reading is linked to increased cognitive processes over time, including greater intellectual progress, both in vocabulary, spelling, and mathematics (A. Sullivan, 2013, para. 3). That is the good news. The bad news is that a 2014–2015 study by Renaissance Learning's Accelerated Reader 360 program "raises some serious questions . . . about whether students' reading habits are preparing them well for study and work after high school" (Gewertz, 2016, para. 4). This study, drawn from the reading habits of 9.8 million American students, indicates that students at every grade level choose reading material below their grade level; in other words, even high schoolers are not challenging themselves by focusing on the "complexity level they'll face in college" (Gewertz, 2016, para. 4). And, according to National Endowment for the Arts data, young people are simply reading less; in 2007, "nearly half of all Americans ages 18 to 24 read no books for pleasure," "less than one-third of 13-year-olds are daily readers," and "58 percent of middle and high school students use other media while reading" (National Endowment for the Arts, 2007, p. 7). This is concerning given that research (Renaissance Learning, 2015) clearly indicates the importance of reading in building not only vocabulary, fluency, comprehension, writing, and higher-order thinking skills (Anderson, Wilson, & Fielding, 1988; Baker, Simmons, & Kameenui, 1998; Greenfield, 2009; Guthrie, Wigfield, Metsala, & Cox, 1999) but also visual-information processing and speech perception (Dehaene et al., 2010; McBride-Chang et al., 2011), among other skills.

The state of writing and math preparedness is not much better. A recent National Assessment of Educational Progress (NAEP) report indicates that "three-quarters of both 12th and 8th graders lack proficiency in writing. And 40 percent of those who took the ACT writing exam in the high school class of 2016 lacked the reading and writing skills necessary to successfully complete a college-level English composition class . . ." (Goldstein, 2017, para. 10). Mathematics achievement results are similarly dismal; 2017 NAEP data on eighth-grade students show that only 34 percent perform at or above the proficient level (McFarland et al., 2018), and recent data on ACT college-entrance exams from 1.9 million graduates (about one-half of the 2018 graduating class) indicate that "only 40 percent of 2018 graduates taking the ACT met a benchmark indicating they could succeed in a first-year college algebra class," down from a high of 46 percent in 2012 (Hobbs, 2018, para. 2).

Our brief discussion of this college preparedness issue is not meant to cast aspersions on secondary education, which operates with many constraints; rather, colleges and universities must address the learning needs of the students we get, not the students we wish we had.

Perceived Skills Gap. For those who *do* gain access and graduate with a degree, the narrative sometimes remains negative. Many surveys of employers continue to indicate that college graduates lack some of the fundamental skills needed for success

21

across jobs and industries (Chronicle of Higher Education, 2012; Hart Research Associates, 2015; Selingo & Werf, n.d.). These include the set of what we think of as "intellectual skills": critical thinking, analytical reasoning, and effective communication (oral and written) with people inside and outside the organization, as well as the ability to solve complex problems, deal with ambiguity and complexity, apply knowledge in real-world settings, and locate, organize, and evaluate information from multiple sources (Carnevale, Smith, & Strohl, 2013). Most, if not all, academics would tell you that these fundamental skills are *deeply embedded* in their respective curricula, which we believe they are—hence the problem. Because faculty are experts in their fields, they often fall victim to "expert blind spot" (Nathan & Koedinger, 2000, p. 209)—they are so far away from novices in their knowledge, skills, and experience that they do not even realize that they are skipping or combining steps, for example, sometimes resulting in inadequate explanations. This unconscious competence (Sprague & Stuart, 2000) means that experts often are not as explicit or transparent in illuminating the thinking process and intellectual skills, which, in many fields and disciplines, are even more important than the content, given that content is always changing and expanding. As a result, students are gaining a set of skills that they are not cognizant of, and even if they are, they are learning those skills within narrow contexts of courses and disciplines, making it difficult for them to then activate and transfer those skills to new contexts, such as their first job (Ambrose et al., 2010). We believe that the skills gap perception is real but that graduates actually do possess these skills: they just don't know they possess them and therefore they do not access and use them.

The story with the set of "professional skills" noted in skills gap surveys and other research is similar. These skills often include such things as (a) adaptability, (b) the ability to collaborate and work well in teams, (c) self-awareness, (d) empathy,

(e) the ability to continue to learn, build relationships, advocate, and negotiate, and (f) the ability to plan, organize, and prioritize work. Students who participate in civic engagement, service learning, on-campus employment in paraprofessional roles (such as coaches, referees, peer advisers, and resident assistants), or who lead campus organizations frequently develop and practice many of these professional skills. But once again, they are not cognizant that they are developing and honing the skills, and hence do not consciously transfer those skills to other contexts. By the way, the top 10 list of skills recognized by the World Economic Forum as most important in the workforce merge these two sets of "intellectual" and "professional" skills (Centre for the New Economy and Society, 2018), further validating the importance of both.

Any discussion about skills seems to trigger the age-old debate regarding the relevance of a liberal arts degree. We would be remiss here if we did not point out, given the continual attack on the liberal arts, that liberal arts degrees often engage students in both the intellectual and professional skills that employers desire, among other things (Dix, 2016). This debate creates a false dichotomy between "knowing" and "doing" that would be better served if it were replaced with dialogue about pedagogical approaches that would ensure relevance and outcomes, designed to align learning with workforce development needs and the development of requisite knowledge, skills, and commitment to constructively engage in civic activities within our global society. In fact, a recent report by the American Enterprise Institute and Burning Glass Technologies indicated that of the 3.8 million entry-level jobs they analyzed, a liberal arts major could qualify for 1.4 million of them. They went on to say that they see the issue to be less about academic major and more one of the need to cluster desired skills in order to improve job prospects (Schneider & Sigelman, 2018). Additionally, the role of the liberal arts is undeniable in enhancing students' ability to creatively express their views, discover beauty, and uncover new interests, all of which contribute to helping learners maintain a healthy life balance (discussed in more detail in chapter 2).

Unfortunately, this narrative about misalignment with workforce needs sometimes results in calls for higher education to abandon nonprofessional degrees, ignoring the skill set honed in those degrees that directly align with what employers say they need in employees (e.g., adaptability, collaboration, self-awareness, empathy, effective communication, problem solving). In other words, matching skills to jobs is just as important (or maybe more important in some areas) as matching degrees to jobs. In his book *You Can Do Anything: The Surprising Power of a "Useless" Liberal Arts Education*, George Anders (2017) translates what employers are looking for when they say, for example, they want to hire employees with critical thinking skills: they want individuals who can (a) work on the frontier (e.g., bring imagination to tackling uncharted areas, think outside the box, adapt to a changing environment, thrive on challenges), (b) find insights (e.g., spotting the less obvious, connecting the dots, filtering and distilling information, dealing with ambiguity), (c) choose the right approach (e.g., synthesize insights to make complex decisions, act on opportunities, find creative solutions), (d) read the room (e.g., understand group dynamics and others' motivations, see the big picture, manage through influence, balance different perspectives and agendas), and (e) inspire others (e.g., energize others to embrace change, convey information effectively, inspire confidence). Anders points out that these are exactly the skills developed and honed in the liberal arts, and he then connects these skills with the kinds of skills employers are seeking. For example, Deloitte, Humana, and the Federal Reserve are looking for that explorer's mindset (working on the frontier); Sony, Dropbox, and Johnson Controls are looking for those who can find insights; FedEx, McKinsey, and PayPal hire those who can engage in choosing the right approach; BlackRock and eBay want employees who know how to satisfy multiple agendas and keep moving forward by reading the room; and American Express, Cox Communications, and Genentech want those who can be persuasive (Anders, 2017). In other words, the liberal arts do align with workforce needs.

Data provided by the Brookings Institution's Hamilton Project also support this argument; they tracked lifetime earnings by college majors. While acknowledging that liberal arts graduates often earn less than those in some other majors (e.g., engineering, computer science, business, nursing) initially (0 to 5 years out), they fare better in annual earnings with 10–20 years' experience and represent half of the top tenth by major in high achievers' lifetime earnings (Anders, 2017). This is not surprising when you recognize the three "proven paths" high-achieving liberal arts graduates take: in the public sector and at nonprofit organizations; in the money trade, such as venture capital, hedge funds, and private equity; and as entrepreneurs (Anders, 2017). So, the world of work validates the skills gained in the liberal arts in a very concrete way.

The fine and performing arts are as much under attack as the liberal arts when it comes to the value in the workplace and society, despite their many contributions. Although many hold the arts in high esteem because they "illuminate our inner lives and enrich our emotional world" (Mowlah, Niblett, Burn, & Harris, 2014, p. 1), we need to remember that they also impact, in a positive way, the economy, people's health and well-being, society, and the growth and development of our youth. In one study by Arts Council England, which focused on synthesizing research and evaluation studies that presented examples of the impact of the arts, they found, for example, that the arts and culture industry generated billions of dollars through tourism, book publishing, performing arts, and so forth; that "those who attended a cultural place or event in the previous 12 months were almost 60 percent more likely to report good health compared to those who had not"; that "high school students who engage in the arts at school are twice as likely to volunteer than those who do not engage in the arts and are 20 percent more likely to vote as young adults"; that "taking part in structured music activities improves attainments in math, early language acquisition and early literacy" (Mowlah et al., 2014, p. 35). Data exist within the United States to validate these claims as well; as far back as 1991, The President's Committee on the Arts and Humanities issued a report that presented data to substantiate the value and worth of the arts and humanities as they ". . . contribute to our wealth and longer-term economic growth; their special ability to create innovations and new environments which advance civilizations; the wide variety of ways the arts stimulate learning; and their unique power for interactions with societies around the world and with the rich diversity of groups within this country" (Murfee, 1991, para. 1). In fact, according to the U.S. Bureau of Economic Analysis and the National Endowment for the Arts, in 2015 the arts contributed "$763.6 billion to the U.S. economy, more than agriculture, transportation, or warehousing. The arts employ 4.9 million workers across the country with earnings of more than $370 billion . . . the arts export $20 billion more than imported . . ." (National Endowment for the Arts, 2018, para. 1). Furthermore, the arts can contribute to the livability of cities and attract investors. So public interest is served in a variety of ways in ensuring that we continue to educate those whose interests and passions lie in the arts (Murfee, 1991).

If you are still not convinced of the value of the arts to practical matters related to employment, read the article "Appreciating the Beauty of Science Ideas: Teaching for Aesthetic Understanding," in which the authors convincingly describe the "beauty inherent in scientific ideas and scientific discovery" that inspires scientists to explore the world (Girod, Rau, & Schepige, 2003, p. 575). They, like others, recommend "educating the artist within young scientists"—what they call aesthetic understanding, and cite numerous accomplished scientists who embraced this notion (e.g., Jane Goodall, Dian Fossey, Ernst Mach, Barbara McClintock, Temple Grandin).

Furthermore, engineering educators around the world have been discussing the value of including more right brain experiences to enhance the professional success of engineers to create and innovate. In fact, in 2017 the National Academy of Engineering awarded the Bernard M. Gordon Prize for Innovation in Engineering and Technical Education to Dr. Julio M. Ottino, the dean of engineering at Northwestern University for his "Whole-Brain Engineering" philosophy and practice, which "merges the analytical and technical components of engineering (left brain) with creativity, design and divergent thinking (right brain)" (Fellman, 2017, para. 1). This recognition of the importance of fields like art and design to science, technology, engineering, and mathematics (STEM) is represented in the rise of STEAM (science, technology, engineering, arts, and mathematics), a movement spearheaded by the Rhode Island School of Design, which both encourages the integration of the arts into education and inspires employers to recognize the value of arts to innovation and hire accordingly. In fact, in May 2018, the National Academies of Science, Engineering, and Medicine issued a report that concluded that integrating the humanities and arts into STEAM is, based on an emerging body of evidence, "associated with positive learning outcomes that may help students enter the workplace, live enriched lives, and become active and informed citizens" (Skorton & Bear, 2018, p. 5).

To be fair, universities are starting to come around and respond to the needs of employers. For example, the University of California, Berkeley announced in October 2018 that they were creating an interdisciplinary Division of Data Science and Information to "meet the needs of the booming data science field," after launching a bachelor of arts in data science in fall 2018

(Dimeo, 2018, para. 1). The Massachusetts Institute of Technology announced the creation of a College of Computing in fall 2018 as well, which would initially include 50 new faculty positions housed in a new building (Paterson, 2018). According to a report in the Pew Foundation's Stateline, about 90 two-year colleges across 19 states are now offering baccalaureate degrees that often are closely aligned with local industry needs, providing a highly cost-effective option leading to good-paying jobs (Povich, 2018). In August 2018, the Georgia Board of Regents approved the offering of "nexus degrees," which are "college credentials that emphasize hands-on experiential learning and skilled knowledge and connections with industry in high-demand career fields" (University of Georgia, 2018, para. 2). The curricula for these degrees are being developed in partnership with industry experts to ensure that they meet current and anticipated workforce needs in high-demand fields. Another example that attracted the attention of the Aspen Institute was the recipient of the 2017 Aspen Prize for Community College Excellence, the Lake Area Technical Institute (LATI) in eastern South Dakota. LATI, in consultation with approximately 300 businesses within their catchment area, have developed 30 two-year programs customized to the specific needs and specifications of local employers (Runnion & Gibson, 2018). There are also several examples of partnerships at the graduate level. To regain public trust, higher education must address both the perception and reality of the skills gap.

Misalignment with Workforce Needs and Public Interest. Beyond the skills gap, there is growing alarm that higher education is simply not meeting and will not be able to meet the needs of the workforce. For example, we continually hear about current job vacancies in STEM fields; a Georgetown study projected 2.6 million STEM job vacancies by 2020, including both new and replacement jobs (Carnevale et al., 2013). In manufacturing alone, the expectation is that 2.7 million employees will retire over the next decade and that 700,000 additional skilled employees will be needed to meet industry growth—that is a total of 3.4 million workers (Josephs, 2017).

The Georgetown study also indicates that we will see 54.8 million new and replacement jobs by 2020 across all sectors of the economy, with 30.8 million of those due to retirements. For example, the financial services industry will lead with 10 million job vacancies, of which some 50 percent will be new; wholesale and retail trade will experience 7 million job vacancies; government and public education, 6.7 million; and leisure and hospitality, 5 million (Josephs, 2017).

According to the Bureau of Labor Statistics, the health-care industry is experiencing faster than average employment growth, which is projected to continue (Bureau of Labor Statistics, 2017). Given the aging population globally and longer life expectancies, health-care support occupations are projected to grow globally by 80 million to 130 million by 2030 (Manyika et al., 2017), health-care practitioners and technical occupations by 15.3 percent, and personal care and service occupations by 19.1 percent, including nurses, occupational therapists, physical therapists, and speech language pathologists. According to the Economic Policy Institute, there is a shortage of 389,000 K–12 teachers as well (Gould, 2018). These numbers beg the question of how aligned our program offerings are with the needs of the workplace.

Finally, misalignment represents not only knowledge and skills, but also access and time. We already live in a world in which employees need to upskill continually, and many do not have the time, interest, or means to either earn or "go back" for another bachelor's or a master's degree. Hence we have the rise of the "shadow learning economy," which represents "a new set of providers offering education in short spurts, either online or in face-to-face classes" (Selingo, 2018, para. 1). Think boot camps, Coursera, YouTube, and Khan Academy, among others. According

29

to Selingo, "this behavior in education mimics that of the broader economy, with consumers increasingly seeking alternatives to legacy businesses—take Uber and Airbnb as examples of this phenomenon" (Selingo, 2018, para. 2). Certainly, there are disruptors of all kinds, including companies such as SpaceX, WeWork, GitHub, Udacity, and Amazon, among several others, emerging across a variety of industries. CNBC believes that these disruptors are an expected part of the landscape evidenced by their annual list, six years running, of Top Fifty Disruptors whose "innovations are changing the world" (McGraw-Hill Education, 2018).

Aligning with the needs of employers, employees, and the broader public interest is vital for the future of the higher education sector.

Political and Social Context. The current political climate also impacts higher education, and not in a positive way. It has contributed to a rise in anti-intellectualism, anti-science, anti-data, and anti-evidence-based decision making (e.g., climate change, "clean coal," fracking), hitting the very heart of what educators believe matters most in order to educate graduates who can address the global challenges of this generation.

As we write this chapter, the current U.S. president is attacking the methodology and motives of a study by researchers at George Washington University that puts the death toll of Hurricane Maria (which hit the island of Puerto Rico in September 2017) at approximately 3,000 (Stripling, 2018). Criticisms like these are often used to cast aspersions on all of higher education, creating a hostile environment that questions the validity and veracity of scientific findings of all university-driven research. Not helping the situation are the actual cases of research misconduct that periodically surface as the academy polices the rigor of research and the ethics of researchers. We have seen legitimate cases of plagiarism, use of inappropriate research methods, unacceptable manipulation of data, falsification or fabrication of data, destruction of data, and so forth that exacerbate the situation, despite the fact that these cases are anomalies, not the norm. As a result of just such cases, universities and the federal government have created processes to both identify and address allegations of research misconduct. In fact, the Office of Research Integrity at the U.S. Department of Health and Human Services maintains a list of those who ". . . CURRENTLY [sic] have an imposed administrative actions against them" (Office of Research Integrity, n.d., para. 1). Further fueling of the fire comes from headlines such as this one from the *Orlando Sentinel*: "UCF lambasted after admitting misusing state funds for new $38 million academic building" (A. Martin, 2018). Sadly, these occasional transgressions erode public confidence in higher education.

This negative political narrative also invokes the "liberal bias" allegedly silencing conservative perspectives on college campuses, cautioning potential parents and students about the free exchange of ideas that some of us view as vital to preparing graduates to become citizens ready to engage in the democratic process. Add to that the growing concern about the number of international students (raised by the anti-immigrant sentiment and xenophobia), particularly in graduate education, and especially in STEM-related fields, who some fear might eventually use that education against the United States. Unfortunately, the polarization we are seeing in America today is being replicated on many college campuses, leading to intolerance and incivility that disrupts university operations, stresses already tight budgets, and negatively impacts learners' growth and development. This condition is creating a chilling effect on freedom of expression and the open exchange of ideas.

Some people, like physicist, television personality, and head of the Hayden Planetarium Neil deGrasse Tyson, partially blame the academy for the lack of respect for higher education,

31

specifically because we do not prioritize communication with the public. In an interview with the Chronicle of Higher Education (Patel, 2018), Tyson criticizes higher education's incentive system, which does not value explaining science to the masses; he rightly suggests that anything that is not done in a laboratory (for scientists, but this holds true in other disciplines as well) does not count professionally in academia. Tyson's assertion is bolstered by a recent study examining the metrics and incentives for public scholarship, which does indicate that our traditional reward system in higher education often hinders researchers from impacting public perception and policy (Alperin et al., 2018).

Fierce Competition and Confusion in the Marketplace. Given all of the concerns and challenges discussed above, collaboration across colleges and universities is vital in addressing these issues. While there are organizations that follow policy developments and advocate for change on behalf of higher education—American Council on Education (ACE), Association of American Colleges and Universities (AAC&U), Council of Graduate Schools, Institute of International Education (IIE), National Association of Student Personnel Administrators (NASPA), American Association of Collegiate Registrars and Admissions Officers (AACRAO), American Association of Community Colleges (AACC), American Association of State Colleges and Universities (AASCU), Association of Public & Land-Grant Universities (APLU), and the Education Commission of the States—the current situation has led to fierce competition for survival. For example, some private colleges are now offering price-matching with public in-state tuition, and some public universities offer in-state tuition to out-of-state students (Korn, 2018). For institutions that can afford it, both low- and middle-income students can receive full-tuition scholarships and grants, along with fees and room and board to low-income students (Lewis, 2018). In fact, in November 2018, Michael Bloomberg donated $1.8 billion to Johns Hopkins University for the express purpose of financial aid for low-income students to make the admissions process "forever need blind" (N. Anderson, 2018). Furthermore, enrollment of international students continues to decline; American universities realized a 3.3 percent decrease in 2017 and another 6.6 percent decrease in 2018, and we are all vying for those students (Hackman & Belkin, 2018).

This Darwinian mentality to "save themselves" pits institutions against one another in a quest to address declining undergraduate enrollments and continuous decrease in public funding, resulting in a losing proposition for all, because resources go toward this competition rather than other initiatives that might solve the longer-term problems that threaten higher education. Additionally, this circumstance for those colleges focused primarily on traditionally aged students will likely worsen since the number of high school graduates is expected to drop by 9 percent between 2026 and 2031, representing nearly 280,000 students (Selingo, n.d.). Furthermore, these actions confuse prospective parents and students, as well as critics of higher education, about what college really costs, as tuition, fees, and room and board differ from the net price paid (Korn, 2018). In fact, one might see the practices of tuition discounting at private colleges and universities as a direct competitive effort for students. The National Association of College and University Business Officers (NACUBO), who prepares an annual tuition discounting report, indicated that in 2016–2017 the average discount rate for first-time freshmen climbed to 48.2 percent, and NACUBO projected that it would rise to 49.9 percent during the 2017–2018 academic year (Valbrun, 2018). When the 2018 NACUBO report was released for the 2017–2018 academic year, it showed that the actual freshman discount rate exceeded the original projections, climbing to a record 50.5%, with projections for academic year 2018–2019 estimated to climb further and likely be 52% (National Association of College and University Business Officers, 2019). This tuition-discounting arms race has often resulted in reduced net tuition revenue for institutions to invest in needed programs and services and reduced access for some students, especially in cases where institutional funds are directed to merit rather than need-based aid. In the past, this financial aid "arms race" has benefited high-achieving and high-income students and exacerbated the competition among institutions. The good news, however, is that a recent analysis from the American Enterprise Institute indicates that the practice of need-based (as opposed to merit-based) institutional aid is benefiting low-income students; in fact, their data show an increase in total financial aid to low-income students between 2003–2004 and 2015–2016 (Delisle & Christensen, 2019).

The truth of the matter is that this phenomenon of competition is relatively new as higher education in the United States becomes more homogeneous. Variety was a hallmark of our educational system for many years, as liberal arts colleges, women's colleges, minority-serving institutions (MSIs), land-grant universities, tribal colleges, research universities, religiously affiliated colleges, and so forth offered unique experiences to different student populations based on their respective institutional missions. Eventually, however, a hierarchy surfaced, and "a consensus emerged about what universities were the most prestigious, and others tried to emulate these top schools and thus to climb up an informal hierarchy" (Altbach, 2010, para. 3).

On top of this "internal" competition among nonprofit institutions of higher education lies the entrance of for-profit institutions, which, as of this writing, are experiencing deregulation under the current administration, likely resulting in an uptick of competition with for-profit universities. In fact, there is optimism in private equity firms as the Department of Education under Secretary DeVos seeks to rescind numerous Obama-era safeguards, including the Gainful Employment Rule (Star, 2018). For example, the secretary restored status to the Accrediting Council for Independent Colleges and Schools (ACICS), a for-profit college accreditor that oversaw the collapse of for-profit chains like Corinthian Colleges and ITT Tech (Kreighbaum, 2018). As of this writing, this situation remains fluid; however, should more of the rules be rescinded, one might reasonably speculate that growth in the for-profit sector, including those with suspect practices, are likely to be the result.

This is why the moment has come, according to Selingo, to link "multiple institutions to create a modern model of higher education," which he calls the Networked University, by moving beyond the "loosely coupled federations of independent campuses that typically cooperate only at the margins of the institution on matters where there is low risk and clear agreement on solutions"; think athletics, mission, and geographic alliances (Selingo, 2017b, p. 11). This is the only way that we will, as an industry, solve the problems that we all face and better serve learners, employers, and society. The good news is that networks are emerging. For example, the University Innovation Alliance is a group of public research universities who serve large numbers of first-generation, low-income students, coming together to test and scale solutions to problems of access and graduation in higher education (University Innovation Alliance, n.d.). Like Selingo, they believe that while some competition can be healthy, institutions need to collaborate in order to achieve collective impact, diffuse innovation, and drive needed changes in higher education (University Innovation Alliance, n.d.). Similarly, the Association of Public and Land-Grant Universities has launched an initiative called "Powered by Publics: Scaling Student Success," which brings together 130 institutions serving 3 million undergraduates, including 1 million Pell Grant recipients, to "focus on solving different

35

pieces of the student success puzzle" (Association of Public & Land-Grant Universities, n.d., para. 3).

State legislators as well as education commissions and boards are increasingly attempting to create ways to enhance student success through institutional collaboration and alignment. According to a 2018 report by the Education Commission of the States, at least 30 states have enacted policies designed to improve articulation between postsecondary institutions, degree completion, and student success across their states (e.g., community technical and 4-year colleges). These policies take many forms, including things such as requiring transferability of general education core credits and/or associate degree acceptance, common course numbering systems, and reverse transfer policies that retroactively award an associate degree (L. Anderson, 2018). These efforts signal a frustration that educators are not leading the way in achieving these goals in support of the degree completion agenda and workforce development. Nevertheless, these efforts should serve as a catalyst for educators to actively engage and innovate new alliances and solutions rather than struggle under the manifestations of imperfect permutations that legislative and mandated solutions often bring.

The tensions and forces for change we have just laid out, both internal and external to the academy, seem to be reaching a feverish pitch. In fact, in October 2018, Gallup reported that American adults with a "'great deal' or 'quite a lot' of confidence in higher education" fell from 57 percent in 2015 to 48 percent in 2018 (Jaschik, 2018, para.1–2). Gallup also notes that "no other institution has seen as large a decline in confidence" between those years, including, for example, the military, the church, the medical system, banks, and public schools (Jaschik, 2018, para. 5). This does not bode well for higher education.

RADICALLY CHANGING EMPLOYMENT LANDSCAPE

On the heels of the second industrial revolution, American philosopher and educator John Dewey is often quoted as having said, "If we teach today's students as we taught yesterday's, we rob them of tomorrow" (goodreads, n.d.) While these words were certainly applicable at the time, they unfortunately remain true as we rapidly transition into a global economy fueled by rapidly changing technologies and knowledge in all domains; some refer to this as Industry 4.0. This emerging and fast-paced service and knowledge economy opens new frontiers of opportunity and challenge. As with other major economic transitions over the course of history, the political and social impact of these transitions are significant and will continue to unfold into the future.

Accelerating Pace of Change. In his 2016 book *Thank You for Being Late: An Optimist's Guide to Thriving in the Age of Accelerations*, Thomas L. Friedman convincingly explains why the world seems to be moving at a faster pace of historical change than we have experienced before. He attributes this to three interacting forces that speed up one another: (1) the market and its expansion and speed of globalization, (2) Moore's law of exponential acceleration of computing power, and (3) Mother Nature—for example, climate change, the extinction of biodiversity, and population growth (Friedman, 2016). According to Friedman, this acceleration is impacting the workplace, politics, geopolitics, ethics, and community, resulting in the need for us to continuously change and adapt, a process that draws on a concept from mechanics known as *dynamic stability*.

Dynamic stability will be a challenge for higher education, a sector regarded as being slow to change. Compounding this challenge is the nature of how people respond and adapt (or not) to

37

change, a subject well researched. It will be no small feat to overcome the fear of the unknown, the feeling of loss of control, concerns about competence, worry about going outside one's comfort zone, anxiety about losing face for those strongly associated with how things have been done in the past, comfort with the status quo, and so forth (Kanter, 2012). Thankfully, the research on change also includes data on how to effectively lead and manage it. The good news is that some of the research indicates that people do have the capacity to act as change agents because "people are not just products of their environment, they have a deep-rooted desire and capacity to self-regulate their behavior and to participate in crafting the world around them based on their present needs and hopes for the future" (Tams, 2018, para. 6). This is good news given how profoundly the world of work will change. This mentality and accompanying behaviors will be increasingly important as we move through the 21st century.

Automation. The pace of technological change, according to Friedman, has been in nonlinear acceleration not only in terms of the computational speed of the microchip, but also in the five basic components of every computing device: integrated circuits, memory units, networking systems, software applications, and sensors (Friedman, 2016). The results of this steady acceleration, resulting in robots, artificial intelligence, machine learning, and so forth, are and will continue to impact the world at large as well as the world of work.

Although headlines often exaggerate the impact of technology by announcing that large numbers of people will be out of jobs, we find the 2017 McKinsey Global Institute (MGI) reports to present a balanced view across sectors of the economy and countries. Their analysis indicates that one-half of work activities globally have the *potential* to be automated using *current* technology, which obviously varies across sectors of the economy and among occupations within those sectors, but that fewer than 5 percent of occupations can be automated entirely (Manyika et al., 2017). Put another way, about 60 percent of jobs have at least 30 percent automatable activities, translating to automation replacing 9 to 26 percent of work hours. So, for example, healthcare occupations are not likely to disappear, but technology will help medical practitioners in new ways.

So, while only 3 to 14 percent of the global workforce will need to switch occupations, the majority of other workers will have to adapt by upskilling. The good news, however, is that these workers will spend more time on activities that are difficult to automate and that many will find more rewarding and fulfilling—creativity, high-level cognitive capacities, and activities that require social-emotional skills (discussed in more detail in chapter 2).

Lest panic set in, however, these MGI reports clearly articulate that the proportion of work that will *actually* be displaced by 2030 will likely be lower because of technical, economic, and social factors that affect adoption. This is how they describe the current and future state:

> Automation will not happen overnight, and five key factors will influence the pace and extent of its adoption. First is technical feasibility, since the technology has to be invented, integrated and adapted into solutions that automate specific activities. Second is the cost of developing and deploying solutions, which affects the business case for adoption. Third are labor market dynamics, including the supply, demand, and costs of human labor as an alternative to automation. Fourth are economic benefits, which could include higher throughput and increased quality, as well as labor cost savings. Finally, regulatory and social acceptance can affect the rate of adoption even when deployment makes business sense. Taking all of these factors into account, we estimate it will take decades for automation's effect on the current work activities to play out fully. (Manyika et al., 2017, p. 2)

It is worth noting that, historically, while technological changes have always wiped out jobs and occupations, they have also always created far more new jobs, which is likely to continue to happen (Paul, 2018; Stewart, De, & Cole, 2015). For those of us in higher education, this means working with employers to anticipate new job frontiers. According to the World Economic Forum (2016, p. 1), "65 percent of children entering primary school today will ultimately end up working in completely new jobs that don't yet exist." Further, new technologies do not immediately impact all work environments in the same way or at the same pace. Consequently, the integration of new technologies will vary across industries and workplace impact will be much more like an evolution rather than a "big bang." Nevertheless, preparation for the changing nature of work is something that cannot be underestimated. In an interview on Charlie Rose's PBS show, Friedman captured the kind of impact this will have when he said the "social contract of the future" between companies and employees is "you can be a lifelong employee, but only if you're a lifelong learner" (Falzon, 2016, para. 5).

While the direct impact of technology alone is relevant, so too is its indirect impact in reshaping the global community. New technologies have enabled a myriad of connections and interconnections to develop, crossing borders and opening up new opportunities, resulting in competition and challenges to economies, regulators, politics, and workers.

Globalization. Since Thomas Friedman made famous the phrase "the world is flat" in his 2005 book of the same name, it has become increasingly clear that physical and geographical boundaries no longer matter in the world of work—the playing field has been leveled and the interdependencies have become more pronounced (Friedman, 2005). Through expanded developments in communication and shipping, the free flow of goods and services across the globe has flourished. These new means of connectivity have resulted in an expanded number of places and people participating in the world's economy. This has several consequences, including an increase in job competition for our graduates (e.g., young people in remote villages with bandwidth can compete for jobs around the world) and an increasing need to be culturally agile with the ability to understand, communicate, and work with people from around the globe, which is where higher education enters the picture.

According to the *Financial Times*, "cultural agility is the ability to understand multiple local contexts and work within them to obtain consistent business results" (Financial Times, n.d., para. 1). Paula Caligiuri tells us that "cultural agility is a practice, not an achievement, and building it is a process, not an event" (Caligiuri, 2012, p. 5). It requires the ability to (1) question our own cultural assumptions, values, and beliefs, (2) view the world from other perspectives, (3) recognize differences among cultures (e.g., communication styles, relationships, personal space, power dynamics, decision making, role of individual and group), and (4) respond accordingly. Depending on the situation and context, response may mean adapting (e.g., to the buyer's culture, to the need for greater autonomy for workers in some cases and direct leadership in others), holding firm to the standards of your company (e.g., safety, ethics), or integrating (e.g., coming up with a new approach), and leveraging the appropriate response at the right time is key to success (Caligiuri, 2012).

Because interest, curiosity, and openness are key to cultural agility, both traveling outside of one's country and learning another language can help to develop and hone this important set of skills. The good news is that the number of U.S. citizens with passports has been increasing—from 15 percent in 1997 to 27 percent in 2007 to 42 percent in 2017, although many believe the uptick since 2007 is the result of a change in U.S. law, which now requires a passport for Americans traveling to Canada, Mexico, the Caribbean, Bermuda, and Central and South America (McCarthy, 2018). For comparison purposes, 66 percent of Canadian citizens have passports and 76 percent of UK citizens as of 2016 (McCarthy, 2018). In November 2018, the Institute of International Education reported that the number of students studying abroad is still increasing, which is promising, although the number is not very impressive; they estimate that about 16 percent of American students earning a bachelor's degree will study abroad at some point during their undergraduate years (Redden, 2018). Additionally, given students' use of social media, they remain closely connected to their home communities, further eroding the benefits of immersion in another culture.

The data on passports are far better than those on Americans with second language skills. According to a 2013 survey, "three-quarters of Americans speak only their mother tongue" (Palmer, 2013, para. 1). In comparison, in 2014, some 54 percent of Europeans were able to hold a conversation in at least one additional language, 25 percent could do so in at least two additional languages, and 10 percent were conversant in at least three (Nardelli, 2014).

Interestingly enough, according to research by Lu et al., at MIT (2017), while working and living abroad might be helpful, that is not as powerful as having close relationships (both romantic and friendships) with people from a different culture, which can happen even if students do not travel abroad. Caligiuri (2012) agrees that working and even living abroad can create an inaccurate assumption that the person has been fully immersed in the culture, which we know is not the case given that many live in expatriate communities, send their children to international schools, and join international clubs, for example. The MIT researchers have found that close relationships lead to higher creativity, innovation, and entrepreneurship because they result in "cultural learning at a deep level" (Lu et al., 2017, p. 1104).

42

Although recent developments with Brexit and the election of Donald Trump on a platform of isolationism and protectionism have suggested a potential retreat by major economic powers from globalization, leading economists are not inclined to signal that globalization is in reverse (Ghemawat, 2017).

Changing Nature of Organizations. It is not only globalization that has changed the employment landscape, but also changes in the nature of organizations responding to a variety of converging forces, including the rise of the gig economy (see the next section), the desire for more flexibility in the workplace, and the need to address increasing complexity in the world.

We are increasingly seeing a transition of organizations into agile ways of working, including moving from "rigid command and control structures" to organizing around short-term and ever-changing project and skills workgroups, discussed in General Stanley McChyrstal's book *Team of Teams: New Rules of Engagement for a Complex World* (McChrystal, Siverman, Collins, & Fussell, 2015). He asserts that F. W. Taylor's *The Principles of Scientific Management* (1911)—which "drew a hard-and-fast line between thought and action: managers did the thinking and planning, while workers executed"—drove enterprises, for 150 years, to a commitment to efficiency and reductionist planning that simply does not make sense in today's world (McChrystal et al., 2015, p. 42). This epiphany happened for McChyrstal when he took over command of the Joint Special Operations Task Force in 2003 and recognized that though our military was stronger, more efficient, and more robust, Al Qaeda was agile and resilient, and more successful! In his words:

> We had to tear down familiar organizational structures and rebuild them along completely different lines, swapping our sturdy architecture for organic fluidity . . . we restructured our force from the ground up on principles of extremely

transparent information sharing (what we call "shared consciousness") and decentralized decision-making ("empowered execution"). We dissolved the barriers—the walls of our silos and the floors of our hierarchies—that had once made us efficient . . . We became what we called "a team of teams": a large command that captured at scale the traits of agility normally limited to small teams. Almost everything we did ran against the grain of military tradition and of general organizational practice. We abandoned many of the precepts that had helped establish our efficacy in the twentieth century, because the twenty-first century is a different game with different rules. Adaptability, not efficiency, must become our central competency. (McChrystal et al., 2015, p. 20)

So, what does this have to do with the changing nature of organizations beyond the military? They too, live in a world that has moved from complicated to complex: complicated defined as things that "have many parts, but those parts are joined, one to the next, in relatively simple ways . . ." and complexity defined as "a diverse array of connected elements that interact frequently," with the density of linkages resulting in extreme fluctuations and unpredictability (McChrystal et al., 2015, pp. 56–57). According to the 2018 Deloitte Global Human Capital Trends, companies are responding by becoming more team-centric, networked, and agile (Agarwal, Bersin, Lahiri, Schwartz, & Volini, 2018). McChyrstal provides examples outside the military, including NASA's movement to embrace complexity through systems engineering/systems management, an approach built on systems thinking, as well as Boeing and Ford (at a time—2009—when GM and Chrysler were filing for bankruptcy) (McChrystal et al., 2015). These "early adopters" of a new approach embraced such notions as collaboration, transparency, and trust by breaking down silos, sharing information, building relationships across teams, promoting cooperative adaptability, and ensuring a holistic understanding among all the moving parts.

At this point in time, many organizations are talking about new ways to organize and distribute work both within and across organizations, including, for example, distributed and interdisciplinary teams and networks (National Academies of Sciences, Engineering and Medicine, 2017) and reduced hierarchical structures and decision authority (Heerwagen, Kelly, & Kampschroer, 2016). For example, Walmart and Target have been focusing on "taming" their respective bureaucracies, with Walmart giving its workers "more say in how their store operates and what it stocks" (Wahba, 2015, para. 8). Zappos has gone even further by embracing holacracy (Zappos, n.d., para. 1) (defined as "a new way of structuring and running your organization that replaces the conventional management hierarchy. Instead of operating top-down, power is distributed throughout the organization, giving individuals and teams more freedom to self-manage, while staying aligned to the organization's purpose" (HolacracyOne LLC, n.d., para. 1). Deloitte is calling for more cross-functional collaboration as well, including in the C-suite (they call this a symphonic C-suite), invoking the team of team's approach described by McChrystal (Agarwal et al., 2018).

Agility has also become increasingly important in the business world, typically defined as the ability to respond to change quickly, without losing momentum. Spotify and Netflix are among companies "born agile," while companies like Amazon, USAA, 3M, and Bosch are embracing the agile approach (Rigby, Sutherland, & Noble, 2018) and launching dozens of teams. National Public Radio, John Deere, Intronis, and Mission Bell Winery are doing so as well (Rigby, Sutherland, & Takeuchi, 2016). After studying the scaling up of agile at hundreds of companies, Rigby and colleagues (p. 40) report that "companies can scale up agile effectively and that doing so creates substantial benefits" in terms of productivity, morale, faster time to market, better quality, and lower risk, but it is important to know which functions will benefit from being agile. As Cappelli and Tavis (2018) indicate, the agile approach has finally moved from tech to product development, manufacturing, marketing, and human resources.

Along with agility, many organizations are looking to also address employees' desire for flexibility in a variety of ways. A 2017 Gallup survey found that the number of employees working remotely rose from 39 percent in 2012 to 43 percent in 2016, and that those "employees working remotely spent more time doing so" (Mann & Adkins, 2017, p. 4). For those millennials working full time, an increasing number indicate they already have some degree of flexibility in their workplace; a recent Deloitte report indicates that 84 percent of millennials surveyed cite this reality (Deloitte University Press, 2017). This appears to be a trend as well in the world of work, given that flexibility can increase morale, broaden the talent pool, breed loyalty, and increase satisfaction (Biro, 2013). The Gallup survey also reports that 51 percent of U.S. employees are "actively looking for a new job or watching for openings" (Mann & Adkins, 2017, p. 14) and reinforces that the top five reasons people leave their jobs voluntarily are career growth opportunities, pay and benefits, manager or management, company culture, and job fit. Company culture (e.g., embracing flexibility, agility) can play a large part in losing potentially talented employees. At Zapier, a company with 170 employees living and working in dozens of states and countries, they build relationships across the organization in a variety of ways to "re-create the watercooler," including a bot that "pairs up two random people each week to do a call, so employees across the organization can get to know one other," themed internal channels that are not work related (e.g., gardening, World Cup, homeownership, movies), and remote dance parties (Belanger, 2018, para. 19–23). Creating some kind of organizational response to adapt to the changing nature of work will become increasingly important to attract and retain employees.

The Rise of the Gig Economy. Some of this change in organizational structure is the result of the nature of project-based work aligning with the interest of young people to engage in the gig economy as freelance and contract workers. This agile talent is also often more cost-effective for companies, and it allows continued new creative energy to enter the organization and provides access to difficult-to-find technical or functional expertise (Younger, 2016). According to the 5th Annual Guardian Workplace Benefits study, some 40 million adults are already engaged in the gig economy, representing nearly 25 percent of the total working population (Guardian Life Insurance, 2017); Deloitte puts the number of people engaged in contingent, part-time, or gig work at 40 percent (Agarwa et al., 2018). And the Guardian survey indicates that 31 percent of employers responding said that they expect to increase their agile workforce (part-time and contingent workers) over the next few years (Guardian Life Insurance, 2017).

Millennials, too, are embracing the gig economy concept, as indicated by the 2018 Deloitte Millennial Survey: "Among those millennials who would willingly leave their employers within the next two years, 62 percent regard the gig economy as a viable alternative to full-time employment . . ." (Deloitte, 2018, p. 20). This sentiment also rings true for millennials in senior management positions: 7 in 10 of those employees report that they would "take on short-term contracts or freelance work as an alternative to full time employment" (Deloitte, 2018, p. 20). These respondents find the gig economy attractive because of its ability to provide increased income, flexibility, and freedom.

Increasingly Diverse Workplaces. The demographics of the workforce will also continue to change the world of work as the workforce becomes more diverse across cultural and generational lines. In 2017, there were 56 million millennials, 53 million Gen Xers, and 41 million baby boomers in the workforce

(Fry, 2018). This dynamic will likely continue for a while, given that "more than 40 percent of households headed by people aged 55 through 70 lack sufficient resources to maintain their living standard in retirement," translating to approximately 15 million households (Gillers, Tergesen, & Scism, 2018, para. 4). Currently, nearly 20 percent of Americans 65 and older are employed in regular jobs (Desilver, 2016). Add to this dynamic the projection that the length of career is expected to expand to 60–70 years, and we will continue to see a multigenerational workforce with all its implications (Gratton & Scott, 2017).

These changing demographics have many implications for the world of work. For example, millennials and Gen Z employees continue to want to work for employers who are focused on improving society and the environment; innovating ideas, products, and services; being inclusive and diverse in the workplace; and providing flexibility (Deloitte, 2018). Smart employers understand these desires and are creating strategies to attract top talent by making learning and development a top priority, establishing an agile workforce strategy, preparing for the demographic shifts, and evolving their organizational culture, among other things (Deloitte University Press, 2017; Guardian Life Insurance, 2017).

Furthermore, according to Irving (2018), though more Americans over 65 will not be retiring, many companies have not prepared for this demographic. In fact, some view it as a crisis rather than an opportunity, not appreciating that these workers' talents "complement those of younger workers . . . they provide emotional stability, complex problem-solving skills, nuanced thinking, and institutional know-how" (Irving, 2018, para. 6). Based on research from the Milken Institute Center for the Future of Aging at Harvard University, Irving has developed a "longevity strategy" to help companies "create a vibrant multigenerational workforce" (Irving, 2018, para. 8). Researchers at the Stanford Center on Longevity could not agree more:

[T]ypical 60-something workers today are healthy, experienced, and more likely than younger colleagues to be satisfied with their jobs. They have a strong work ethic and loyalty to their employers. They are motivated, knowledgeable, adept at resolving social dilemmas, and care more about meaningful contributions and less about self-advancement. They are more likely than their younger counterparts to build social cohesion and to share information and organizational values. (Irving, 2018, para. 11)

There are many benefits to working in a multigenerational and multicultural workplace. The different life experiences and varying knowledge and skill sets can lead to broader perspectives that may result in new approaches to solving a problem, designing a product or service, and building capacity to lead. A 2011 study of some of the largest U.S. employers conducted by the Sloan Center of Aging at Boston College found multiple benefits for both employers and employees in multigenerational settings. Employer benefits included (a) increased and diversified work experiences, (b) retention, and (c) increased feelings of company loyalty, sense of value, motivation, and team spirit. Increased sales and profitability were noted along with improved customer service, business savings, and organizational reputation as being among the company benefits they cite (Roundtree, 2011). A 2016 study done by McDonald's UK Division found that multigenerational teams were 10 percent happier than same-age teams. One might speculate that happier workers are more motivated and productive (Gartner, 2016; McDonald's Corporation UK, 2016).

Some companies like CVS, The National Institutes of Health, Steelcase, Home Depot, and Michelin have begun to recognize and leverage the value of older employees by offering, among other things, flexible schedules, seasonal work, rehiring retirees, telecommuting, and phased retirement. Other companies like Xerox, BMW, and Nissan have adjusted physical workspaces

49

to accommodate the aging population of workers. Still others, like PNC Financial Group, Airbnb, and Pfizer, are focusing on intergenerational collaboration, including intentional multigenerational teams and pairings, along with intergenerational mentoring (Irving, 2018).

The presence of multiple generations creates a richer environment within which a broader collection of skill sets is available that can lead to greater creativity and innovation. In fact, the opportunity to create mutual mentorship programs, wherein team members of different generations might be intentionally paired with the goal of each learning and/or mentoring the other in some way, is presenting new opportunities for employee development. As one executive at a digital design firm observed, "Business is much more than trends and technology. It's applied intuition that takes years of experience to develop" (Gay, 2017, para. 11).

Employer View of the Future. All of the changes just discussed lead employers to ask how to prepare for, lead, and manage in a world summed up in the "trendy managerial acronym" (discussed more in chapter 2) VUCA: volatility, uncertainty, complexity, and ambiguity (Bennett & Lemoine, 2014). How does one hire employees who can function effectively in this environment? What will it take to ensure that current employees can "get up to speed" as the roles and skills they (and the organization) need to be successful continually change around them? And how can employers keep talent who are drawn to the gig economy (when that makes sense for the organization)?

Rethinking the hiring process is vital, and unfortunately those doing research in this area do not believe that most employers have yet acted on this reality (Chamorro-Premuzic & Swan, 2016). The employers who are actively changing their strategies are, in fact, hiring for "learnability," defined as "curious and inquisitive individuals who are genuinely interested in acquiring new knowledge" (Chamorro-Premuzic & Swan, 2016, para.

7). For example, a major pillar in Google's recruitment strategy is to hire "versatile learning animals" who thrive on continuous learning because "when you're in a dynamic industry where the conditions are changing so fast, then things like experience and the way you've done a role before isn't nearly as important as your ability to think" (Schmidt & Rosenberg, 2014, para. 9). According to Business Insider, "smart companies are now asking the bigger question in interviews, 'How are you keeping your ability to learn new things up, now that school is over?'" (O'Donnell Inc., 2016, para. 5). Ernst and Young recruiters say that "to be a standout, candidates need to demonstrate technical knowledge in their discipline, but also a passion for asking the kind of insightful questions that have the power to unlock deeper insights and innovation for our clients" (Chamorro-Premuzic & Swan, 2016, para. 3).

Along with changing the hiring process, we must address the short shelf life of knowledge and skills with current employees, whether through internal learning and development programs or partnerships with colleges and universities. In this new world, learning becomes a continuous need. A recent McKinsey survey reports that executives see "investing in retraining and 'upskilling' existing workers as an urgent business priority" (Illanes, Lund, Mourshed, Rutherford, & Tyreman, 2018, para. 1). Unfortunately, research indicates that "despite spending approximately $164.2 billion on learning and development programs, many executives still grapple with how to improve and enhance their effectiveness" (Ferrazzi, 2015, para. 2). According to the Association for Talent Development's "State of Industry Report," this translates, on average, to companies spending $1,252 per employee on training and development in 2015, which represents an increase every year since 2010 (Association for Talent Development, 2016).

There are those who are also focusing on how learning and development needs to change within organizations. One BCG Henderson Institute report recommends that

51

CEOs should initiate what we call "learning in the work-flow," and these efforts must be adaptive and personalized to individual users and their specific needs, always-on, with real-time support and feedback, "gamified" with social elements that create "learner pull" to encourage learners to participate, measurable, translating to outcomes for both the learners and for the enterprise. (Dyer, Barybkina, Erker, & Sullivan, 2018, para. 10)

Dyer and colleagues also suggest that it is imperative for organizations to create new learning ecosystems where, among other things, learning becomes experiential as knowledge and skills are developed on the job and where managers must "transform from taskmasters to learning coaches" (2018, para. 25).

The good news for employers is that they do not need (nor do they have the capability, expertise, and so forth) to address all of the learning requirements of their employees. They have begun to recognize this and are increasingly partnering with colleges and universities in new and unique ways. For example, General Electric has partnered with Northeastern University to provide an accelerated Advanced Manufacturing degree, which is delivered in a hybrid way at GE facilities and online (Krantz, 2016). In 2014, Georgia Tech pioneered an online master's degree in computer science in collaboration with AT&T, who made a $2 million investment to help launch the low-cost program. By spring 2018, more than 6,300 students were enrolled in the program. Given the success of the initiative, AT&T and Accenture collaborated with Georgia Tech to launch another online master's degree in analytics, another emergent area where talent is needed (McKenzie, 2018). Motorola partnered with Northwestern University to enhance its leadership development, and Caterpillar Manufacturing maintains relationships with Bradley University, University of Illinois, Georgia Institute of Technology, Purdue, and others (Rio, 2018).

These emerging partnerships, designed to enhance employee skills and develop workforce pipelines, are also expanding in technical and vocational programs. For example, Bluegrass Community and Technical College and Toyota developed an Advanced Manufacturing Technician Program, where students receive an associate's degree by taking their classes in the Toyota manufacturing plant (Martin & Samels, 2015). These examples represent the variety of learners with diverse needs and life situations.

All of these factors in the radically changing employment landscape should impact how we design education for the future, as should the diversity of learners and needs, discussed in the next section.

EXPANDING LEARNER BASE AND CHANGING LEARNER NEEDS

If higher education is going to remain relevant and be successful in the future, we need to clearly understand and address the diverse learners' needs as they continue to learn, develop, and grow across their lives. The main groups—which themselves are not homogeneous—include traditional-age college students and the post-traditional and lifelong learners.

A simple review of the most recent statistics from the National Center for Educational Statistics (NCES) shows significant shifts in the demographics of those enrolled and projected to enroll in postsecondary institutions of all kinds (2- and 4-year, public, private, profit, nonprofit). There has been an increase in the number of women, Hispanics, and African Americans since 2000, with a projected increase of 25 percent for Hispanics and 34 percent for African Americans by 2023 (Hussar & Bailey, 2016).

It is no secret that the only constant for "traditional" college students is that they are 18–24 years old. Like all generations before them, the millennial and Gen Z learners are unique in their own ways, as will be those who come after them. It behooves those of us in higher education to understand the ideals, values, desires, and needs of this population, because they have been shaped by the environment in which they grew up, one that is vastly different from those of us responsible for their continued learning, growth, and development.

There is also another large and diverse group of "post-traditional" learners who will need continual learning throughout their lives and careers in order to stay active in the labor market (Soares, 2013). Some of these people have already earned a credential or degree, some have credits toward a credential but no credential, and others have nothing beyond a high school diploma. The latter group numbers about 80 million (ages 25 through 65) (Blumenstyk, 2018a; Selingo, n.d.). In a report completed by the American Council on Education and based on data from the National Postsecondary Student Aid Study (2011–2012), they state "post-traditional learners have been a consistent and significant presence in higher education, making up close to 60 percent of the undergraduate population in each of the previous three years of the study" (Soares & Gagliardi, 2017, p. 11). Of course, given the discussion earlier in the chapter, everyone in the workforce will become a post-traditional and lifelong learner at some point(s) in their lives and careers. Our responses to successfully educate future learners will have to take many forms depending on their different needs and life situations.

Traditional Learners. Many forces have shaped the current and upcoming college population, among them the post-9/11 world, school shootings, climate change, recession, social media, marriage equality, and the first black U.S. president. All of these forces combined result in college students who have had the world at their fingertips (for better *and* worse) through increasingly sophisticated technologies, and yet come from a secondary school system that, for many, has not fostered curiosity, creativity, or innovation, let alone the reading, writing, problem-solving, and computing skills colleges and universities expect incoming students to possess.

The most recent national data from the University of California, Los Angeles Cooperative Institutional Research Program (CIRP) survey, administered each fall to incoming freshmen across the nation, shows changes in both beliefs and behaviors (Eagan, et al., 2017). For example, the 2016 incoming class indicated rising levels of civic engagement as well as being the most politically polarized cohort "in the 51-year history of the Freshmen Survey" (Eagan et al., 2017, p. 4). We also see in these students an increased concern about global climate change, interest in influencing the political structure, desire to address the world's grand challenges (e.g., poverty, clean water, race relations), commitment to maintain a work–life balance, and belief that they possess a pluralistic orientation, which includes the ability to see the world from someone else's perspective (almost 80 percent) and a tolerance of others with different beliefs (almost 80 percent). These socially, environmentally, and politically conscious learners have multiple interests and are already changing the nature of the way colleges and universities operate, for example, by (a) pushing against disciplinary boundaries, (b) eschewing learning as listening/being lectured to, (c) demanding more connection to the real world during their course of study, (d) wanting to design their own programs of study, and (e) yearning for opportunities to learn about entrepreneurship. And despite the presence of technology in their lives, one survey indicates that only 15 percent of Gen Zs prefer social media to in-person interactions with friends (Northeastern University News, 2014).

Gen Z, often referred to as iGen, like other generations before them, have some very interesting characteristics, beliefs, and attitudes that impact their behavior. Jean M. Twenge (2017) identifies iGens as those born between 1995 and 2012 and has studied them extensively by drawing on four longitudinal survey databases in order to examine changes among the different generations over time. This generation, representing 24 percent of the population (some 74 million), is the most ethnically diverse in American history and is already having an impact on higher education given that iGens began to arrive at college a few years ago. The 10 trends that Twenge's research indicates are shaping these young people (with both positive and negative repercussions) include that they

· are in no hurry to grow up, and they embrace their parents' overprotection,
· spend more time online and texting,
· spend less time face to face with friends and thus do not hone in-person social skills,
· are experiencing more mental health issues (discussed in more detail below),
· are being raised in nonreligious households,
· are risk averse given their desire for safety, including not just physical but also intellectual, social, and emotional risks,
· are practical in terms of work and income and less interested in entrepreneurship (unlike the millennials, who want jobs that are interesting and want to follow their dreams),
· possess cautious attitudes toward relationships and do not prioritize marriage and family,
· are inclusive, and
· are politically independent. (Twenge, 2017)

What impact are they already having on higher education? iGens (a) are less interested in the amenities discussed earlier in the chapter (e.g., climbing walls, lazy rivers, movie theaters) and more interested in safe spaces and trigger warnings, (b) want hands-on and job relevant educational experiences, (c) want to be treated as individuals, (d) have less experience with alcohol and sex, (e) fear failure, (f) crave face-to-face communication, (g) are less confident and entitled, (h) are more hesitant to talk in class, (i) are afraid to make mistakes, (j) have a strong work ethic, (k) are less independent and want more guidance, and (l) come to college to get a better job and make money, not necessarily to improve their minds (Pappano, 2018; Twenge, 2017).

As mentioned earlier, along with the impressive interests and vast opportunities in front of current traditional-aged students comes increasing stress. According to the American College Health Association, in spring 2018, 87 percent of students reported feeling overwhelmed, 63 percent reported feeling lonely, and more than 80 percent reported feeling exhausted at times (American College Health Association, 2018). The Center for Collegiate Mental Health (2019) tells us that anxiety and depression levels are also on the rise and are taking a toll on students' well-being. And longitudinal data from the CIRP survey indicates a concerning trend, as self-rated emotional health of college freshmen has steadily declined from 1985 to 2015 (Eagan et al., 2017). One source of that stress may very well be that college students are increasingly gravely concerned about their ability to pay for college and the debt they will incur. Over half (55.9 percent) of 2016 CIRP respondents who were incoming students had "some concern about their ability to finance college while 13.3 percent report that they have major concerns about their ability to finance college" (Eagan et al., 2017, p. 7).

Sadly, the picture does not look any better when you consider the next generation coming to college. According to the National Alliance on Mental Illness, citing data from the National Institute of Mental Health, 20 percent of youth ages 13 to 18 are living with a mental health condition, 11 percent have a mood disorder, and 8 percent have an anxiety disorder (National Alliance on Mental Illness, 2019). Although every generation has its shared stressors,

57

some are unique to the digital natives, particularly the stressors connected to social media. For example, some young people report anxiety about clogging their friends' feeds with a barrage of low-quality pictures that might annoy them, not having the right caption for Instagram photos, and not getting enough likes on their posts (which leads them to delete the post before embarrassment sets in) (Dougherty, 2016). Others in certain socioeconomic groups find the continual scheduling of school, homework, sports practices, band rehearsals, tournaments, and so forth exhausting and stressful, especially because "[e]ach activity is seen as a step on the ladder to a top college, an enviable job and a successful life" (Abeles, 2016, para. 5). In a 2013 study by the American Psychological Association, one in three teenagers reported that "stress drove them to sadness or depression—and their single biggest source of stress was school" (Abeles, 2016, para. 7). This phenomenon becomes increasingly concerning as "A growing body of medical evidence suggests that long-term stress is linked not only with a higher risk of adult depression and anxiety, but with poor physical health outcomes as well" (Abeles, 2016, para. 12).

In August 2018, the American Psychological Association launched its 12th annual "Stress in America" survey and found, not surprisingly, that for young Gen Zs gun violence is a significant source of stress—especially school and mass shootings—along with the political climate, the state of the nation, and their family's financial well-being. Overall, the report found that stress generally is very high across all generational age groups, and while money and work have typically topped the list, this most recent survey placed "future of the nation" at the top of the list for the first time (American Psychological Association, 2018).

Obviously these mental and emotional states are a cause for concern and impact the learning, growth, and development of traditional-aged college students, hence the need for a more holistic, integrated, and student-centered approach to higher education.

As we think about what learners need (chapter 2) and how we design educational experiences to meet those needs (chapter 3), we have to keep in mind the characteristics of these traditional-aged college students.

Post-traditional and Lifelong Learners. Besides the traditional-aged learners who will continue to enroll in colleges and universities, tens of millions of adults will be driven by the demands of the economy as well as their own ambitions to engage in further/continued learning. This population is diverse in terms of their motives and life situations, but "finances, family obligations, and even fear can keep them from college" (Blumenstyk, 2018a). This population will continue to grow as the world of work continues to change and as the high school population decreases in coming decades (projected to decrease between 2026 and 2031 by 9 percent, or some 280,000 students) (Field, Fischer, Young, & Selingo, 2018).

This group of post-traditional learners includes (a) 63.9 million adults between the ages of 25 and 64 who have never pursued any type of higher education (Lumina Foundation, 2017), (b) 31 million adults (as of 2014) with some college and no degree (Shapiro et al., 2014), (c) career enhancers who recognize the need for upskilling, and (d) career switchers who either "see the writing on the wall" per the technological impact on their job role and responsibilities or simply decide to move in a new direction.

For those who never pursued a college education, the news continues to be dire. According to Pew Research Center (2014, para. 20), there has been a "dramatic decline in the value of a high school education ... the typical high school graduate's earnings fell by more than $3,000, from $31,384 in 1965 to $28,000 in 2013." This drop in real dollars is considerably worse when adjusted for inflation between the two years.

According to the National Student Clearinghouse Research Center, among the 31 million *some college-no degree population* are

59

learners who have stopped out, enrolled part time, enrolled as adults (not college age), and enrolled at multiple institutions (Shapiro et al., 2014). This heterogeneous group includes, for example, learners who have two or more years' worth of college experience, those who have enough credits for an associate's degree but do not have the degree, those who attended 2-year institutions exclusively, and those who attended two or more institutions during their educational journey. In other words, the enrollment pathways of this population vary significantly. The majority of multiple-term enrollees are between 24 and 29 years of old, and women are represented more than men in the 30-years-or-older cohorts (Shapiro et al., 2014). We know that completing a degree will impact this population's financial situation, including salary as well as in employer health insurance and pension coverage (Shapiro et al., 2014). In fact, "college graduates with a bachelor's degree typically earn 66 percent more than those with only a high school diploma" and "over the course of a lifetime . . . earn approximately $1 million more . . ." (U.S. Department of Education, 2015, para. 3).

These first two groups (no higher education at all and some college–no degree) have become increasingly visible through the agendas of state governments, multiple foundations, and new organizations as well as new institutions and older universities and colleges that focus specifically on adult learners. This is why the Institute for Higher Education Policy (IHEP), along with the Lumina, Kresge, and ECMC foundations and Great Lakes Higher Education Corporation & Affiliates, has launched (in 2018) a campaign to help colleges and universities with what it calls "degree reclamation" (in the past referred to as "reverse transfer"). This campaign will focus on helping those who have earned enough credits but who do not have a degree to obtain the degree and, for those who are a few credits short of earning a degree, work toward helping them complete those final courses (Blumenstyk, 2018b). This $5.8 million initiative will "train college officials—teams of registrars, marketers, institutional researchers, advisers and IT experts—in the skills they will need to identify and counsel students eligible to earn a reclaimed degree or return for their final credits" (Blumenstyk, 2018b, para. 7). A lot of data exist for these 31 million people, data that college and universities will find enlightening as we think about the future of higher education. For example, the New Jersey legislature recently voted to make reverse transfer a statewide policy, as have other states, according to the Education Commission of the States (Blumenstyk, 2018b; Education Commission of the States, 2018). The Lumina Foundation's goal is to increase "the proportion of Americans with high-quality degrees, certificates and other credentials to 60 percent by 2025," and their strategic plan includes increasing attainment for *returning adult students* by 2 million by 2020 and increasing by 3.4 million *adults with no recognized postsecondary education* (Lumina Foundation, 2017, pp. 3-4). The Bill & Melinda Gates Foundation has invested nearly $4 billion since 2000 to "improve high school graduation and college readiness rates, and expanding access to college" (Bill & Melinda Gates Foundation, 2008, para. 13).

Both new and existing universities also support adult learners. For example, College Unbound, founded in 2009, is designed for adults who want to *reenter* college and earn a degree. Their strategy is that "the academic content and instruction build on earlier studies and life experience" (College Unbound, n.d., para. 1). Thomas Edison State University has served the needs of adults since 1972 (Thomas Edison State University, n.d.), as have universities like University of Maryland University College, which was founded to serve adults more than 70 years ago (University of Maryland, n.d.), and Brandman University, which spun off from Chapman University in 2009 and now focuses on adult learners. Furthermore, the Tennessee Reconnect program provides adults over the age of 25 with free tuition (and no fees) at community college for those interested in earning an associate's degree or a technical certificate (Gonzalez, 2018). Complementing these programs are new advocacy groups that have emerged recently to promote the agenda of adult learners, including the National Adult Learner Coalition (UPCEA, n.d.), Higher Learning Advocates (Higher Learning Advocates, n.d.), and the Council for Adult and Experiential Learning (CAEL, n.d.).

The other two groups that comprise post-traditional learners are the career enhancers and career switchers, who seek to move either horizontally or vertically in their current job or change to another career. McKinsey Global Institute estimates that, by 2030, some 14 percent of the global workforce (about 375 million) "will likely need to transition to new occupational categories and learn new skills" (Manyika et al., 2017, p. 1).

The *enhancers* will need to identify specific skills and knowledge that they lack and look for educational opportunities that align with their needs, finances, and life situations. In a Pew Research Center (2016) survey, 87 percent of employees responding believed that it will be necessary for them to develop new skills throughout their career in order to keep up with ongoing changes in their job and industry. Current graduates also recognize the reality; Accenture reports that 97 percent of 2017 graduates said they will need on-the-job training to further their careers (Lyons, Lavelle, & Smith, 2017). In fact,

> Millennials and Generation Z have a different view of workplace learning. They understand more than the rest of us that rapid and discontinuous change in products, services and ways of working mean that life-long learning is a critical element of the workplace. Deloitte points out that for millennial professionals, ongoing development support trumps all other "benefits." (Younger, 2016, para. 8)

As we discussed in earlier sections, if 60 percent of jobs have at least 30 percent of automatable activities per tasks that are repetitive, mundane, and rote, the numbers of those needing continual education will not be small.

Lest we think that continuous learning is important only for employees generally, Risto Siilasmaa, the chairman of Nokia, explains in a piece he wrote for the Harvard Business Review why and how he engaged in gaining a basic understanding of machine learning as well as ensuring that every employee has the same basic knowledge. According to Siilasmaa,

> . . . as a longtime CEO and Chairman, I had fallen into the trap of being defined by my role: I had grown accustomed to having things explained to me. Instead of trying to figure out the nuts and bolts of a seemingly complicated technology, I had gotten used to someone else doing the heavy lifting. Why not study machine learning myself and then explain what I learned to others who were struggling with the same questions? That might help them and raise the profile of machine learning in Nokia at the same time. (Siilasmaa, 2018, para. 3)

While Siiasmaa turned to a series of massive open online courses (MOOCs) on machine learning, deep learning, and convolutional neural networks, followed by extensive reading on the topics, McKinsey research indicates that chief executive officers' primary methods of continual learning include turning to peers outside their company; engaging mentors who have experience; and gaining, practicing, and embedding new skills intentionally (Dotiwala & Kumra, 2014). These practices, particularly turning to peers and mentors, may be outdated given the fast pace of change in the world, which means these individuals may not have the requisite experience to share.

Understanding *career switchers* might be difficult, because the Bureau of Labor Statistics (within the U.S. Department of Labor) does not report on how often people change careers or how many different jobs individuals have over the course of their work life (despite data we often see cited in the popular press). So, we have no historical data to work from. We do have data, however, from various surveys that ask the question of current employees from which to work. For example, a Harris Interactive Survey reported in 2013 that "[n]early 80 percent of workers in their 20s said they wanted to change careers, followed by 64 percent of 30-somethings and 54 percent in their 40s" (Reaney, 2013, para. 5). More recently, a survey by the University of Phoenix (2017, para. 1) indicated that 58 percent of working adults were "somewhat interested" in a career change. Given both the interest these surveys indicate and the data we cited earlier in the chapter about the impact of technology on the world of work, we need to anticipate and prepare for this group as well. Some universities have already begun to address the needs of career switchers. In fact, the state of Virginia has aligned this reality with their needs, creating the Virginia Career Switcher Alternative Route to Licensure Program, which recognizes and builds on the life experience of these individuals and prepares them for a teaching career in the state (Virginia Department of Education, n.d.).

What we do know about *older* post-traditional learners in general, despite which of the four categories they fall into, is that their continued education and training must look different from that of younger workers given such things as their life experience and life commitments. Shih, Rudnick, and Tapen (2018) recommend shorter work-based programs, stackable credentials, wraparound support, and maybe most importantly, helping older learners recognize their potential as they often underestimate what their capabilities are.

Recognizing and embracing the needs of these diverse learners is both an imperative and an opportunity for higher education. But it means that we must do some things radically different, which is no small order for a system steeped in tradition.

CONCLUSION

The belief persists that postsecondary education provides a promising path to the middle class and can also provide an opportunity for individuals in pursuit of career advancement at any stage of life. The link between work, success, and education is a well-worn path that has been traveled by an expanding and diversifying demographic over the history of American higher education, beginning most notably with the signing of the first Morrill Act in 1862 (Library of Congress, n.d.). This act was intended "to support the needs of Agriculture and Mechanical Arts" and more notably provide a "college in every State upon a sure and perpetual foundation, accessible to all, but especially to the sons of toil" (Loss, 2012, para. 3). This trajectory of expansion and inclusivity is well documented across the growth of American higher education and, as Martin Trow observed in 1999, new technologies have freed education from the constraints of time and place, consequently contributing significantly to changing the nature and potentialities toward creating universal access and participation in postsecondary education. He goes on to say that this "will surely have revolutionary consequences for existing institutions and systems of higher education, as well as for the larger societies which sustain and depend on them" (Trow, 2000, p. 308).

If one accepts that the world will continue to change (even if the pace slows down a bit) and that people will live longer, resulting in expanded work lives, then it is obvious that a college degree, even advanced degrees, will not be enough to sustain our graduates throughout their lives. Continuous learning will be essential, and those colleges and universities that adapt will succeed whereas those that choose not to, do so at their own peril.

What will this entail? We will need to fundamentally question all of the assumptions under which we have been operating, about our learners and how we prepare them for their lives and work, as well as the ecosystem that supports this endeavor, in order to design an education that is robot-proof (Aoun, 2017). This includes rethinking such things as (a) the 4-year degree, (b) the semester or trimester system, (c) credit hours and seat time, (d) pedagogy, (e) overemphasis on content at the expense of skills, (f) how financial aid works, (g) the tenure system, (h) business practices, and (i) how we deliver student services. While the 4-year degree for 18–23-years-olds will most likely continue to exist for a subpopulation of learners, the larger need will be for new and/or expanded knowledge and skills for those already in the workforce.

In the next chapter, we explore what all of these different learners require to align with both workforce needs and prepare them for their roles as citizens of a flat world who need to address the grand challenges they will take on, such as poverty, clean water, clean fuel, and inequality. In chapter 3, we discuss how higher education might change to help accomplish that.

REFERENCES

Abeles, V. (2016, January 2). *Is the drive for success making our children sick?* Retrieved from The New York Times: https://www.nytimes.com/2016/01/03/opinion/sunday/is-the-drive-for-success-making-our-children-sick.html

ACT. (2006). *Reading between the lines: What the ACT reveals about college readiness in reading.* Iowa City: ACT.

ACT. (2013). *The condition of college & career readiness 2013*. Iowa City, IA: ACT.

Agarwal, D., Bersin, J., Lahiri, G., Schwartz, J., & Volini, E. (2018, March 28). *Introduction: The rise of the social enterprise*. Retrieved from Deloitte Insights: https://www2.deloitte.com/insights/us/en/focus/human-capital-trends/2018/introduction.html#

Alperin, J., Nieves, C., Schimanski, L., Fischman, G., Niles, M., & McKieman, E. (2018). *How significant are the public dimensions of faculty work in review, promotion, and tenure documents?* Retrieved from Humanities Commons: http://dx.doi.org/10.17613/M6W950N35

Altbach, P. (2010, August 12). *Competition's impact on higher education*. Retrieved from Forbes: https://www.forbes.com/2010/08/01/higher-education-competition-opinions-best-colleges-10-altbach.html#e3cd722722ae

Ambrose, S., Bridges, M., Dipietro, M., Lovett, M., & Norman, M. (2010). *How learning works: 7 research-based principles for smart teaching*. San Francisco, CA: Jossey-Bass.

American College Health Association. (2018). *Spring 2018: Reference Group Executive Summary*. Retrieved from https://www.acha.org/documents/ncha/NCHA-II_Spring_2018_Reference_Group_Executive_Summary.pdf

American Psychological Association. (2018, October). *Stress in America: Generation Z*. Retrieved from https://www.apa.org/news/press/releases/stress/2018/stress-gen-z.pdf

Anders, G. (2017). *You can do anything: The surprising power of a "useless" liberal arts education*. New York, NY: Little, Brown and Company.

Anderson, L. (2018, June 12). *50-state comparison: Transfer and articulation policies*. Retrieved from Education of the States ECS.org: https://www.ecs.org/transfer-and-articulation-policies-db/

Anderson, N. (2018, November 18). Bloomberg gives Johns Hopkins a record $1.8 billion for student financial aid. *The Washington Post*.

Anderson, R., Wilson, P., & Fielding, L. (1988). Growth in reading and how children spend their time outside of school. *Reading Research Quarterly 23(3)*, 285–303.

Andriotis, A. (2019, February 2). *Over 60, and crushed by student loan debt.* Retrieved from The Wall Street Journal: https://www.wsj.com/articles/over-60-and-crushed-by-student-loan-debt-11549083631?ns=prod/accounts-wsj

Aoun, J. (2017). *Robot-proof: Higher education in the age of artificial intelligence.* Cambridge, MA: The MIT Press.

Association for Talent Development. (2016, December 8). *ATD releases 2016 State of the Industry Report.* Retrieved from https://www.td.org/insights/atd-releases-2016-state-of-the-industry-report

Association of Public & Land-Grant Universities. (n.d.). *Powered by publics.* Retrieved from http://www.aplu.org/projects-and-initiatives/center-for-public-university-transformation/powered-by-publics/index.html

Baker, S., Simmons, D., & Kameenui, E. (1998). Vocabulary acquisition: Research bases. In D. Simmons & E. Kameenui (Eds.), *What reading research tells us about children with diverse learning needs: Bases and basics* (p. 183). Mahwah, NJ: Erlbaum.

Bauman, D. (2018, March 1). *Is student debt big enough to hold back the economy? What the research says.* Retrieved from the Chronicle of Higher Education: https://www.chronicle.com/article/Is-Student-Debt-Big-Enough-to/242719

Belanger, L. (2018, September 20). *This company hosts virtual dance parties to help its 170 remote employees feel connected.* Retrieved from Entrepreneur: https://www.entrepreneur.com/article/320411

Bennett, N., & Lemoine, G. J. (2014). *What VUCA really means for you.* Retrieved from Harvard Business Review: https://hbr.org/2014/01/what-vuca-really-means-for-you

Bill & Melinda Gates Foundation. (2008). *New initiative to double the number of low-income students in the U.S. who earn a postsecondary degree – Bill & Melinda Gates Foundation.* Retrieved from https://www.gatesfoundation.org/Media-Center/Press-Releases/2008/12/New-Initiative-to-Double-the-Number-of-LowIncome-Students-in-the-US-Who-Earn-a-Postsecondary-Degree

Bill & Melinda Gates Foundation. (n.d.). *Postsecondary success: Making a difference.* Retrieved from https://postsecondary.gatesfoundation.org/making-difference/

Biro, M. M. (2013, August 18). *5 reasons why workplace flexibility is smart talent strategy*. Retrieved from Forbes: https://www.forbes.com/sites/meghanbiro/2013/08/18/5-reasons-why-workplace-flexibility-is-smart-talent-strategy/#677c471c18ff

Black, H. (2018, October 9). *Cal State system is dropping remedial classes*. Retrieved from Education Dive: https://www.educationdive.com/news/cal-state-system-is-dropping-remedial-classes/539236/

Bleemer, Z., Brown, M., Lee, D., & van der Klaauw, w. (2017). *Tuition, jobs, or housing: What's keeping millennials at home?* New York, NY: Federal Reserve Bank of New York, Staff Reports No. 700.

Blumenstyk, G. (2018a). *The adult student: The population colleges—and the nation—can't afford to ignore*. Washington, DC: The Chronicle of Higher Education.

Blumenstyk, G. (2018b, September 24). *What's the value in helping students "reclaim" their degrees?* Retrieved from the Chronicle of Higher Education: https://www.chronicle.com/article/what-s-the-value-in-helping/244614

Bureau of Labor Statistics. (2017, October 24). *Employment projections 2016–26*. Retrieved from U.S. Department of Labor, Bureau of Labor Statistics: https://www.bls.gov/news.release/pdf/ecopro.pdf

Burning Glass Technologies. (2014). *Moving the goalposts: How demand for a bachelor's degree is reshaping the workforce*. Boston, MA: Burning Glass Technologies.

CAEL. (n.d.). *Linking learning and work to help adults succeed*. Retrieved from https://www.cael.org

Caligiuri, P. (2012). *Cultural agility: Building a pipeline of successful global professionals*. San Francisco, CA: Jossey-Bass.

Cappelli, P., & Tavis, A. (March–April 2018). HR goes agile. *Harvard Business Review*, 3–9.

Carnevale, A. P., Smith, N., & Strohl, J. (2013). *Recovery: Job growth and education requirements through 2020*. Retrieved from Georgetown University: https://cew.georgetown.edu/cew-reports/recovery-job-growth-and-education-requirements-through-2020/#powerpoint

Cataldi, E. F., Bennett, C. T., & Chen, X. (2018). *First-generation students: College access, persistence, and post-bachelor's outcomes*. Institute of

Education Sciences, National Center for Education Statistics. Washington, DC: U.S. Department of Education.

Cataldi, E. F., & Staklis, S. (2018). *Four years later: 2007–08 college graduates' employment, debt, and enrollment in 2012*. Washington, DC: U.S. Department of Education, National Center for Education Statistics.

Cataldi, E., Woo, J., & Staklis, S. (2017). *Four years after a bachelor's degree: Employment, enrollment, and debt among college graduates*. Washington, DC: U.S. Department of Education, National Center for Education Statistics.

Center for Collegiate Mental Health. (2019). *Center for Collegiate Mental Health 2018 Annual Report*. Retrieved from Center for Collegiate Mental Health, Penn State Counseling & Psychological Services: https://ccmh.psu.edu/files/2019/02/2018-Annual-Report-2.11.18-FINAL-y2nw3r.pdf

Centre for the New Economy and Society. (2018). *The future of jobs report* 2018. World Economic Forum. Cologny/Geneva: World Economic Forum.

Chamorro-Premuzic, T., & Swan, M. (2016, July 18). *It's the company's job to help employees learn*. Retrieved from Harvard Business Review: https://hbr.org/2016/07/its-the-companys-job-to-help-employees-learn

Chronicle of Higher Education. (2012). *The role of higher education in career development: Employer perceptions*. Concord, MA: Chronicle of Higher Education and American Public Media's Marketplace.

CNBC. (2018, May 22). Meet the 2018 CNBC Disruptor 50 companies. Retrieved from https://www.cnbc.com/2018/05/22/meet-the-2018-cnbc-disruptor-50-companies.html

College Unbound. (n.d.). *Welcome to a college designed for adults*. Retrieved from https://www.collegeunbound.org/apps/pages/impact

Cowen, S., & Seifter, B. (2018). *Winnebagos on Wednesdays: How visionary leadership can transform higher education*. Princeton: Princeton University Press.

Dehaene, S., Pegado, F., Braga, L. W., Ventura, P., Filho, G. N., Jobert, A., . . . Cohen, L. (2010, November 11). How learning to read changes the cortical networks for vision and language. *Science, 330*(6009), 1359–1364.

Delisle, J. D., & Christensen, C. (2019). The merit aid illusion: The hidden winners in a competition for affluent students. Washington, DC: American Enterprise Institute. Retrieved from http://www.aei.org/wp-content/up;oads/2019/The-Merit-Aid-Illusion.pdf

Deloitte. (2018). *2018 Deloitte Millennial Survey: Millennials disappointed in business, unprepared for Industry 4.0.* Retrieved from https://www2.deloitte.com/content/dam/Deloitte/global/Documents/About-Deloitte/gx-2018-millennial-survey-report.pdf

Deloitte University Press. (2017, February 27). *Rewriting the rules for the digital age.* Retrieved from Deloitte Global Human Capital Trends: https://www2.deloitte.com/content/dam/insights/us/articles/HCTrends_2017/DUP_Global-Human-capital-trends_2017.pdf

Desilver, D. (2016, June 20). *More older Americans are working, and working more, than they used to.* Retrieved from Pew Research Center: https://www.pewresearch.org/fact-tank/2016/06/20/more-older-americans-are-working-and-working-more-than-they-used-to/

Dickler, J. (2016, July 13). *College costs are out of control.* Retrieved from CNBC: https://www.cnbc.com/2016/07/12/college-costs-are-out-of-control.html

Dimeo, J. (2018, November 2). *UC Berkeley launching data science division on heels of fast-growing major.* Retrieved from Education Dive: https://www.educationdive.com/news/uc-berkeley-launching-data-science-division-on-heels-of-fast-growing-major/541238/

Dix, W. (2016, November 16). *A liberal arts degree is more important than ever.* Retrieved from Forbes: https://www.forbes.com/sites/willarddix/2016/11/16/a-liberal-arts-degree-is-more-important-than-ever/#154fa91e339f

Dotiwala, F., & Kumra, G. (2014, March 11). *How CEOs learn.* Retrieved from McKinsey Perspectives on CEO Leadership: https://www.mckinsey.com/~/media/McKinsey/Business%20Functions/Strategy%20and%20Corporate%20Finance/Our%20Insights/How%20CEOs%20learn/How-CEOs-learn.ashx

Dougherty, C. (2016, January 1). *App makers reach out to the teenager on mobile.* Retrieved from The New York Times: https://www.nytimes.com/2016/01/03/business/app-makers-reach-out-to-the-teenager-on-mobile.html

71

Dyer, A., Barybkina, E., Erker, C. P., & Sullivan, J. (2018, September 5). *A CEO's guide to leading and learning in the digital age.* Retrieved from BCG Henderson Institute: https://www.bcg.com/en-us/publications/2018/ceo-guide-leading-learning-digital-age.aspx

Eagan, K., Stolzenberg, E. B., Zimmerman, H. B., Aragon, M. C., Sayson, H. W., & Rios-Aguilar, C. (2017). *The American freshman: National norms fall 2016.* Los Angeles, CA: Cooperative Institutional Research Program at the Higher Education Research Institute at UCLA.

Education Commission of the States. (2018, June). *50-state comparison: Transfer and articulating statewide reverse transfer.* Denver, CO: Education Commission of the States.

Education Trust. (n.d.). *The state of higher education equity.* Retrieved from https://edtrust.org/the-state-of-higher-education-equity/

Engle, J. (2016). *Answering the call: Institutions and states lead the way toward better measures of postsecondary performance.* Seattle, WA: Bill & Melinda Gates Foundation.

Esch, M. (2018, April 18). *Free food for thought: Campus food pantries proliferate.* Retrieved from AP News: https://www.apnews.com/0200d850a4f9461584518c0dcfbeb752

Falzon, K. (2016, December 22). *Thomas Friedman's guide for thriving in an accelerated workforce.* Retrieved from Working Nation: https://workingnation.com/thomas-friedmans-guide-thriving-accelerated-workforce/

Fellman, M. (2017, January 5). *Julio Ottino awarded top National Academy prize for innovative education.* Retrieved from Northwestern University–McCormick School of Engineering: https://www.mccormick.northwestern.edu/news/articles/2017/01/julio-ottino-awarded-top-national-academy-prize-for-innovative-education.html

Ferrazzi, K. (2015, July 31). *7 Ways to improve employee development programs.* Retrieved from Harvard Business Review: https://hbr.org/2015/07/7-ways-to-improve-employee-development-programs

Field, K., Fischer, K., Young, J. R., & Selingo, J. (2018). *Beyond the horizon: What's next for higher education.* Stony Brook, NY: Academic Intelligence.

Financial Times. (n.d.). *Definition of cultural agility.* Retrieved from http://lexicon.ft.com/Term?term=cultural-agility

Friedman, T. (2005). *The world is flat: A brief history of the twenty-first century*. New York: Farrar, Straus and Giroux-Macmillan Publishers.

Friedman, T. (2016). *Thank you for being late: An optimist's guide to thriving in the age of accelerations*. New York, NY: Farrar, Straus and Giroux.

Fry, R. (2017, May 5). *It's becoming more common for young adults to live at home—and for longer stretches*. Retrieved from Pew Research Center: http://www.pewresearch.org/fact-tank/2017/05/05/its-becoming-more-common-for-young-adults-to-live-at-home-and-for-longer-stretches/

Fry, R. (2018, April 11). *Millennials are the largest generation in the U.S. labor force*. Retrieved from Pew Research Center: https://www.pewresearch.org/fact-tank/2018/04/11/millennials-largest-generation-us-labor-force/

Gartner. (2016, August 30). Changes are coming: How to stay ahead of workplace disruptions. Retrieved from Talent Daily: https://www.cebglobal.com/talentdaily/changes-are-coming-how-to-stay-ahead-of-workplace-disruptions/

Gay, W. (2017, October 20). *Why a multligenerational workforce is a competitive advantage*. Retrieved from Forbes: https://www.forbes.com/sites/wesgay/2017/10/20/multigeneration-workforce/#1ca559c24bfd

Gewertz, C. (2016, November 17). *What are students reading in middle and high school?* Retrieved from Education Week: http://blogs.edweek.org/edweek/high_school_and_beyond/2016/11/what_are_students_reading_in_middle_and_high_school.html

Ghemawat, P. (2017, July–August). *Globalization in the age of Trump*. Retrieved from Harvard Business Review: https://hbr.org/2017/07/globalization-in-the-age-of-trump

Gillers, H., Tergesen, A., & Scism, L. (2018, June 22). *A generation of Americans is entering old age the least prepared in decades*. Retrieved from The Wall Street Journal: https://www.wsj.com/articles/a-generation-of-americans-is-entering-old-age-the-least-prepared-in-decades-1529676033

Girod, M., Rau, C., & Schepige, A. (2003). Appreciating the beauty of science ideas: Teaching for aesthetic understanding. *Science Education, 87*(4), 574–587.

Goldstein, D. (2017, August 2). *Why kids can't write*. Retrieved from The New York Times: https://www.nytimes.com/2017/08/02/education/edlife/writing-education-grammar-students-children.html

Gonzalez, J. (2018, August 27). *Free Tennessee community college for adults program shatters expectations in its first year*. Retrieved from Tennessean: https://www.tennessean.com/story/news/education/2018/08/27/tennessee-reconnect-community-college/1109159002/

goodreads. (n.d.). John Dewey Quotes. Retrieved from https://www.goodreads.com/author/quotes/42738.John_Dewey

Gould, E. (2018, October 5). *Back-to-school jobs report shows a continue shortfall in public education jobs*. Retrieved from Economic Policy Institute: https://www.epi.org/press/back-to-school-jobs-report-shows-a-continue-shortfall-in-public-education-jobs/

Gratton, L., & Scott, A. (2017). *The 100-year life: Living and working in an age of longevity*. London: Bloomsbury.

Greeley, M. (2018, October 2). *3 nontraditional ways to get a bachelor's degree*. Retrieved from U.S. News: https://www.usnews.com/education/best-colleges/articles/2018-10-02/how-to-get-a-bachelors-degree-using-new-alternatives

Greenfield, P. M. (2009, January 2). Technology and informal education: What is taught, what is learned? *Science, 323*(5910), 69–71.

Guardian Life Insurance. (2017). *The next generation of work: Guardian Workplace Benefits Study 5th Annual*. New York, NY: Guardian Life Insurance.

Guthrie, J. T., Wigfield, A., Metsala, J. L., & Cox, K. E. (1999). Motivational and cognitive predictors of text comprehension and reading amount. *Scientific Studies of Writing, 3*(3), 231–256.

Hackman, M., & Belkin, D. (2018, November 13). *Fewer international students heading to the U.S.* Retrieved from The Wall Street Journal: https://www.wsj.com/articles/fewer-international-students-heading-to-the-u-s-1542105004

Hart Research Associates. (2015). *Falling short? College learning and career success*. Washington, DC: Hart Research Associates.

Heerwagen, J., Kelly, K., & Kampschroer, K. (2016, October 5). *The changing nature of organizations, work, and workplace*. Retrieved from WBDG

Whole Building Design Guide: https://www.wbdg.org/resources/changing-nature-organizations-work-and-workplace

Higher Education Compliance Alliance. (n.d.). *Compliance matrix*. Retrieved from https://www.higheredcompliance.org/compliance-matrix/

Higher Learning Advocates. (n.d.). *Who are today's students?* Retrieved from Higher Learning Advocates: https://higherlearningadvocates.org

Hillman, N., & Wiechman, T. (2016). *Education deserts: The continued significance of "place" in the twenty-first century*. American Council on Education and Center for Policy Research and Strategy. Washington, DC: American Council on Education.

Hobbs, T. D. (2018, October 17). *ACT scores show drop in college readiness, especially in math*. Retrieved from The Wall Street Journal: https://www.wsj.com/articles/act-scores-show-drop-in-college-readiness-especially-in-math-1539768600

HolacracyOne LLC. (n.d.). *What is Holacracy*. Retrieved from Holacracy: https://www.holacracy.org/what-is-holacracy

Hussar, W., & Bailey, T. (2016). *Projections of education statistics to 2023*. Washington, DC: U.S. Department of Education, National Center for Education Statistics.

Illanes, P., Lund, S., Mourshed, M., Rutherford, S., & Tyreman, M. (2018, January). *Retraining and reskilling workers in the age of automation*. Retrieved from McKinsey & Company: https://www.mckinsey.com/featured-insights/future-of-work/retraining-and-reskilling-workers-in-the-age-of-automation

Irving, P. (2018). *When no one retires*. Retrieved from Harvard Business Review: https://hbr.org/cover-story/2018/11/when-no-one-retires

Jaschik, S. (2018, October 9). *Falling confidence in higher ed*. Retrieved from Inside Higher Ed: https://www.insidehighered.com/news/2018/10/09/gallup-survey-finds-falling-confidence-higher-education

Jerald, C. (2006, July). *"Teach to the test"? Just say no*. Washington, DC: The Center for Comprehensive School Reform and Improvement. Retrieved September 2018 from The Center for Comprehensive School Reform and Improvement, Issue Brief: https://files.eric.ed.gov/fulltext/ED494086.pdf

Josephs, M. (2017, March 15). *U.S. manufacturing labor shortage: How to make your company a happy exception.* Retrieved from Forbes: https://www.forbes.com/sites/maryjosephs/2017/03/15/u-s-manufacturing-labor-shortage-how-to-make-your-company-a-happy-exception/#2d3e83f17e13

Kanter, R. M. (2012, September 25). *Ten reasons people resist change.* Retrieved from Harvard Business Review: https://hbr.org/2012/09/ten-reasons-people-resist-chang.html

Kitroeff, N. (2018, May 25). *How student debt can ruin home buying dreams.* Retrieved from The New York Times: https://www.nytimes.com/2018/05/25/business/how-student-debt-can-ruin-home-buying-dreams.html

Koch, J. V. (2018, January 9). *No college kid needs a water park to study.* Retrieved from The New York Times: https://www.nytimes.com/2018/01/09/opinion/trustees-tuition-lazy-rivers.html

Korn, M. (2018, September 3). *In race for students, colleges offer to match tuition at rival schools.* Retrieved from The Wall Street Journal: https://www.wsj.com/articles/in-race-for-students-colleges-offer-to-match-tuition-at-rival-schools-1535972400

Krantz, L. (2016, August 16). *Northeastern, GE partner on accelerated manufacturing degree program.* Retrieved from The Boston Globe: https://www.bostonglobe.com/metro/2016/08/16/northeastern-partner-create-accelerated-manufacturing-degree/SyFu2kflRK-b3nglJ6f2qUO/story.html

Kreighbaum, A. (2018, November 26). *DeVos restores recognition for troubled for-profit accreditor.* Retrieved from Inside Higher Ed: https://www.insidehighered.com/news/2018/11/26/devos-restores-authority-profit-accreditor

Lederman, D. (2017, October 12). *The new, improved IPEDS.* Retrieved from Inside Higher Ed: https://www.insidehighered.com/news/2017/10/12/new-federal-higher-ed-outcome-measures-count-part-time-adult-students

Lerner, M. (2017, para. 2, October 19). *Report: Student loan debt delays home-ownership by seven years.* Retrieved from The Washington Post: https://www.washingtonpost.com/news/where-we-live/wp/2017/10/19/

report-student-loan-debt-delays-homeownership-by-seven-years/?noredirect=on&utm_term=.423924408bfb

Lew, I. (2015, November 13). *Student loan debt and the housing decisions of young households*. Retrieved from Joint Center for Housing Studies of Harvard University: http://www.jchs.harvard.edu/research-areas/working-papers/student-loan-debt-and-housing-decisions-young-households

Lewis, B. A. (2018, September 18). *Rice University announces free tuition for middle income undergraduate students*. Retrieved from Houston Chronicle: https://www.chron.com/news/houston-texas/houston/article/Rice-University-announces-free-tuition-for-middle-13236823.php?elqTrackId=12086e9d15784001849718dc196328f3&elq=f5ab0cc84e2c4f599af06e7625f6e89f&elqaid=20576&elqat=1&elqCampaignId=9690

Library of Congress. (n.d.). *Morrill Act*. Retrieved from Web Guides: Primary Documents in American History: https://www.loc.gov/rr/program/bib/ourdocs/morrill.html

Long, B. T. (2014, June 19). *Addressing the academic barriers to higher education*. Retrieved from Brookings: https://www.brookings.edu/research/addressing-the-academic-barriers-to-higher-education/

Loss, C. P. (2012, July 16). *Why the Morrill Land-Grant Colleges Act still matters*. Retrieved from the Chronicle of Higher Education: https://www.chronicle.com/article/Why-the-Morrill-Act-Still/132877

Lu, J. G., Hafenbrack, A. C., Eastwick, P. W., Wang, D. J., Maddux, W. W., & Galinsky, A. D. (2017). "Going out" of the box: Close intercultural friendships and romantic relationships spark creativity, workplace innovation, and entrepreneurship. *Journal of Applied Psychology, 102*(7), 1091–1109.

Lumina Foundation. (2017). *Lumina Foundation strategic plan for 2017–2020*. Indianapolis, IN: Lumina Foundation.

Lyons, M., Lavelle, K., & Smith, D. (2017). *Gen Z Rising, U.S. Edition*. Retrieved from Accenture Strategy: https://www.accenture.com/t20170901T082427Z__w__/us-en/_acnmedia/PDF-50/Accenture-Strategy-Workforce-Gen-Z-Rising-POV.pdf#zoom=50

Mann, A., & Adkins, A. (2017, March 15). *America's coming workplace: Home alone*. Retrieved from Gallup: https://news.gallup.com/businessjournal/206033/america-coming-workplace-home-alone.aspx

Manyika, J., Chui, M., Miremadi, M., Bughin, J., George, K., Willmot, P., & Dewhurst, M. (2017, January). *Harnessing automation for a future that works*. Retrieved from McKinsey & Company: https://www.mckinsey.com/featured-insights/digital-disruption/harnessing-automation-for-a-future-that-works

Manyika, J., Lund, S., Chui, M., Bughin, J., Woetzel, J., Batra, P., . . . Sanghvi, S. (2017, December). *Jobs lost, jobs gained: Workforce transitions in a time of automation*. Retrieved from McKinsey Global Institute: https://www.mckinsey.com/~/media/mckinsey/featured%20insights/future%20of%20organizations/what%20the%20future%20of%20work%20will%20mean%20for%20jobs%20skills%20and%20wages/mgi-jobs-lost-jobs-gained-report-december-6-2017.ashx

Martin, A. (2018, September 13). *UCF lambasted after admitting misusing state funds for new $38 million academic building*. Retrieved from Orlando Sentinel: https://www.orlandosentinel.com/features/education/school-zone/os-ucf-funds-misappropriation-20180913-story.html?elqTrackId=386a8a7e9beb4a49aafa87ea45bc4f6e&elq=33fc2d7893aa405b8f10a20b8ebbd5a5&elqaid=20515&elqat=1&elqCampaignId=9651

Martin, J., & Samels, J. E. (2015, March 17). *Corporate university partnerships: No longer barbarians at the gate*. Retrieved from University Business: https://universitybusiness.com/corporate-university-partnerships-no-longer-barbarians-at-the-gate/

Martin, S. (2017, April 4). *Unfunded federal mandates cost Virginia universities*. Retrieved from The Commonwealth Times: https://commonwealthtimes.org/2017/04/04/unfunded-federal-mandates-cost-virginia-universities/

McBride-Chang, C., Zhou, Y., Cho, J. R., Aram, D., Levin, I., & Tolchinsky, L. (2011). Visual spatial skill: A consequence of learning to read? *Journal of Experimental Child Psychology, 109*(2), 356–262.

McCarthy, M. (2018, January 11). *The share of Americans holding a passport has increased dramatically in recent years [Infographic]*. Retrieved from Forbes: https://www.forbes.com/sites/niallmccarthy/2018/01/11/the-share-of-americans-holding-a-passport-has-increased-dramatically-in-recent-years-infographic/#5f6f083c1675

McChrystal, S., Siverman, D., Collins, T., & Fussell, C. (2015). *Team of teams: New rules of engagement for a complex world*. London, UK: Portfolio.

McDonald's Corporation UK. (2016). *Bridging the generation gap: The impact of multigenerational working on business, people and customers*. Retrieved from https://www.mcdonalds.co.uk/content/dam/McDonaldsUK/press_release/McDonald%27s%20Bridging%20the%20Generation%20Gap%20exec%20summary.pdf

McFarland, J., Hussar, B., Wang, X., Zhang, J., Wang, K., Rathbun, A., . . . Mann, F. B. (2018). *The condition of education 2018 (NCES 2018-144)*. National Center for Education Statistics. Washington, DC: U.S. Department of Education.

McKenzie, L. (2018, March 20). *Online, cheap—and elite*. Retrieved from Inside Higher Ed: https://www.insidehighered.com/digital-learning/article/2018/03/20/analysis-shows-georgia-techs-online-masters-computer-science

Mowlah, A., Niblett, V., Burn, J., & Harris, M. (2014). *The value of arts and culture to people and society: An evidence review*. Manchester, UK: Arts Council England.

Murfee, E. (1991, December 31). *The value of the arts*. Retrieved from Americans for the Arts: https://www.americansforthearts.org/by-program/reports-and-data/legislation-policy/naappd/the-value-of-the-arts

Myers, B. (2018, July 17). *Who lives in education deserts? More people than you think*. Retrieved January 2019, from the Chronicle of Higher Education: https://www.chronicle.com/interactives/education-deserts

Nardelli, A. (2014, September 26). *Most Europeans can speak multiple languages. UK and Ireland not so much*. Retrieved from The Guardian: https://www.theguardian.com/news/datablog/2014/sep/26/europeans-multiple-languages-uk-ireland

Nathan, M., & Koedinger, K. (2000). An investigation of teachers' beliefs of students' algebra development. *Journal of Cognition and Instruction, 18*(2), 209–237.

National Academies of Sciences, Engineering and Medicine. (2017). *Information technology and the U.S. workforce: Where are we and where do we go from here?* Committee on Information Technology, Automation & The U.S. Workforce. Washington, DC: The National Academies Press.

National Alliance on Mental Illness. (2019). *Mental health by the numbers*. Retrieved from https://www.nami.org/Learn-More/Mental-Health-By-the-Numbers

National Association of College and University Business Officers. (2019, May 9). *Private colleges now use nearly half of tuition revenue for financial aid*. Retrieved from https://www.nacubo.org/Press-Releases/2019/Private-Colleges-Now-Use-Nearly-Half-of-Tuition-Revenue-For-Financial-Aid

National Center for Education Statistics. (n.d.). *Fast facts: Graduation rates*. Retrieved from https://nces.ed.gov/fastfacts/display.asp?id=40

National Center on Safe and Supportive Learning Environments. (n.d) *Federal mandates*. Retrieved from https://safesupportivelearning .ed.gov/training-technical-assistance/education-level/higher-education/strategic-planning/federal-mandates

National Endowment for the Arts. (2007). *To read or not to read: A question of national consequence*. Washington, DC: National Endowment for the Arts.

National Endowment for the Arts. (2018, March 6). *The arts contribute more than $760 billion to the U.S. economy*. Retrieved from https://www.arts.gov/news/2018/arts-contribute-more-760-billion-us-economy

Newlon, C. (2014, July 31). *The college amenities arms race*. Retrieved from Forbes: https://www.forbes.com/sites/caranewlon/2014/07/31/the-college-amenities-arms-race/#32a2c8e74883

Northeastern University News. (2014, November 18). "Generation Z" is entrepreneurial, wants to chart its own future. Boston, MA: Northeastern University News.

O'Donnell, J., Inc. (2016, July 26). *Companies like Google and Ernst & Young have found that one trait is more important than the rest when recruiting new employees*. Retrieved from Business Insider: https://www.businessinsider.com/this-one-trait-will-help-you-get-hired-by-google-2016-7

Office of Planning, Evaluation and Policy Development. (2016). *Advancing diversity and inclusion in higher education: Key data highlights focusing on race and ethnicity and promising practices*. Washington, DC: Office of the Under Secretary,U.S. Department of Education.

Office of Research Integrity. (n.d.). *Case summaries*. Retrieved from The Office of Research Integrity: U.S. Department of Health and Human Services: https://ori.hhs.gov/content/case_summary

Palmer, K. (2013, July 31). *75% of Americans have no second language*. Retrieved from YouGov: https://today.yougov.com/topics/lifestyle/articles-reports/2013/07/31/75-americans-have-no-second-language

Pandey, E. (2018, October 11). *The future of student debt: How employers might help*. Retrieved from Axios: https://www.axios.com/student-loans-debt-assistance-401k-28f36662-fa66-42f5-9650-110f0fcd02d1.html

Pappano, L. (2017, January 31). *Colleges discover the rural student*. Retrieved from The New York Times: https://www.nytimes.com/2017/01/31/education/edlife/colleges-discover-rural-student.html

Pappano, L. (2018, August 2). *The iGen shift: Colleges are changing to reach the next generation*. Retrieved from The New York Times: https://www.nytimes.com/2018/08/02/education/learning/generationz-igen-students-colleges.html

Patel, V. (2018, September 16). *What Neil deGrasse Tyson thinks higher ed gets wrong*. Retrieved from the Chronicle of Higher Education: https://www.chronicle.com/article/What-Neil-deGrasse-Tyson/244522?cid=wb&utm_source=wb&utm_medium=en&elqTrackId=06b414533b79491cb93c3a9b6585dbca&elq=be1d1bcf613c48138713fac8b2c97314&elqaid=20622&elqat=1&elqCampaignId=9715

Paterson, J. (2018, October 16). *MIT plans $1B computing college, AI research effort*. Retrieved from Education Dive: https://www.educationdive.com/news/mit-plans-1b-computing-college-ai-research-effort/539761/

Paul, M. (2018, June 12). *Don't fear the robots: Why automation doesn't mean the end of work*. Retrieved from Roosevelt Institute: http://rooseveltinstitute.org/dont-fear-robots/

Pew Research Center. (2014, February 11). *The rising cost of not going to college*. Retrieved from Pew Research Center: http://www.pewsocialtrends.org/2014/02/11/the-rising-cost-of-not-going-to-college/

Pew Research Center. (2016, October 6). *The state of American jobs*. Retrieved from http://www.pewsocialtrends.org/2016/10/06/the-state-of-american-jobs/

Phillips, E., McDaniel, A., & Croft, A. (2018). Food insecurity and academic disruption among college students. *Journal of Student Affairs Research and Practice 55*(4), 353–372.

Povich, E. (2018, April 26). More community colleges are offering bachelor's degrees—and four-year universities aren't happy about it. Retrieved from PEW Stateline: https://www.pewtrusts.org/en/research-and-analysis/blogs/stateline/2018/04/26/more-community-colleges-are-offering-bachelors-degrees

Reaney, P. (2013, July 1). *Dream job? Most U.S. workers want to change careers – poll*. Retrieved from Reuters: https://www.reuters.com/article/us-usa-work/dream-job-most-u-s-workers-want-to-change-careers-poll-idUSBRE96015Z20130701

Redden, E. (2018, November 13). *Study abroad numbers grow*. Retrieved from Inside Higher Ed: https://www.insidehighered.com/news/2018/11/13/study-abroad-numbers-continue-grow-driven-continued-growth-short-term-programs

Redford, J. A. (2017). *First-generation and continuing-generation college students: A comparison of high school and postsecondary experiences*. U.S. Department of Education. Washington, DC: National Center for Education Statistics.

Renaissance Learning. (2015). *The Research Foundation for Accelerated Reader 360*. Wisconsin Rapids, WI: Renaissance Learning. Retrieved from http://doc.renlearn.com/KMNet/R0057375D0FDD7A8.pdf

Rigby, D. K., Sutherland, J., & Noble, A. (2018). Agile at scale. *Harvard Business Review*, *96*(3), 88–96.

Rigby, D., Sutherland, J., & Takeuchi, H. (2016). Embracing agile. *Harvard Business Review*, *94*(5), 40–50.

Rio, A. (2018, March 19). *Corporate universities and academic institutions: Symbiotic relationship or broken system?* Retrieved from Chief Learning Officer: https://www.clomedia.com/2018/03/19/corporate-universities-academic-institutions-symbiotic-relationship-broken-system/

Ripley, A. (2018, September 11). *Why is college in America so expensive?* Retrieved from The Atlantic: https://www.theatlantic.com/education/archive/2018/09/why-is-college-so-expensive-in-america/569884/

Roundtree, L. (2011). *Age: A 21st century diversity imperative.* Chestnut Hill, MA: Boston College The Sloan Center on Aging & Work.

Runnion, T., & Gibson, I. (2018, June 4). Companies can address talent shortages by partnering with educators. Retrieved from Harvard Business Review: https://hbr.org/2018/06/companies-can-address-talent-shortages-by-partnering-with-educators

Sankar, A. (2018, April 4). *A rising mountain of student debt.* Retrieved from Federal Reserve Bank of Minneapolis: https://www.minneapolisfed.org/publications/fedgazette/a-rising-mountain-of-student-debt

Schanzenback, D. W., Bauer, L., & Breitwieser, A. (2017, April 26). *Eight economic facts on higher education.* Retrieved from Brookings: https://www.brookings.edu/research/eight-economic-facts-on-higher-education/

Schmidt, E., & Rosenberg, J. (2014, September 25). How Google manages talent. (S. Green, Interviewer) Retrieved from Harvard Business Review: https://hbr.org/2014/09/how-google-manages-talent

Schneider, M. A. (2018). *Saving the liberal arts: Making the bachelor's degree a better path to labor market success.* Boston: American Enterprise Institute and Burning Glass Technologies.

Selingo, J. J. (2017a, August 21). *Why universities are phasing out luxury dorms.* Retrieved from The Atlantic: https://www.theatlantic.com/education/archive/2017/08/why-universities-are-phasing-out-luxury-dorms/537492/

Selingo, J. J. (2017b). *The networked university: Building alliances for innovation in higher education.* Retrieved from Pearson: https://www.pearson.com/content/dam/one-dot-com/one-dot-com/global/Files/about-pearson/innovation/the-networked-university/Pearson_The_Networked_University_v22-1_WEB.pdf

Selingo, J. J. (2018, September 19). Is there an alternative to college? Retrieved from The Washington Post: https://www.washingtonpost.com/education/2018/09/15/how-are-we-learning-today-only-shadow-knows/?utm_term=.fe36af7730d4

Selingo, J. J. (n.d.). *The future learners: An innovative approach to understanding the higher education market and building a student-centered university.* Retrieved from Pearson: https://www.pearson.com/corporate/about-pearson/innovation/future-learners.html

Selingo, J. J., & Werf, M. V. (n.d.). *The future of work and what it means for higher education part three: The colleges and universities already filling the needs of the next economy.* Retrieved from Workday: https://resources. workday.com/c/higher-ed-futureofwo?x=LXBfjV&lx=4ajE1Q& mkt_tok=eyJpIjoiWVRJMFlUSTVNRFl5WlRKbCIsInQiOiJYMGd-VOGhFWnptb3VSdjA2cEYyaFUzYUxnbU11SWJJOGhMblliYWpC RGtoK1YrOENrUnc5K3BwNFFLSFpGSVhjUG5YNFNiblpFbDl5c-GxtNmRNZk5CaHltTWU3ak5cLzRSOFhpZkp

Seymour, D. (2016, November 6). *Higher education has lost control of its own narrative.* Retrieved from the Chronicle of Higher Education: https:// www.chronicle.com/article/Higher-Education-Has-Lost/238321

Shapiro, D., Dundar, A., Huie, F., Wakhungu, P. K., Bhimdiwali, A., Nathan, A., & Youngsik, H. (2018). *Transfer and mobility: A national view of student movement in postsecondary institutions, fall 2011 cohort. (Signature Report No. 15).* Herndon, VA: National Student Clearinghouse Research Center.

Shapiro, D., Dundar, A., Yuan, X., Harrell, A., Wild, J., & Ziskin, M. (2014). *Some college, no degree: A national view of students with some college enrollment, but no completion (Signature Report No. 7).* Herndon, VA: National Clearinghouse Research Center.

Shih, W. C., Rudnick, H., & Tapen, C. (2018, November 9). *Rethinking retraining.* Retrieved from Harvard Business Review: https://hbr. org/2018/11/rethinking-retraining

Siilasmaa, R. (2018, October 4). *The chairman of Nokia on ensuring every employee has a basic understanding of machine learning—including him.* Retrieved from Harvard Business Review: https://hbr.org/2018/10/ the-chairman-of-nokia-on-ensuring-every-employee-has-a-basic-understanding-of-machine-learning-including-him

Singletary, M. (2018, October 3). *U.S. student loan debt reaches a staggering $1.53 trillion.* Retrieved from The Washington Post: https://www.washingtonpost.com/business/2018/10/04/

us-student-loan-debt-reaches-staggering-trillion/?utm_
term=.0b147eba121c

Skorton, D., & Bear, A. (2018). *The integration of the humanities and arts with
sciences, engineering and medicine in higher education: Branches from the same
tree.* Washington, DC: The National Academies Press.

Smith, A. A. (2018, October 3). *Tackling poverty to increase graduations.*
Retrieved from Inside Higher Ed: https://www.insidehighered.com/
news/2018/10/03/college-administrators-meet-find-solutions-
reduce-student-poverty

Soares, L. (2013, January). *Post-traditional learners and the transformation
of postsecondary education: A manifesto for college leaders.* Retrieved from
American Council on Education: https://www.acenet.edu/news-
room/Documents/Post-Traditional-Learners.pdf

Soares, L. & Gagliaridi, J. S. (2017). *The post traditional learners manifesto
revisited.* Retrieved fron ACENET: https://www.acenet.edu/news-room/
Documents/The-Post-Traditional-Learners-Manifesto-Revisited.pdf

Sprague, J., & Stuart, D. (2000). *The speaker's handbook.* Fort Worth, TX:
Harcourt College Publishers.

Sreenivasan, H. (2018, October 9). Aging Maine repays college debts to
attract younger workers. *PBS Podcast.*

Star, M. G. (2018, October 15). *For-profit postsecondary education M&A poised
for quiet comeback.* Retrieved from Forbes: https://www.forbes.com/sites/
mergermarket/2018/10/15/for-profit-postsecondary-education-
ma-poised-for-quiet-comeback/#778e185c7729

Stewart, I., De, D., & Cole, A. (2015). *Technology and people: The great job-
creating machine.* London, UK: Deloitte.

Stripling, J. (2018, September 13). *Hurricane Trump bears down on science.*
Retrieved from the Chronicle of Higher Education: https://www
.chronicle.com/article/Hurricane-Trump-Bears-Down-on/244518?cid
=db&elqTrackId=a5984aa7548d4c6d94998eceb51d8895&elq
=33fc2d7893aa405b8f10a20b8ebbd5a5&elqaid=20515&elqat=1&
elqCampaignId=9651

Student Loan Hero. (2017). *2017 student loan debt statistics.* Retrieved January
2019 from Student Loan Hero: https://cdn.studentloanhero.com/wp-
content/uploads/Student-Loan-Hero-2017-Student-Loan-Statistics.pdf

Sullivan, A. (2013, September 16). *Reading for fun improves children's brains, study confirms.* Retrieved from The Guardian: https://www.theguardian.com/books/booksblog/2013/sep/16/reading-improves-childrens-brains

Sullivan, P. (2016). *An open letter to high school students about reading.* Retrieved from American Association of University Professors: https://www.aaup.org/article/open-letter-high-school-students-about-reading#.XEeDPs9KjOQ

Sullivan, P. (2017, November 13). *Shaping the public narrative about teaching and learning.* Retrieved from Association of American Colleges & Universities: https://www.aacu.org/liberaleducation/2017/summer-fall/sullivan

Swartz, J. (2014, May 19). *Is college tuition paying for essentials, or lavish amenities?* Retrieved from USA Today: https://www.usatoday.com/story/college/2014/05/19/is-college-tuition-paying-for-essentials-or-lavish-amenities/37391309/

Tams, C. (2018, January 26). *Everybody is a change agent: A new anthropological foundation for change management.* Retrieved from Forbes: https://www.forbes.com/sites/carstentams/2018/01/26/everybody-is-a-change-agent/#3b7895914bb2

Thomas Edison State University. (n.d.). *Thomas Edison State University.* Retrieved from https://www.tesu.edu/

Trow, M. (2000). *From mass higher education to universal access: The American advantage.* Berkeley, CA: University of California, Berkeley Center for Studies in Higher Education.

Twenge, J. M. (2017). *iGen: Why today's super-connected kids are growing up less rebellious, more tolerant, less happy—and completely unprepared for adulthood—and what that means for the rest of us.* New York: Atria Books.

University Innovation Alliance. (n.d.). *University Innovation Alliance.* Retrieved from http://www.theuia.org/

University of Georgia. (2018, August 14). *Board of Regents approve first nexus degrees.* Retrieved from https://www.usg.edu/news/release/board_of_regents_approve_first_nexus_degrees

University of Maryland. (n.d.). *Earn a degree at the university made for you.* Retrieved from https://www.umuc.edu/

University of Phoenix. (2017, July 13). *The majority of the American workforce is interested in changing careers, but risks of starting over may be holding them back*. Retrieved from https://www.phoenix.edu/about_us/media-center/news/uopx-releases-career-change-survey.html

UPCEA. (n.d.). *National Adult Learner Coalition*. Retrieved from https://upcea.edu/news/national-adult-learner-coalition/

U.S. Department of Education. (2015, July 27). *Fact sheet: Focusing higher education on student success*. Retrieved from https://www.ed.gov/news/press-releases/fact-sheet-focusing-higher-education-student-success

Valbrun, M. (2018, April 30). *Tuition conundrum*. Retrieved from Inside Higher Ed: https://www.insidehighered.com/news/2018/04/30/nacubo-report-finds-tuition-discounting-again

Valletta, R. (2016). *Recent flattening in the higher education wage premium: Polarization, skill downgrading, or both?* San Francisco, CA: Federal Reserve Bank of San Francisco.

Virginia Department of Education. (n.d.). *Career switcher program*. Retrieved from http://www.doe.virginia.gov/teaching/educator_preparation/career_switcher/index.shtml

Wahba, P. (2015, June 5). *Walmart's CEO calls on staff to be like Han Solo, other Star Wars rebels*. Retrieved from Fortune: http://fortune.com/2015/06/05/walmart-star-wars/

World Economic Forum. (2016). *The future of jobs: Employment, skills and workforce srategy for the fourth industrial revolution*. Retrieved from https://sisr.swissinformatics.org/the-future-of-jobs-employment-skills-and-workforce-strategy-for-the-fourth-industrial-revolution-january-2016-wef/

Younger, J. (2016, October 11). *How learning and development are becoming more agile*. Retrieved from Harvard Business Review: https://hbr.org/2016/10/how-learning-and-development-are-becoming-more-agile

Zappos. (n.d.). *Holacracy and self-organization*. Retrieved from Zappos Insights: https://www.zapposinsights.com/about/holacracy

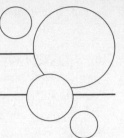

CHAPTER 2

Leveraging Complexity: Illuminating Compelling Outcomes

This chapter explores 10 major areas that define aspects of higher education that should be continually nurtured in both our traditional and post-traditional and lifelong learners. As graduates leave our programs, at any stage of their lives, they should be prepared to

- Address the world's political, economic, and social challenges
- Reflect the human experience and imagine the future
- Respond to volatility, uncertainty, complexity, ambiguity (VUCA)
- Engage a multigenerational and multicultural workforce
- Continue to learn in a workplace environment
- Take control of their own career development
- Learn to work in human–robot partnerships
- Navigate access to expanding information
- Become responsible citizens of their country and the world
- Design lives that achieve balance, fulfillment, and well-being

INTRODUCTION

Although some may see chapter 1 as describing a frightening set of challenges, we see the exciting potential of vast opportunities for higher education to reshape and reinvent itself in order to both remain and becoming increasingly more relevant—for example, to (a) more closely align our programs with market needs, (b) address the expanding diversity of learners' goals and desires, (c) prepare graduates to work in an increasingly multicultural and multigenerational workplace, (d) groom future engaged citizens for an ever increasing volatile environment, (e) use learning science to drive the educational experiences we create, and (f) flexibly redesign the learning environment—time available, preferred venue, price point, goals and desired outcomes—to meet learners where they are in their lives. Reshaping higher education in those ways would alleviate many of the issues identified in chapter 1. The first step in doing so, however, is to identify what we expect learners to be able to do as they engage with higher education over the course of their lifetimes. That is the focus of this chapter.

The good news is that we do have some time to be thoughtful and purposeful about our transformation, because the changes upon us will not significantly alter the world of work overnight. This is especially true of the technological advances that are driving much of the change. At least five factors will affect the pace and extent of adoption of new technologies: (1) technical feasibility, (2) cost of developing and deploying hardware and software, (3) labor market dynamics (including the cost of labor and related supply and demand dynamics), (4) economic benefits (including higher levels of output, better quality, and fewer errors), and (5) the capacity to mediate ethical and policy dilemmas associated with new technologies (e.g., even if we can genetically modify people, does it mean we should?) along with the associated regulatory and social acceptance (Manyika, Chui, & Miremadi, 2017). The time required to address these factors allows colleges and universities to gather data and make decisions that align with our respective current and/or future missions.

One simple example is facial recognition software. In July 2018, Amazon's facial recognition software incorrectly identified 28 lawmakers as people charged with crimes, including members of the Congressional Black Caucus. In a test conducted by the American Civil Liberties Union (ACLU), the software "disproportionally misidentified African-American and Latino members of Congress" when comparing photos of federal lawmakers with those of mug shots (Singer, 2018, p. B-4). Their conclusion was that the technology is not yet perfected; in fact, they called it "flawed, biased and dangerous" (Singer, 2018, p. B-4). The same is true, as of this writing, of self-driving cars. Although the technology is progressing, it is not yet ready, nor has it gained public confidence and acceptance.

Make no mistake, however, that there *will* be a tipping point when business processes are redesigned, investments are made, regulations are created, people accept and trust the technology, and so forth, at which time most workers' lives will be disrupted to some degree. Because of this—and the fact that people will be engaged in the labor market longer (Scott & Gratton, 2016) and workforce training programs as a percent of gross domestic product (GDP) has been steadily falling in the United States, moving from 0.08 in 1993 to 0.03 in 2015 (Manyika, Chui et al., 2017)—higher education has an exciting opportunity to not only remain relevant, but to become increasingly more relevant.

Taking a macro view, we should begin by thinking about the longer-term outcomes of a college education. We are fans of the Gallup-Purdue Index (now known as Strada-Gallup Alumni

Survey), which represents how people live their lives (in an integrated and holistic way) and what makes them happy and engaged. Their research has identified five areas of well-being that contribute to that happiness and engagement:

1. *Purpose Well-being:* Liking what you do each day and being motivated to achieve your goals.
2. *Social Well-being:* Having strong and supportive relationships and love in your life.
3. *Financial Well-being:* Effectively managing your economic life to reduce stress and increase security.
4. *Community Well-being:* The sense of engagement you have with the areas where you live, liking where you live, and feeling safe and having pride in your community.
5. *Physical Well-being:* Having good health and enough energy to get things done on a daily basis.

More information about this survey is available at https://www.gallup.com/education/194264/measuring-college-university-outcomes.aspx

For those interested, Gallup connects these general outcomes with experiences that undergraduate learners had in college. For example, this is where you see the impact of such things as mentoring, caring professors, experiential learning opportunities, and co-curricular activities. Additionally, since these five areas represent fundamental human needs, we can assume that those adult learners who are upskilling, changing professions, and so forth would also view these well-being goals as desirable and continue to work toward them.

What does this mean as we design education for the future needs of a diverse set of learners? We address this larger question with a set of goals that can drive how faculty, staff, and leaders of colleges and universities might think about their own path forward as they make decisions about their learner audiences and foci: learners need to be prepared to

- Address the world's political, economic, and social challenges
- Reflect the human experience and imagine the future
- Respond to volatility, uncertainty, complexity, ambiguity (VUCA)
- Engage a multigenerational and multicultural workforce
- Continue to learn in a workplace environment
- Take control of their own career development
- Learn to work in human–robot partnerships
- Navigate access to expanding information both accurate and inaccurate
- Become responsible citizens of their country and the world
- Design lives that achieve balance, fulfillment, and well-being

We structure this chapter around this set of goals: *what* we believe our learners need in order to respond to some of the challenges laid out in chapter 1. (In chapter 3, we discuss *how* colleges and universities might choose to achieve these outcomes.) In this chapter, we also share different sets of intellectual and professional skills (some call them competencies, attributes, hard and soft skills) noted by various entities (e.g., World Economic Forum; LinkedIn; Association of College & Research Libraries [ACRL]; and researchers from various disciplines, like Peter Drucker, Michael Arthur, and Denise Rousseau). Depending on the perspective of the source, the skill sets are sometimes general and sometimes more focused, and at various levels of concreteness, but combined they promote the successful intellectual, psychological, social, and physical development and well-being of our graduates. Though some overlap exists, there is not one set that by itself fully addresses all of the skills, competencies, and attributes that we believe our graduates will need. Consequently, we will be looking across these sets, because they offer the breadth that learners need to develop and hone to achieve personal and professional success.

ADDRESS THE WORLD'S POLITICAL, ECONOMIC, AND SOCIAL CHALLENGES

Many would agree that one of the most vital purposes of higher education is to prepare graduates to address the big issues or grand challenges facing the world. The notion that higher education is expected to play a role in addressing a changing world is deeply rooted in the history of American higher education, dating back to the Morrill Act of 1862. As President M. Peter McPherson of the Association of Public and Land-Grant Universities (APLU) pointed out in preparation for the sesquicentennial celebration of the land-grant universities in 2012, "The curriculum focused on 'scientific agriculture' to help improve farm productivity, mechanical arts (engineering) as the country was rapidly industrializing, and the humanities were deemed important for everyone" (Penn State University, 2012, para. 11). He went on to point out that "Early on, colleges adopted a model of cutting-edge teaching, discovering of new knowledge and using knowledge to solve problems in their states" (Penn State University, 2012, para. 12). It seems clear to us that dealing with grand challenges has been and continues to be one of the central purposes and roles of higher education.

Government organizations, foundations, professional associations, and nonprofits, among others, have articulated these challenges and, in some cases, provided funding toward addressing them. For example, the National Academy of Engineering identified the need to make solar energy economical, provide access to clean water, restore urban infrastructure, boost cybersecurity, manage the nitrogen cycle, and work to prevent nuclear terrorism, among others as key grand challenges (National Academy of Engineering, 2019). The Bill & Melinda Gates Foundation initially launched their grand challenges initiative in 2003 that focused on global health and, more recently, they expanded their focus to include global development as well as addressing humanitarian crises resulting from conflict and saving lives at birth in hard-to-reach communities (Bill & Melinda Gates Foundation, 2019). The American Academy of Social Work and Social Welfare identified 12 challenges, some of which include the need to stop family violence, eradicate social isolation, end homelessness, build financial capability for all, promote smart decarceration, harness technology for social good, and close the health gap (American Academy of Social Work and Social Welfare, 2019).

Since 2011, the United States Agency for International Development (USAID) has been committed to developing new public-private partnerships that have included governments, foundations, universities, and others to bring innovative solutions to scale in addressing a series of grand challenges to development. These partnerships include Saving Lives at Birth, All Children Reading, Powering Agriculture, Making All Voices Count, Securing Water for Food, Fighting Ebola, Combatting Zika and Future Threats, Scaling Off-Grid Energy, Ensuring Effective Health Supply Chains, and Creating Hope in Conflict (USAID, 2018). The United Nations also issued Millennium Development Goals in 2003, which were superseded by Sustainable Development Goals. Essentially, all of these grand challenges focus on matters related to health, education, sustainability, poverty, and gender equality. Increasingly, however, issues surrounding artificial intelligence (AI), cybersecurity, and privacy are also emerging as new frontiers for grand challenges.

The concept of universities intentionally launching their own grand challenges initiatives is also starting to gain new traction. The University of California, Los Angeles (UCLA) hosted a workshop and strategy session with the goal of developing a new community of practice for university-led grand challenges. The university released a report in February 2018 featuring a number of leading U.S. research institutions that have launched grand challenges, sometimes called "moonshot" (a term referring to President John Kennedy's space program commitment) programs (Popowitz & Dorgelo, 2018). The report summarizes key strategies for success for those who may have interest in launching one of their own. UCLA relates that it has been advising universities across the globe, including in the United Kingdom, Australia, and Germany, that are becoming interested in setting their own grand challenge goals (Popowitz et al., 2018).

The good news about these daunting challenges is that they align with the concerns and interests of millennial graduates and Gen Z learners (Eagan et al., 2017). The other good news is that colleges and universities recognize that we cannot address any of these challenges in a siloed way. In other words, one discipline does not "hold" the answer; rather, integration across disciplines is the key (more about how to do that in chapter 3). Each challenge requires all of these: a technical solution, a policy solution, an economic solution, and a social solution. In this respect, all disciplines will play a role in addressing these global challenges, including the sometimes maligned liberal arts. It is not only the perspectives and methodologies of various disciplines that we need, but also the skills they focus on that provide an integrated and holistic approach to sustainable solutions. According to the World Economic Forum 2016 Report (World Economic Forum, 2016), the top 10 skills graduates need are

· complex problem solving,
· critical thinking,
· creativity,
· people management,

- coordinating with others,
- emotional intelligence,
- judgment and decision making,
- service orientation,
- negotiation, and
- cognitive flexibility.

In the World Economic Forum's Future of Jobs Report, just 2 years later they indicate that other skills are also growing in need for the 2022 outlook, including analytical thinking, innovation, resilience, attention to detail, and leadership. In addition to these and proficiency in new technologies, the report emphasizes the need for "human skills," specifically creativity, initiative, originality, and persuasion (World Economic Forum, 2018).

A well-rounded education addresses the need for some of these integrated skills, as does integrated teams working toward a solution, which means that not all learners necessarily need all skills, perspectives, methodologies, and so forth. Instead, learners with varying interests and backgrounds will all be needed to address the grand challenges that face us. In fact, it's not just in the arena of grand challenges that all disciplines are needed; for example, in the development of Microsoft's AI bot Cortana, a poet, novelist, and playwright were all on the team to ensure the right personality tone was achieved. The same is true of Apple's Siri and Amazon's Alexa—all of these projects engaged similar specialties to create the "right" personality for the machine (Wilson & Daugherty, 2018). So, what learners need is the ability to work collaboratively across disciplinary boundaries, and higher education needs to prepare them to do so.

Increasingly, new cross-disciplinary initiatives demonstrate a commitment to the value added when those in the liberal arts work together with scientists and engineers. One such example is

96

the grand challenges initiative launched by Heidi Bostic, former dean of the College of Liberal Arts at the University of New Hampshire. She explains,

> Scientists and engineers remind us again and again that these matters must be understood within broader realms of human concern, like health, vulnerability, sustainability and the joy of living. These are basic issues of meaning, purpose and value, questions that the humanities and the broad liberal arts confront: Who are we and how ought we live? (Dumais, 2018, para. 3)

Another project designed to acknowledge the value of the liberal arts has been funded by the Teagle Foundation and is under the aegis of the National Academy of Engineering (NAE). The planning grant given to four partnering institutions (Rochester Institute of Technology, Lawrence Technological Institute, Franklin W. Olin College of Engineering, and Worcester Polytechnic Institute) is for the purpose of integrating the liberal arts into engineering curricula by launching the Grand Challenges Scholars Programs (GCSP). In compliance with NAE standards, GCSP students "will complete a curriculum that prepares them to work at the boundary between engineering and non-engineering disciplines" (Van Fleet, 2015, para. 2; Teagle Foundation, n.d.). And Bucknell University boldly identifies itself as "a unique national university where liberal arts and professional programs complement each other" (Van Fleet, 2015, para. 1).

In all of the previous examples, there is evidence of collaboration and integration across disciplines along with preparation of graduates with disciplinary knowledge and skills. Interdisciplinary, multidisciplinary, and cross-disciplinary curricular approaches have been on the rise at colleges and universities across the globe over the past 4 decades as faculty recognized the limitations of trying to innovate or create solutions with a single disciplinary approach (Jacob, 2015). Focusing on teamwork has also garnered much attention at institutions, as has connecting students to real-world problems through experiential learning opportunities like co-ops, internships, undergraduate research, and service learning, among others. Continuing these trends is vital to addressing the nation's and the world's challenges and requires that higher education prepare graduates with the requisite knowledge, skills, attitudes, and perspectives.

REFLECT THE HUMAN EXPERIENCE AND IMAGINING THE FUTURE

Above we articulate the value of the liberal and fine and performing arts in providing perspectives, methodologies, and skills to address some of the world's major problems. Beyond that, however, is another important goal for higher education that draws from the liberal and fine and performing arts: they both reflect the human experience and push us in new directions. The human experience across time, cultures, and civilizations is made clearer and enriched by art, music, literature, and other aesthetic representations or frames of reference (e.g., poetry, sculptures, poems, operas, short stories, theater). Brown and Dissanayake (2009) point out that aspects of the arts (pitch, tone, rhythm, role-playing, image development, and design) may be serving a significant social, rather than aesthetic, role. They suggest that the arts may have more to do with things such as motivating people into action, communicating with gods or other celestial beings, helping people to better understand their cultural lineage, and relieving stress (Brown & Dissanayake, 2009). Greene (1995) sees the arts as key in opening minds to new possibilities, envisioning alternatives, and imagining the world differently than the one we currently see.

The fine and performing arts also convey the texture of the human experience and foster deeper understanding for contemporaneous and historical meaning-making of events and experiences as well as the values of a given culture. For example, as of this writing, Broadway hits include *Hamilton*, *Les Misérables*, *Come from Away*, and *Fiddler on the Roof*, to name a few. These representations provide accessible, textured interpretations of historical events, potentially leading to a more robust and deeper understanding than simply reading textbook accounts. And this historical understanding helps us all to better comprehend current political, economic, and social situations. Another example is the impact of the horror of World War I on the arts, which has helped to provide perspective and insight, especially for those from different generations and experiences. Examining writings such as *All Quiet on the Western Front*, written by Erich Maria Remarque, a German veteran of WWI; Ernest Hemingway's *A Farewell to Arms*; or T. S. Elliot's poem "The Waste Land" evoke rich and powerful understanding of and connection to the human experience. These works serve as a medium and vehicle through which emotion and values might be discovered and expressed—a means through which imagination, introspection, and appreciation of that which is authentically human is enriched and made more complete. In this way, the opportunities to analyze, interpret, create new insights, and broaden understanding and to advance the creation and development of knowledge to envision and discover the future are all furthered. Elliot Eisner (1992) points out that, though we commonly think of the arts in terms of expression that often provides insight and feeling, we also need to recognize the arts for their contributions to learning and discovery. Consequently, attention to the arts is an essential component to expressing and understanding the human experience through time and place, as well as promoting discovery and imagination, all critical elements and attributes for the 21st century.

The creative capacities learned through the liberal and fine and performing arts are becoming increasingly more important in the world of emerging technologies, which we will explore later in this chapter. This is part of the reason STEM (science, technology, engineering, and mathematics) has morphed into STEAM (science, technology, engineering, arts, and mathematics), as we discussed in chapter 1; the skills of entrepreneurship, imagination, creativity, and innovation are more important in a rapidly evolving world. These characteristics and skills are learned and nurtured through the liberal and fine and performing arts, a recognition that continues to lend support to general education and core curriculum (discussed in more detail in chapter 3) as one of several ways to accomplish the goals of reflecting the human experience and imagining the future.

RESPOND TO VOLATILITY, UNCERTAINTY, COMPLEXITY, AMBIGUITY (VUCA)

We established in chapter 1 the confluence of factors that are contributing to the fast pace of change in our world, including the fact that some jobs will end, new occupations and jobs will be created, and most jobs will change in some way due to AI, automation, and/or the Internet of Things (IoT).

Although the term VUCA first appeared in the revised curriculum dealing with strategic leadership established by the United States Army War College in 1987, shortly thereafter decision makers and leaders across all fields adopted the term, believing that the same conditions and principles applied broadly across all industries and professions in the postindustrial 21st century (U.S. Army Heritage & Education Center, 2018). Volatility is not just about the rate of change but concerns the fact that some information or presumed knowledge becomes obsolete, so much so that

100

no program of study in any major can provide students with all of the knowledge and skills they will need to sustain their employability for the duration of their working lives. Therefore, preparing students to become self-directed learners (discussed later in this chapter) is vital to their lifelong success. At a recent University Convocation, the president of Northeastern University, Joseph E. Aoun (2018), expressed to incoming students that at least half of what they would learn would be obsolete by the time they would graduate, and if it was known which half that was, it wouldn't be taught!

One doesn't need to look hard to find evidence of the pace of these dramatic shifts in the employment landscape. Citing a study completed by Lin (2011), who found that 0.56 percent of new jobs in the United States each year were in new occupations, the McKinsey Global Institute said, "[T]his implies that 18 percent of the workforce today is employed in an occupation that essentially did not exist in 1980" (Manyika, Lund et al., 2017, p. 4). Further, the McKinsey Global Institute puts the number of workers who will need to switch occupations by 2030 somewhere between 3 and 14 percent of the global workforce (Manyika, Lund et al., 2017). If we ask the question a bit differently, in terms of what jobs did not exist 10 years ago, it becomes clear that this is not a new phenomenon; for example, we now have application developers, social media managers, Uber drivers, driverless car engineers, cloud computing specialists, big data analysts/data scientists, sustainability managers, YouTube content creators, and drone operators (Hallett & Hutt, 2016).

According to a World Economic Forum 2018 Report on the future of jobs, nearly 50 percent of the responding companies indicated that they expect automation to reduce their full-time workforce by 2022; however, more than 25 percent of them also anticipate an increase in new roles in their enterprises. The same report shares estimates that indicate that 75 million jobs may be displaced, whereas 133 million new roles may emerge. The survey included human resource executives across multiple industries that employed approximately 15 million employees and included both emerging and developed economies representing approximately 70 percent of global GDP. Naturally, they also reported that they expect, by 2022, skills required to perform all jobs will shift significantly (World Economic Forum, 2018).

To prepare our graduates for these changes, we need to help them embrace the concept of a growth mindset (Dweck, 2007) and the development of such skills as *self-awareness* (e.g., knowing what you don't know), *discernment* (e.g., knowing what you need to learn, where you want to go, and what your goals are), *metacognition* (e.g., knowing how to learn), *self-efficacy* (e.g., a sense of empowerment and confidence to act), *resilience* (e.g., the willingness to learn from failure and persist), *nimbleness* (e.g., the capacity to flexibly adapt and adjust to new situations or environmental constraints), *entrepreneurship* (e.g., the ability to assume a creative mindset and to imagine new avenues of discovery or opportunity), and *comfort with ambiguity* (e.g., to be open to and handle risks associated with uncertainty), to name a few. Some business leaders have called for individuals to focus more on developing underlying capabilities such as curiosity, critical thinking, risk-taking, imagination, creativity, and social emotional intelligence rather than simply gaining disciplinary knowledge and skills alone. These attributes will enable employees to continue to evolve their skills more rapidly in the future. It is a widely held belief that acquired knowledge becomes obsolete faster than ever before, and that the amount of knowledge most employees need to effectively carry out their roles is growing at a much faster pace than ever before. Essentially, employees need to be open to new approaches that may require them to unlearn what they think they already know (Hagel & Brown, 2017). These capacities require a flexibility and adaptability that are more important now than ever.

Unfortunately, our younger graduates do not feel confident that they are ready to address VUCA. A survey by Deloitte (2018) indicates that many millennial and Gen Z employees do not believe they are prepared for the changes Industry 4.0 will bring. The McGraw-Hill Education (2018) survey indicates that only 41 percent of college graduates "feel very or extremely prepared for their future careers" (p. 3). Additionally, the Strada-Gallup College Student Survey (2017), which collected the views of more than 32,000 students, found what it described as "a crisis of confidence among most students regarding their readiness to launch careers" (Strada-Gallup Education Network, 2018, para. 3). This observation is based on their finding that only about a third of students believe they will graduate with the skills and knowledge necessary for success in the job market and/or workplace, and a little more than 50 percent report they believe their major will enable them to acquire a good job (Strada-Gallup Education Network, 2018).

There is also ample evidence to indicate that the general public and employers also have a lack of confidence in the workforce readiness of both high school and college graduates (Busteed, 2018). The 2018 Jobs Outlook Survey, conducted by the National Association of Colleges and Employers (NACE), reported substantial differences between employers' perceptions of college graduates' and college graduates' perception of their own readiness across eight competencies—Professionalism/Work Ethic, Oral/Written Communication, Critical Thinking/Problem Solving, Teamwork/Collaboration, Leadership, Digital Technology, Career Management, and Global/Intercultural Fluency (Gray & Koncz, 2018). Essentially, employers viewed graduates as less prepared than graduates viewed themselves. Higher education needs to address both the perception and the reality to ensure our graduates can flourish in a VUCA world.

ENGAGE A MULTIGENERATIONAL AND MULTICULTURAL WORKFORCE

As noted earlier, the demographic shifts in the workplace are and will continue to be dramatic. Individuals' and organizations' success will depend, in large part, on the ability for both employers and employees to be able to connect, communicate, build trust, and gain credibility with people different from them. This begs the question of how higher education contributes to helping its learners gain the competencies and skills necessary to flourish in a multigenerational and multicultural workplace.

Each fall semester since 1997, the Beloit College Freshman Mindset List whimsically brings focus to some of the events or experiences that may have potentially shaped the worldview or mindset of the entering traditionally aged freshman class. We often read these with amusement and trepidation, recognizing the items listed are not scientifically researched and that they can provide a stark reminder of our advancing age. Nevertheless, they provide a realization of the context and frame of reference through which the new cohort of students may see their world. For example, the class of 2022, who entered in 2018, have always had Wikipedia, have never used a spit bowl in a dentist's office, rarely if ever visit a bank, have always seen emotional support animals on airplanes, have always seen films distributed on the Internet, have access to mass market books through E-books, and have grown up with stories of where their parents were on 9/11 (McBride, 2018).

Although we recognize that there are no hard and fast sets of behaviors, values, and characteristics assignable to different generations—and we eschew stereotypes, especially those that state them as if they are universally applicable—attributes associated with different generations can help us to be more sensitive and potentially effective in our interactions with people different from ourselves. It is not uncommon to find some generalizations regarding shared attributes and attitudes drawn about various generations. If one accepts that people's perspectives can be, at least partially, shaped by their experiences and context during their formative years, we can certainly benefit from becoming loosely familiar with current generational categories and consider how it may impact policy and practice within the academy and workforce. Some of the more common generational characterizations include

- Silent or Traditional (born before 1945),
- Baby boomers (born between 1946 and 1964),
- Generation X (born between 1965 and 1980),
- Millennials (born between 1981 and 1996, and
- Postmillennial/Generation Z (born after 1997).

Although the mix of each generation across the labor force shifts over time, millennials currently represent the largest percentage in the workforce (Pew Research Center, 2018). However, given the need for individuals to reskill and upskill throughout their lives, and the growing number of post-traditional learners in higher education, understanding some of the attitudes, beliefs, values, behaviors, and ways of thinking of these different groups is an important part of the mosaic for educators, employers, and employees to consider.

For example, baby boomers are often described as workaholics, optimistic, tolerant, and loyal, believing people should pay their dues to advance at work, and many prefer more formal styles of communication. Gen Xers are described as self-reliant, fiercely independent, skeptical, seeking a good work–life balance, and preferring informal and direct communication. Millennials are said to be goal focused, realistic, independent, and self-directed, whereas Gen Zs possess a uniqueness and authentic presence, with an openness to change and willingness to share, and they generally prefer informal communication styles (American Management Association, n.d.; Matre, 2017; Wall Street Journal, n.d.). These characteristics present new challenges *and* opportunities for educators and employers alike.

Because of these potentially different values and attitudes, it will become increasingly important that *all* employees develop skills to interact with one another across generational lines. For example, millennials differ from baby boomers as they favor collaboration, respond better to coaching rather than a traditional top-down authoritative approach, and view change as a vehicle for new opportunities (Lipman, 2017). Furthermore, younger workers, particularly women, tend to "more often question workplace expectations, such as long work hours or taking work home, and they often are more open about their parenting obligations and commitments" (Dittman, 2005, para. 8). Psychologist Constance Patterson notes the extremes:

> [B]oomers may believe gen Xers are too impatient and willing to throw out the tried-and-true strategies, while gen Xers may view boomers as always trying to say the right thing to the right person and being inflexible to change. Traditionalists may view baby boomers as self-absorbed and prone to sharing too much information, and baby boomers may view traditionalists as dictatorial and rigid. And, gen Xers may consider millennials too spoiled and self-absorbed, while millennials may view gen Xers as too cynical and negative. (Dittman, 2005, para. 10)

Since people are living and working longer, organizations are facing a new epoch in having three to five different generations represented in their workforce. And though it is important not to pigeonhole each generation into a particular mindset or to dwell on differences, enough evidence exists to suggest that employers would be wise to understand the characteristics of their workforce as part of developing their overall human capital management strategies (Stevens, 2010). Most especially, it is important to understand what matters to ones' employees, what motivates them, and where they might be on their life journey (e.g., new to the workforce, kids, mortgage, aging parents) without dwelling on the potential differences that may exist across different generations (R. Knight, 2014). With this in mind, building inclusive and cooperative teams is key and requires strong communication skills, emotional intelligence, flexibility, creativity, and adaptability, among other skills. These skills are often referred to as "soft skills," although we believe them to be foundational and fundamental skills for success. In fact, in a LinkedIn Survey of Workplace Learning, "soft skills" emerged as the top priority for talent development among executives and talent development professionals (LinkedIn Learning, 2018). Higher education needs to prioritize graduates' preparedness in these areas.

Fundamentally, the complexity of both educational and work environments in terms of generational and cultural differences is here to stay. We know that communication styles are continuously shaped and reshaped by shared cultural values, norms, and worldviews of the specific cultural or generational group to which one is affiliated (Liu, 2016). Further, these various communication styles, values, and work habits create changing dynamics to navigate in the workplace, requiring a new constellation of skills and expertise for both employers and employees. Some aspects of the working environment might need additional flexibility to accommodate the needs and interests of this multigenerational, multicultural workforce—for example, benefits expectations, job perks, team structures, communication strategies, and work–life balance. Furthermore, social consciousness of the organization, commitment, or loyalty factors associated with length of stay with an organization may well require innovative approaches (Deloitte, 2018). Millennials want professional development opportunities for growth, whereas other generations may be less interested in professional development (yet need it), and how individuals' belief systems align with a company's profit motives may differ. Millennials, the largest segment of the labor force, have an increased awareness of and commitment to the social consciousness, social justice, and inclusion behaviors of employers than have other segments of the workforce (Deloitte, 2018).

The transfer of organizational knowledge is a critical management challenge that is made more complex by the multiple approaches to learning that each generation embraces. Piktialis and Greenes (2008), while cautioning that typecasting generations whole cloth should be approached with caution, assert that understanding, in broad terms, how each generation prefers to learn is critical to designing an effective knowledge transfer approach. For example, younger employees often embrace technology to both communicate and collaborate, whereas older colleagues prefer face to face for both. Younger employees also yearn for continual, even informal, feedback; their older colleagues prefer the structured annual performance review approach they are accustomed to. Therefore, understanding the learner and designing programs that are most suitable to helping them learn to effectively engage those from different cultures and generations is important to both individual success and organizational health. Real challenges result from cultural and generational differences that, if not recognized and addressed, can mitigate the potential benefits and frustrate the workforce. (We discuss ways to address these issues in chapter 3.) Colleges and universities can begin to help learners hone the necessary skills to be successful in a diverse environment.

Similarly, diversity of gender, race, ethnicity, or nationality is also seen as an opportunity to leverage different worldviews, values, unique histories, and strengths for the benefit of the organization. A number of studies (Cox, 1994; Erhardt, Werbel, & Shrader, 2003;

McLeod & Lobel, 1992; Miller, 2009; Noland, Tyler, & Kotschwar, 2016; Richard, 2017) have explored the impact of diversity in the workplace, arguing multiple perspectives and examining a number of different questions on the benefits, conditions, and/or limitations associated with multicultural workforces. Regardless of these various studies, the case for business necessity to embrace a positive approach (Youssef-Morgan & Hardy, 2014) to building multicultural workforces is made compelling as a result of at least three business realities: changing demographics, globalization, and a clear value-added associated with the inclusion of different perspectives, experiences, and values to all aspects of corporate decision making (e.g., marketing, human resources management, and communications). Convincing evidence exists indicating that organizations that embrace a sincere commitment to developing a positive multicultural climate and workforce outperform those organizations that do not (Von Bergen, Soper, & Parnell, 2005). Consequently, developing the skills necessary to lead and/or work in such environments is integral to both individual and organizational success, and higher education needs to begin the process of helping graduates to develop these skills.

As we discussed in chapter 1, the successful multicultural workplace requires that employees possess some degree of cultural agility, which includes the ability to (1) question one's own cultural assumptions, values, and beliefs, (2) view the world from other perspectives, (3) recognize differences among cultures (e.g., communication styles, relationships, personal space, power structures and dynamics, decision making, role of individual and group), and (4) respond accordingly. Depending on the situation and context, response may mean adapting (e.g., to the client's culture, to the need for greater autonomy for workers in some cases and direct leadership in others), holding firm to the standards of your organization (e.g., safety, ethics), or integrating (e.g., coming up with a new approach), and most

109

importantly, leveraging the appropriate response at the right time (Caligiuri, 2012).

We are fans of Caligiuri's (2012) research on cultural agility, which includes not only a framework and set of competencies, but thoughtful recommendations for helping organizations to build cross-cultural training. Her work can easily be adapted to college and university settings. For example, it can aid us in thinking about how to help learners (a) become more comfortable with ambiguity, (b) develop appropriate self-efficacy, (c) learn to ask questions and gain information to assist in cross-cultural interactions, (d) switch perspectives to view the work, challenge, or task through another lens, and (e) reassign meaning to behaviors that initially could be misunderstood. A lot of research exists that both overlaps and extends Caligiuri's work, so higher education has much to draw on as we think about how to help graduates gain the competencies that can enable them to effectively engage with people different from themselves, positively impacting their confidence, interactions, and decisions (Rasmussen & Sieck, 2015; Spitzberg & Changnon, 2009).

CONTINUE TO LEARN IN A WORKPLACE ENVIRONMENT

To ensure that these work environments are productive for organizations and individuals, ongoing knowledge acquisition and skills development will be key ingredients. Traditionally, learning in the workplace has been oriented to the organization maintaining the locus of control regarding the selection of content (e.g., knowledge, skills, and attributes to be developed) and the manner and structure of delivery. Learning is, however, becoming more controlled by the learner in the workplace, and training models need to reflect the emerging emphasis on person-centered rather

110

than instructor-centered approaches (Noe, Clarke, & Klein, 2014). Although there may be some paradigm shifts in training models, employers will continue to play a role in meeting training and development needs of employees. A 2018 LinkedIn Workplace Learning Report indicated that the talent gap facing most organizations necessitates the creation of learning opportunities for employees in order to remain competitive and ahead of the curve. Further, the report noted that 68 percent of employees prefer to learn at work, with 58 percent reporting they like to learn at their own pace. Ninety-four percent of the employees participating in the survey indicated that they would stay longer with a company if the firm invested in their career development (LinkedIn Learning, 2018).

According to the 2018 Deloitte Millennial Survey, both millennials and Gen Zs expect business employers to take the lead in helping them to prepare for workplace educational needs, yet fewer than 45 percent believe employers are helping them to prepare for changes in the workplace (the next section challenges this expectation and asserts that graduates need to take control of their own career development). Millennials and Gen Zs credit their university studies with only 23 percent and 26 percent, respectively, for providing them with the knowledge and skills they are currently using in their jobs. Perhaps that is why the LinkedIn survey also indicates that these groups are not turning to universities for further learning and development. About 80 percent of millennials say that on-the-job training, continuous professional development, and formal training led by employers will be most important to helping them perform their best (Deloitte, 2018). Ironically, only about a third of the talent-development professionals responding in that same survey indicated that they would recommend their own training programs. Employees also report that manager involvement is critical in encouraging employees to develop new skills, with some 56 percent reporting that they would commit time to learning if their manager identified skills or courses that would be helpful to their advancement or performance (LinkedIn Learning, 2018). We would argue that those graduates or employees who will be most successful are those who do this for themselves—that is, they recognize what they don't know, identify what they need to learn, find appropriate opportunities to do so, and engage in those learning opportunities. These are the self-directed learners we all want in our organizations, and graduates should leave their colleges and universities with the skills to engage in self-directed, lifelong learning. All of this suggests opportunity for considerable improvement in meeting these growing needs across the workplace.

With the half-life of skills now estimated to be about 5 years and the expanded length of time that people are expected to remain in the workforce (some estimate 60–70 years), metacognitive skills (the process of reflecting on and directing one's own thinking and learning) are increasingly more important as employees' continual learning becomes key to individual and organizational success (Scott & Gratton, 2016). As noted in the previous paragraph, these skills help learners to become self-directed, and they include the ability to assess the demands of a new task, evaluate one's own knowledge and skills to successfully complete the task, plan their approach (including addressing shortcomings in knowledge and skills), monitor their progress toward successfully completing the task, and adjust their strategies as needed in response to monitoring progress (Ambrose, Bridges, DiPietro, Lovett, & Norman, 2010).

The LinkedIn Learning at Work report (LinkedIn Learning, 2018) asserts that companies will need to develop a lifelong learning system to ensure the availability of human capital, and that workers will need a "mindset of agile learning" to reskill and or upskill to perform the jobs that will emerge by 2022 (World Economic Forum, 2018). As many have noted, reskilling and lifelong learning are the new normal, and higher education could play an increasingly important role in preparing graduates who are self-directed learners ready to take control of their own learning and career development. As you will see in chapter 3, companies are just beginning to partner with higher education given the realization that they cannot, nor do they want or need to, provide all of the continual learning on their own.

TAKE CONTROL OF THEIR OWN CAREER DEVELOPMENT

The very nature of the VUCA environment discussed earlier in this chapter makes it virtually impossible for clear predictions to emerge or standard assumptions and/or projections to provide the assurances they once did. Lifelong employment within one company or industry is just not what the "social contract" governing the relationship between employers and employees looks like in the 21st century. Rather, employees "must take charge of their own employability, expect to have many jobs and many different employers over their working lifetimes, and create their own security by maintaining their special knowledge and skill set through a lifetime of continuous learning" (Shaffer & Zalewski, 2011, p. 68). In their book *The Boundaryless Career: A New Employment Principle for a New Organizational Era*, Arthur and Rousseau (1996) describe a "boundaryless career" in which people will need to take responsibility for their own career futures; they use the word "boundaryless" to refer to multiple circumstances, including (a) the movement between and across organizational boundaries (changing industries), (b) the marketing of oneself beyond a current employer (freelancing and consulting), (c) establishing and sustaining external networks, (d) the flattening or altering of hierarchical organizational charts, and

113

(e) the choosing of personal demands of one's life over a potential career advancement (work–life balance). Basically, the concept of a boundaryless career shifts the locus of control over one's career away from a structured career ladder that may have individuals be dependent on the organization that employs them to one of independence and personal ownership. In this way, the relationship between the individual and the employer is dramatically altered (Arthur, Claman, & DeFillippi, 1995; DeFillippi & Arthur, 1994, 1996).

Burnett and Evans (2016), Stanford University design educators and cofounders of the Life Design Lab, embrace the notion that people need to take control of their careers, affirming that people will be continually designing and redesigning their lives, including careers. These educators see life design as a generative process that is constantly changing and evolving as life circumstances change and evolve. Their book is a result of very popular courses they teach at Stanford which "help any student to apply the innovation principles of design thinking to the wicked problem of designing your life at and after university" (Burnett & Evans, 2016, p. xviii). They suggest reframing the age-old question "What do you want to be when you grow up?" to "Who or what do you want to grow into?" We resonate with this question for two reasons. First, given previous discussions in this chapter as well as chapter 1, graduates will need to be nimble, agile, flexible, and adaptable throughout their professional lives to respond to the rate and pace of change in the workplace. Second, as we discuss later in this chapter, human beings continue to learn, develop, and grow throughout their lives, potentially resulting in different interests and values that can lead them in new directions. Burnett and Evans view life design as a journey in which an iterative design process is key, much like Caligiuri (as quoted in chapter 1) telling us that "cultural agility is a practice, not an achievement, and building it is a process, not an event" (2012, p. 5).

114

Carter Cast (2018b), in his book *The Right and Wrong Stuff: How Brilliant Careers Are Made and Unmade*, investigates what contributes to a successful career versus those behaviors that contribute to one's demise. Cast calls this an "era of do-it-yourself career development" (2018a, para. 1), acknowledging that many companies offer less training because employees change jobs so frequently, so it falls to the employee to take control. Peter Drucker (2005) calls this "managing oneself" and believes that, in order to do so, you need to clearly understand your strengths, how you perform (which includes how you learn), and what your values are, which will lead you to decisions of where you belong and what you want to contribute. Although he admits that these sound obvious and elementary, he points out that most people believe they know what they are both good at and not good at, and those people are usually wrong on both counts. As a result, graduates need to be thoughtful and purposeful about managing their careers, a skill that colleges and universities should help them hone.

We live in a very different world now, even from the time Drucker wrote the above-cited article in 2005. In that piece, he discusses how to develop a second career in the second half of one's life. If you accept that workers will be in the workforce much longer than in the past (we referenced a projection of 60–70 years in chapter 1) and that technological advances will continue to change the world of work at an increasing rate and pace, then workers have the potential to be engaged in multiple careers, not just two, over the course of their lives. We are already seeing the expectation of movement among younger workers; in the 2018 Deloitte Millennial Survey, 43 percent of millennials envision leaving their jobs within 2 years, whereas only 28 percent seek to stay beyond 5 years. Employed Gen Z respondents express even less loyalty, with 61 percent saying they would leave within 2 years if given the choice (Deloitte, 2018). While this represents changing jobs as opposed to changing careers, will that be far behind? Given the current and future projected state of work, history does not provide guidance as organizations no longer outlive workers and people no longer stay put (Drucker, 2005). Higher education needs to ensure that our graduates and lifelong learners are empowered to take control of their own career development.

LEARN TO WORK IN HUMAN-ROBOT PARTNERSHIPS

Many are quick to create dystopian apocalyptic visions of the future, with robots overtaking the planet and/or replacing humans in just about everything. In fact, a whimsical film by Spike Jonze titled *Her* chronicles a writer's romance with a computer operating system; this is the world that some fear. However, humans possess a number of characteristics that robots, machines, and AI cannot yet replicate. Emotions, most notably empathy, sympathy, and patience—critical in many occupations—are uniquely human. Though machines are capable of the massive processing of data and repetitive precision activities, human creativity, spontaneity, and adaptability remain elusive. Computers are not yet able to read or react to nuance, reason, or establish trust; these, too, remain authentic human attributes (Morgan, 2017).

Often, discussions about automation and AI devolve into a human versus machine dynamic. The real opportunity is in exploring and understanding the unique strengths, talents, and skills that machines and humans possess and bring to the task, which ultimately will simply redesign the work rather than eliminate it. Machines cannot yet improvise, they are not curious, they do not deal well with novel or unexpected phenomena, and they do not parse human or social significance. As Bill McDermott (2018), CEO of SAP, puts it, "machines don't dream, set goals, and are not responsible, they can only learn from the past, they

116

cannot imagine the future" (para. 20)—which is why we need to develop the creative capacities in all of our learners, as noted earlier in this chapter. The potential is more about considering the architecture of work, exploring the components of each aspect, and leveraging the strengths that people bring to the table to create what some refer to as an "augmented humanity." In this way, through partnerships, human and machine intelligence will transform outcomes and create new possibilities. Clearly, machines require human oversight to be effective. Developing the skills necessary to effectively function with this mindset calls for new educational paradigms that promote and strengthen skills, characteristics, and attributes that are uniquely human (McDermott, 2018).

In fact, in a recent article based on research across 1,500 companies, Wilson and Daugherty (2018) assert that those organizations that are using AI to replace workers rather than to complement or augment the work of humans are very short-sighted. They note that the most significant long-term performance improvements were found when efforts to leverage the human skills of creativity, teamwork, leadership, and social skills *were combined with* the speed, scalability, and quantitative capabilities of the machines in a complementary and collaborative way (Wilson & Daugherty, 2018). Further, though it is widely acknowledged that machine learning and artificial intelligence will have a broad impact on the world of work, Brynjolffson, Mitchell, and Rock (2018) found that, while most occupations include some tasks that could be addressed through machine learning, few are able to be fully automated. This is consistent with the research reported by the McKinsey Global Institute (2017) discussed in chapter 1.

Moreover, all workers will need to adapt as their occupations evolve alongside increasingly capable machines. Some of that adaptation will require higher educational attainment or spending more time on activities that require social and emotional skills, creativity, high-level cognitive capabilities, and other skills relatively hard to automate (Manyika, Lund et al., 2017).

In other words, people will remain critical to many facets of work. For example, people are needed to train machines, explain a machine decision that might be an unpredicted or a controversial recommendation, or perhaps find the explanation of unanticipated machine action(s) such as a fatal crash of a self-driving vehicle or financial credit denials. People will also need to sustain the safe use of machines—for example, making sure that employees are recognized by the machines to avoid accidents, in fast-moving industrial settings where machines perform major functions, provide systemic decisions that may present bias, or offer prescription recommendations that are contraindicated. Machines, on the other hand, can amplify skills and achievement by humans in a variety of settings. One such example is the use of generative design software that can produce multiple options given the parameters of a project, allowing the designer to use professional judgment and aesthetic considerations to select from among the many machine-generated alternatives. In this way, the creative process is amplified and augmented, not replaced, by AI (Wilson & Daugherty, 2018).

Industries of all kinds are beginning to utilize machines in novel ways. Marty Linn, principal engineer for robotics at General Motors, said GM is employing robots to do the "dirty, dull, difficult and dangerous tasks" (Shirouzu, Taylor, & Carey, 2018, para. 15). Also from the car industry, Mercedes Benz in Stuttgart, Germany, wanted to improve their ability to customize their highly priced vehicles and achieve flexibility within their plant to better meet their consumers' preferences while still managing costs. Through the use of collaborative robots, or "cobots," they have been able to deliver individualized preferences all from one plant. Although some have seen these developments as a threat, there is broad recognition that AI and robots cannot achieve everything. United Auto

Workers President Dennis Williams said, "It's critical thinking that automation can't replicate." And Tesla CEO Elon Musk recently tweeted, "Excessive automation at Tesla was a mistake . . . Humans are underrated" (Shirouzu, Taylor, & Carey, 2018, para. 32).

As we just noted, technology is playing an ever-expanding role in our society. The benefits associated with automation handling all kinds of tasks with greater efficiency and effectiveness are finding their way into all aspects of modern life. Examples can be found emerging across all fields and professions. In fact, Gartner predicts that by 2021, AI-enabled tools will generate approximately $2.9 trillion in business value and are expected to create more jobs by 2020 than they eliminate (Gartner, 2017). PricewaterhouseCoopers has predicted that AI could contribute nearly $16 trillion to global economy growth and by 2030 increase GDP growth by 26 percent (McDermott, 2018). Whether it is managing the warehouse functions for Amazon, managing supply chain operations of major industries, automating repetitive tasks for financial advisers at Ernst & Young (freeing them to focus on client relations), using virtual reality to improve managerial and customer relations training at Walmart (Matney, 2017), and/or managing and sorting enormous amounts of data to support medical diagnostics, the value and impact of automation are altering all aspects of work and life (Chandrasekaran & Conrad, 2015).

There are clearly benefits in utilizing automation to do the mundane, repetitive tasks, enabling humans to be freed up to do those things that only we can do. We know that automation can usually reduce errors, increase the speed with which repetitive tasks can be accomplished, and identify patterns easily and effectively. Additionally, robots can often conduct activities that are unsafe for humans, such as surveilling hostages, dealing with dangerous hazardous environments (industrial accidents like Chernobyl), tackling natural disasters such as the impact of the tsunami on the Fukushima nuclear power plant, or attending to improvised explosives. Within the field of medicine, the impact of AI, machine learning, and data science is life altering. In October 2018, Google announced that they have developed algorithms that examine biopsies of lymph nodes to determine with 99 percent accuracy metastatic breast cancer (Wiggers, 2018). There has been a lot of press indicating that AI enables better analysis of medical images, leading to questions about the future "need" for radiologists. Researchers at Stanford University have developed a deep learning system that is able to diagnose pneumonia from chest X-rays better than expert radiologists working alone (Kubota, 2017). However, in the spirit of remembering that all jobs are made up of many tasks, it is important to note that radiologists also "decide which images should be taken, confer on tricky diagnoses, discuss treatment plans with their patients, translate the conclusions of research literature into the messy business of real-life practice, and so on" (Economist, 2018, para. 2). In other words, radiologists are not going away any time soon.

Robots can also fill prescriptions to liberate pharmacists. University of California at San Francisco (UCSF) Medical Center has relied on an automated "robot pharmacy" to fill prescriptions for the past 5 years, and the robots have worked with 100 percent accuracy. The work is repetitive and mundane. Now pharmacists can review the full medical record of individuals to make sure they are getting the best medication for their condition. California lawmakers recently authorized pharmacists who have certain levels of training and experience to prescribe some medications. There are dozens of examples of new ways that AI is impacting health-care delivery and outcomes on the quality of life for patients. Many hold the potential for expanding services, reducing costs, and improving patient outcomes.

Higher education is just beginning to leverage the power of AI. For example, AI-powered animated characters help students in a virtual "cognitive immersive room" at Rensselaer Polytechnic

Institute to immerse themselves in Chinese culture to practice their Mandarin language skills. Georgia Institute of Technology has been experimenting with virtual AI-powered teaching assistants, and Carnegie Mellon University is using AI to help students develop cloud computing software and tools (McKenzie, 2018).

The National Science Foundation (NSF), in November 2018, announced the funding of 26 projects to

> . . . advance human-technology collaboration in the workplace and focus on enhancing productivity, innovation and learning. Research goals will focus on advancing the field of embodied intelligent cognitive assistants, systems that harness machine intelligence to enhance human cognitive and physical capabilities. (National Science Foundation, 2018, para. 3-4)

Each project brings together researchers from different disciplines to solve a challenging research problem and integrate knowledge, methods, and expertise to stimulate discovery and innovation (validating the earlier discussion of the importance of equipping learners with inter-, multi-, and cross-disciplinary approaches). According to Arthur Lupia, NSF's assistant director for social, behavioral, and economics sciences: "The impact of emerging technologies goes beyond individual workers to the transformation of occupations and entire industries . . . . This research addresses the effect of future work technologies on workers and provides the means to grow and transmit the requisite skills" (National Science Foundation, 2018). A sampling of the funded projects provides a glimpse into the diversity and potential in human–machine partnerships on the horizon:

· Augmenting and advancing cognitive performance of control room operators for power grid resiliency,

- Augmented cognition for teaching—transforming teacher work with intelligent cognitive assistants,
- The next mobile office—safe and productive work in automated vehicles, and
- Future of firefighting and career training—advancing cognitive, communication, and decision-making capabilities of firefighters.

Although automation has been part of the landscape for a very long time—and there is considerable knowledge about the impact of industrialization in the work, social, and cultural dimensions of the human story—human–robot partnerships represent a completely new frontier. As with the introduction of all previous technological advancements, new strategies, policies, and impacts of their integration into society will unfold. That said, however, the contemporary environment seems to be distinguished by the speed and depth of change. Concern for our collective capacity to keep pace with the related ethical, legal, and social questions and implications of these advances are important for us to prepare for and consider. While history and experience has taught us that technological advancements always result in the creation of new jobs, it is also typical that the location and kinds of jobs are often difficult to fully and accurately project or anticipate. Nevertheless, it is clear that emerging changes in big data, AI, and machine learning are converging in ways that will strain all existing systems and structures.

However exciting these opportunities, we must remember that there are a number of ethical and policy issues that we need to grapple with across this evolving field of human–robot partnerships. As social roboticist Heather Knight notes: "Human cultural response to robots has policy implications. Policy affects what we will and will not let robots do. It affects where we insist on human primacy and what sort of decisions we will delegate to machines"

(H. Knight, 2014). Indeed, we are moving into uncharted territory with human–robot partnerships; as a result, higher education must prepare all graduates to deal with the volatility, uncertainty, complexity, and ambiguity discussed here and in the previous section on VUCA.

NAVIGATE ACCESS TO EXPANDING INFORMATION

The amount of new information generated daily is truly astonishing. According to Forbes,

> There are 2.5 quintillion bytes of data created each day at our current pace, but that pace is only accelerating with the growth of the Internet of Things (IoT). Over the last two years alone, 90 percent of the data in the world was generated . . . . Google now processes more than 40,000 searches EVERY second (3.5 billion searches per day). (Marr, 2018, para. 1–2)

This is truly astounding.

Add to this the fact that some percentage of that information falls into the category of misinformation, making it even more important for our graduates to be able to "tell a truth from a falsehood" (Gooblar, 2018, para. 2). Unfortunately, many studies indicate that thus far we have not been very successful in this realm. In fact, a 2017 study focusing on evaluating digital information found that even Ph.D. historians' as well as Stanford University history students' validation methods paled in comparison to professional fact checkers, because the historians and students read vertically within the site to validate it, whereas the fact checkers read horizontally, exiting the site in order to validate its accuracy (Wineburg & McGrew, 2017). Another study that focused on college students using academic databases concluded that "the majority of students . . . exhibited significant difficulties that ranged across nearly every aspect of the search process" (Asher & Duke, 2012, p. 73).

Clearly, this means that information literacy skills will become increasingly more important in our daily lives, both personally and professionally. Information literacy emerged as a critical skill for the 21st century concurrent with the expansion of information technology in the early 1970s. Despite the general agreement that these skills are important, there is little agreement on all of the activities that might be construed to lead to information literacy, as well as little agreement on the appropriate metrics to measure information literacy (Saracevic, 2016).

Additionally, evidence exists that employers are surprised at the lack of information literacy skills that graduates possess when they enter the workforce. Employers see these information literacy skills as having value because they relate to critical thinking, problem solving, communication, and innovation (Raish & Rimland, 2016; Sokoloff, 2012). Employers also report that effective information management requires both technological and social competencies— the use of multiple sources that are both online as well as in more traditional formats such as annual reports and/ or other print materials. In a study by Head, Van Hoeck, Eschler, and Fullerton (2013), the information management gap areas most reported by employers included (a) engaging team members during a research process, (b) retrieving information using a variety of formats, (c) finding patterns and making connections, and (d) exploring a topic thoroughly. These findings are consistent with survey findings of NACE (Head et al., 2013). All of this begs the question of how colleges and universities can do a better job of equipping graduates with these skills.

In 2016, ACRL revised and expanded their original thinking on information literacy standards (Association of College

Research Libraries, 2016), defining what it called the "Framework for Information Literacy for Higher Education." This updated framework is organized into six frames, which include

· Authority Is Constructed and Contextual,
· Information Creation as a Process,
· Information Has Value,
· Research as Inquiry,
· Scholarship as Conversation, and
· Searching as Strategic Exploration.

The framework revises the earlier vision of information literacy, advancing the notion that learners are both consumers and creators of information and knowledge. This new approach conveys a more dynamic, flexible, and community-based notion of learning and information literacy, relying more heavily on critical self-direction and metacognitive skills of learners. In this new framework, the ACRL defines information literacy as "a set of integrated abilities encompassing the reflective discovery of information, the understanding of how information is produced and valued, and the use of information in creating new knowledge and participating ethically in communities of learning" (201, para. 6).

The work of Mackey and Jacobson (2011) was instrumental in this shift in the ACRL standards by advancing the concept of information literacy as a metaliteracy building on the notion that multiple literacies—such as digital literacy, media literacy, visual literacy, and cyber literacy, among others types of literacy—are all at play in our media-rich and dynamic environments (Mackey & Jacobson, 2011). They also asserted that the fundamental skills to determine, access, evaluate, incorporate, use, understand, produce, share, and collaborate are necessary and important, regardless of the medium within which the information is found. They brought to light that shifting formats, often the result of new technologies and delivery systems (e.g., social media, Rich Site Summary [RSS] feeds, blogs, and websites), require learners to be adaptive and skillful across these various mediums. Further, the role each information consumer plays in contributing to the expansion and development of knowledge and information in the contemporary environment is a game changer. This new reality requires information consumers to develop greater capacity in the discernment for accuracy, legitimacy, and credibility of available information and sources. Also, as participant contributors to the knowledge community, people have a new and more active, rather than passive recipient only, role.

Discerning fact from fiction has become even more central during recent years with "fake news" and "alternative facts" emerging on an almost daily basis. The rate and volume of misinformation that circulates through multiple social media outlets, both intentionally and unintentionally, have become a matter for concern worldwide. Allegations of election tampering and inciting violence and hate can be found across the globe, with policy makers and legislators considering approaches to best grapple with what is perceived as a significant threat to governing. The field of third-party fact checkers is somewhat nascent but growing rapidly. In fact, by June 2018, the number of fact-checking organizations tripled around the world. Yet despite the growth in numbers, the field remains overwhelmed and somewhat chaotic in terms of common and accepted practices. The business of fact checking and concern for fake news has been highlighted frequently, with Facebook, Google, Bing, Twitter, Mozilla, and others seeking out new strategies and fact checkers in an effort to curb the negative impact of this misinformation (Kessler, 2018). In fact, Facebook continuously removes fake news accounts (Frier, 2018).

A number of initiatives have been cropping up across the nation in an attempt to better equip learners and educators in developing information literacy skills. In 2007, the School of

Journalism at State University of New York (SUNY) at Stony Brook, with funding from the James L. Knight Foundation, launched the Center for News Literacy. Since its inception, the center has been committed to helping students learn how to use critical thinking skills to judge the reliability and credibility of news sources and reports. The center has taught news literacy skills to more than 10,000 undergraduates from all academic disciplines at Stony Brook. Additionally, the work of the center has grown significantly and now includes partnerships with at least 18 other U.S. and global universities as well as a massively open online course (MOOC) in partnership with Coursera. Recognizing the need for this type of education to begin earlier, and with additional funding from the Ford and McCormick foundations, the center has been able to host national meetings as well as a high school teacher training program. The online digital resource center also provides curriculum materials and other resources for teachers at both middle and high schools nationwide (Stony Brook University School of Journalism, 2016).

In October 2018, the University at Albany and SUNY Empire State College announced a partnership to launch a MOOC on the EdX platform titled "Empowering Yourself in a Post-Truth World." The course is intended to "explore issues related to the post-truth era" (University at Albany State University of New York, 2018, para. 3). Others, such as the University of Maryland's Terrapin Learning Commons and Penn State University, have been exploring the use of digital badges as a micro-credential across the various skill areas associated with information literacy (Raish & Rimland, 2016). Developing these metaliteracies is a critical area for educators and learners alike and spans all aspects of people's lives in the knowledge age. Thoughtful integration designed to develop these multifaceted skills presents rich opportunities and challenges across all disciplines and is important because the consumption and construction of

127

information and knowledge are at the foundation of a free and democratic society. Higher education needs to do a much better job at preparing graduates in this area.

BECOME RESPONSIBLE CITIZENS OF THEIR COUNTRY AND THE WORLD

A fundamental purpose of postsecondary education in the United States has been eloquently and routinely tied to developing an educated citizenry who would be prepared to assume the responsibilities associated with a democratic society (Dewey, 2004). Numerous writings, spanning decades, link education to political and civic engagement, asserting that education enables the populace to exercise the rights and responsibilities of a democratic society (Hillygus, 2005). This connection between education and democracy is also not unique to the United States. Furthermore, there is no dearth of language that also links education to the economic well-being and growth of the economy. Any major federal legislation designed to expand postsecondary education (e.g., Morrill Act, G.I. Bill, Higher Education Act) is routinely steeped in rhetoric extolling the political, social, and economic benefits to both individuals and the nation as the rationale for the legislation. For that matter, a scan of institutional mission statements will often be filled with language such as "civic-minded, socially conscious, responsible citizens, contributions to society or the public good." We agree that these are important purposes and goals for all levels of education, especially for a society facing the acceleration and proliferation of knowledge growth and rapid change, as well as a world faced with inequality, the demise of democracy, assaults on free speech, violence against minorities, and other challenges. This aspect of higher education's role in creating an educated citizenry is even more important in a world that has seen elections manipulated, and the rise of nationalistic and widespread global populist movements.

Referring to an essay titled "Better Outcomes through Radical Inclusion" by Lin Wells, Tom Friedman (2016, p. 201) asserts that we are facing a "full-on societal reinvention challenge" brought on by the rates of technological change that is overtaking our capacity to keep pace with our "learning, governing and regulating systems." Developing learners' awareness, skills, and capacity both as consumers and advocates to deal with the ethical and regulatory matters brought about by technological change, among other changes, is yet another area demanding focus for educators in the 21st century. One does not have to look far to uncover a number of policy, ethical, and regulatory issues that require innovation and resolution, whether it is a discussion about cloning animals or humans, or developing war-related robots, personal care assistants, or self-driving cars. At one time, the advances in technology were focused solely on doing things more quickly and efficiently. Now, however, there is also the goal of having intelligent, "smart" machines, able to make good decisions that can align to a human-like value system (Rossi, 2015), reinforcing our earlier discussion about preparing graduates to create effective and robust human–robot partnerships.

According to Amitai Etzioni (1988), all decisions have a moral dimension, so even in the case of a driverless car, also known as an autonomous vehicle (AV), when deciding whether swerving to avoid a collision at the risk of killing a puppy or a mother and child in a baby carriage, the decision tree needs to reflect choices and values that were written into its code. There are some who assert that the passenger should be able to "set an ethical knob" in order to select the option and/or path the AV would/should take (Contissa, Lagioia, & Sartor, 2017). Naturally, this discussion can raise significant legal and ethical questions, ones that higher education should prepare graduates to tackle.

129

Currently, it is possible to clone (for a $50,000 fee) your dog, cat, horse, or other animal with a company in Texas named Per-PETuate. Its founder, Ron Gillespie, reports that they have received many requests to clone humans but have refused to accept human cells (Regalado, 2018). In November 2018, reports emerged from China of a scientist who genetically altered the genes of babies. Although his work has not been verified, it has raised many eyebrows and stimulated backlash across the global scientific and human communities (Kolata, Wee, & Belluck, 2018). Regardless of the veracity of this report, it drew attention to the lack of ethical and regulatory standards in this arena. The prospect of "designer babies" is certainly an intense topic of debate among ethicists, scientists, and religious and laypeople alike. How will cultural differences and norms become integrated and mediated across these ethical dilemmas? Developing the schemas and frameworks to navigate the legal and ethical aspects of these technological advances as well as other innovations is a complex and major challenge, one that higher education must be mindful of in preparing learners to identify and address.

Issues surrounding privacy and cybersecurity also abound. Barely a month goes by without the report of a new "breach of data security" occurring at some major organization. From the giant credit reporting agency Equifax (Clemens, 2018), to web services provider Yahoo (Reints, 2018), or retailers such as Target and Home Depot, these breaches have occurred across all kinds of institutions and organizations. The financial fallout and brand damage when these occur is daunting and costly. In Target's case, they settled by agreeing to pay $18.5 million to 47 states and the District of Columbia (Abrams, 2017). In his book *Understanding Privacy*, Daniel Solove aptly gave his first chapter the title "Privacy: A Concept in Disarray," stating that "[w]idespread discontent over conceptualizing privacy persists even though privacy is an essential issue for freedom and democracy" (Solove, 2008, p. 2).

130

Despite thousands of laws, both domestic and international, that have attempted to protect personal information, individuals' personal data are at risk. These risks are not just limited to the storage of data, but also include things such as wearable technology like fitness trackers and smart watches (Saa, Moscoso-Zea, & Lujan-Mora, 2018), surveillance systems (there are cameras everywhere, it seems), consumer behavior tracking systems, and communications through social media—all represent some exposure to people and their information. Determining how to regulate and manage this brave new world will require, among other things, innovative approaches to policy development that graduates must be prepared to employ.

DESIGN LIVES THAT ACHIEVE BALANCE, FULFILLMENT, AND WELL-BEING

We began this chapter by invoking the well-being framework from the Strada-Gallup Alumni Survey, which measures long-term "college graduates' success in their pursuit of great jobs and great lives" (Gallup, n.d., para. 1). Their work represents interviews over a period of 10 years (2008–2018) with more than 2.6 million people about their daily lives. What we like about this framework is that it is holistic in nature and represents the integrated way we live our lives. The Greek physician Herophilus, around 300 BC, declared, "When health is absent, wisdom cannot reveal itself, art cannot manifest, strength cannot fight, wealth becomes useless, and intelligence cannot be accepted." To put it in terms of the well-being framework, if you have enough money to feel secure but no strong relationships and poor health, are you fulfilled and happy? Or if you have your health but live in a violent neighborhood without enough food, are you fulfilled and happy?

131

Many years ago, Arthur Chickering (1969) defined *seven vectors of development* for traditional-age college students, which he and a colleague revisited in 1993 to make relevant to college students of all ages (Chickering & Reisser, 1993; Dillard, 2017; Pascarella & Terenzini, 2005). Student affairs professionals, among others, have long embraced these areas of growth and development because many of these areas are central to their work. The vectors include (a) developing competence, (b) learning to manage emotions, (c) moving through autonomy to interdependence, (d) cultivating mature relationships, (e) establishing identity, (f) defining purpose, and (g) building integrity. Like the well-being framework, Chickering's work represents the integrated and full scope of growth and development that we begin to nurture in college and that no doubt goes beyond college since human beings continue to grow in developing those vectors throughout their lives. In some respects, this growth and development may become increasingly important as people live and work longer, and as they change jobs and/or professions more frequently, hence continually "redesigning" their lives, as discussed earlier in this chapter.

The Centers for Disease Control and Prevention (CDC) working definition of well-being aligns with the Strada-Gallup framework and Chickering's research: "a dynamic and relative state where one maximizes his or her physical, mental and social functioning in the context of supportive environments to live a full, satisfying, and productive life" (Kobau, Sniezek, Zack, Lucas, & Burns, 2010, p. 274). Not surprisingly, the CDC believes that understanding well-being is critical to understanding disease prevention (Gallup, 2017). Some of their research has focused on capturing people's experiences as they live their lives, particularly those *experiences that track with well-being* scales, including the quality of relationships, emotion, physical and mental functioning, and the realization of their potential. In fact, there are efforts under way by many organizations and researchers to "develop

132

national indicators of well-being for policy purposes" (Kobau et al., 2010, p. 274).

Why is this so important, and why should colleges and universities help learners on their path to balance, fulfillment, and well-being? Because human beings work to both gain and maintain well-being across ages and stages of life and career, and it is a continuous search for equilibrium as we recalibrate balance in response to changing life events and circumstances. As we discussed in the VUCA section of this chapter, *adapting to continuous change*—as well as finding happiness and well-being—*requires some of the same skills and attributes* that we can help learners to gain and hone, including such skills as self-awareness (e.g., knowing what you don't know), discernment (e.g., knowing what your goals are), self-efficacy (e.g., a sense of empowerment and confidence to act), resilience (e.g., the willingness to learn from failure and persist), nimbleness (e.g., the capacity to flexibly adapt and adjust to new situations or environmental constraints.), and comfort with ambiguity (e.g., to be open to and handle risks associated with uncertainty). Equally important is helping our traditional-age college students to understand some of the key research on happiness and well-being, as their limited life experience may result in them believing that money, material items, and a title lead to happiness and well-being—the reverse of what research has actually shown (e.g., happiness is derived from meaning and purpose, satisfying relationships, and a sense of accomplishment).

Leading balanced and fulfilling lives—to find happiness and well-being—requires aligning behavior with personal values and beliefs to find meaning and purpose in life; building and sustaining meaningful relationships; living in community with others; having financial stability; and optimizing emotional and physical health. Higher education must prepare our younger learners to value and work toward balance in their lives and remind our adult learners of the same.

CONCLUSION

Obviously, colleges and universities will address these 11 goals in various ways. As part of their thinking about preparing diverse learners for the many areas identified in this chapter, within the complex context described in chapter 1, Northeastern University (n.d.) in Boston defined five cross-cutting dimensions of learning, growth, and development to drive their educational mission. This university framework is holistic in its conceptualization and is designed to acknowledge the diversity of learning experiences that occur through both the formal and informal (curricular and co-curricular) offerings of the university and beyond, as well as the diversity of learners. These five dimensions provide all learners and educators within the university's ecosystem with a shared framework and language around which to organize, connect, integrate, and develop knowledge, skills, attributes, and characteristics. Most especially, the framework is intended to facilitate learners' ability to recognize *what* they are learning from each experience, *integrate and transfer* what they learn across experiences, *communicate* how they know what they know, and *identify* where they may need additional learning, development, and growth. The major goal is to help graduates become self-directed, lifelong learners. These dimensions are as follows:

- **Intellectual agility** that responds to the ways in which the world of work is changing and enables graduates to continually use knowledge, behaviors, skills, and experiences flexibly in new and unique situations to innovatively contribute to their job, field, and/or career.
- **A global mindset** that addresses the fact that physical and geographical boundaries no longer matter in the world of work, compelling our graduates to develop knowledge, skills, and

behaviors to live, work, and communicate with people whose backgrounds, experiences, and perspectives are different from their own, and to consider the global impact of their decisions.

- **Personal and professional effectiveness** that requires graduates to develop the confidence, skills, behaviors, and values to effectively and *continuously* discern life goals, form relationships, and shape their personal and professional identities to achieve fulfillment. This work will continue throughout our graduates' lifetime as they upskill and switch jobs to continuously keep themselves relevant in the workplace.
- **Social consciousness and commitment,** which enables learners to develop the confidence, skills, and values to effectively recognize the needs of individuals, communities, and/or societies and to make a commitment to constructively engage in social action.
- **Well-being** that supports the cognitive, physical, emotional, and social growth and development, which will enable our graduates to live balanced and fulfilling lives by equipping them with the knowledge, skills, and behaviors necessary to do so.

This framework provides a schema that aligns with the Strada-Gallup areas of well-being and creates a way to map the diversity of skills, characteristics, and attributes identified across the spectrum of societal and employer needs discussed earlier. Other valuable frameworks are available (e.g., the Association of American Colleges & Universities' VALUE Rubrics, University of Central Oklahoma's Central Six, Indiana University-Purdue University Indianapolis [IUPUI] Profiles of Learning for Undergraduate Success). These and other models can help direct the efforts of all educators in the planning and delivery of programs and services designed to prepare their institutions and learners to respond to the 10 areas discussed in this chapter.

REFERENCES

Abrams, R. (2017, May 23). *Target to pay $18.5 million to 47 states in security breach settlement*. Retrieved from The New York Times: https://www.nytimes.com/2017/05/23/business/target-security-breach-settlement.html

Ambrose, S. A., Bridges, M. W., DiPietro, M., Lovett, M. C., & Norman, M. K. (2010). *How learning works: 7 research-based principles for smart learning*. San Francisco, CA: Jossey-Bass.

American Academy of Social Work and Social Welfare. (2019, January). *Grand challenges for social work*. Retrieved from http://grandchallenges-forsocialwork.org/grand-challenges-initiative/

American Management Association. (n.d.). *Leading the four generations at work*. Retrieved from https://www.amanet.org/training/articles/leading-the-four-generations-at-work.aspx

Aoun, J. E., Ph.D. (2018, September 4). *President's Convocation*. Speech presented at President's Convocation at Northeastern University, Boston, MA.

Arthur, M., Claman, P., & DeFillippi, R. (1995). Intelligent enterprise, intelligent careers. *Academy of Management Executive, 9*(4), 7–22.

Arthur, M., & Rousseau, D. (1996). *The boundaryless career: A new employment principle for a new organizational era*. New York, NY: Oxford University Press.

Asher, A. D., & Duke, L. M. (2012). Searching for answers: Student research behavior at Illinois Wesleyan University. In A. D. Asher, & L. M. Duke, *College libraries and student culture: What we now know* (pp. 71–86). Chicago, IL, Washington, DC: American Library Association.

Association of College Research Libraries. (2016). *Information literacy competency standards for higher education*. Retrieved from http://www.ala.org/Template.cfm?Section=Home&template=/ContentManagement/ContentDisplay.cfm&ContentID=33553#stan

Association of College and Research Libraries. (2016). *Framework for information literacy for higher education*. Retrieved from http://www.ala.org/acrl/standards/ilframework

Bill & Melinda Gates Foundation. (2019). *About grand challenges*. Retrieved from https://gcgh.grandchallenges.org/about

Brown, S., & Dissanayake, E. (2009). The arts are more than aesthetics: Neuroaesthetics as narrow aesthetics. In *Foundations and frontiers in aesthetics: Neuroaesthetics* (pp. 43–57). Amityville, NY: Baywood Publishing Co.

Brynjolffson, E., Mitchell, T., & Rock, D. (2018). What can machines learn, and what does it mean for occupations and the economy? *AEA Papers and Proceedings, 108*, 43–47.

Burnett, B., & Evans, D. (2016). *Designing your life: How to build a well-loved joyful life*. New York, NY: Alfred A. Knopf.

Busteed, B. (2018, April 25). *Americans have little confidence in grads' readiness for work, college*. Retrieved from Gallup: https://news.gallup.com/opinion/gallup/233153/americans-little-confidence-grads-readiness-work-college.aspx

Caligiuri, P. (2012). *Cultural agility: Building a pipeline of successful global professionals*. San Francisco, CA: Jossey-Bass.

Cast, C. (2018a). *6 Ways to take control of your career development if your company doesn't care about it*. Retrieved from Harvard Business Review: https://hbr.org/2018/01/6-ways-to-take-control-of-your-career-development-if-your-company-doesnt-care-about-it

Cast, C. (2018b). *The right and wrong stuff: How brilliant careers are made and unmade*. New York, NY: Public Affairs.

Chandrasekaran, B., & Conrad, J. M. (2015). *Human–robot collaboration: A survey*. Fort Lauderdale, FL: Institute of Electrical and Electronics Engineers.

Chickering, A. (1969). *Education and identity*. San Franciso, CA: Jossey-Bass.

Chickering, A., & Reisser, L. (1993). *Education and identity* (Vol. 2). San Francisco, CA: Jossey-Bass.

Clemens, N. (2018, March 5). *Equifax's enormous data breach just got even bigger*. Retrieved from Forbes: https://www.forbes.com/sites/nickclements/2018/03/05/equifaxs-enormous-data-breach-just-got-even-bigger/#78da5e0153bc

Collings, D. G., Scullion, H., & Caligiuri, P. M. (2018). *Global talent management*. New York, NY: Routledge.

Contissa, G., Lagioia, F., & Sartor, G. (2017, September 11). The ethical knob: Ethically-customisable automated vehicles and the law. *Artificial Intelligence and Law, 25*(3), 365–378.

Cox, T. (1994). *Cultural diversity in organizations: Theory, research and practice.* San Francisco, CA: Berrett-Kochler Publishers, Inc.

DeFillippi, R., & Arthur, M. (1994). Boundaryless contexts and careers: A competency-based perspective. *Journal of Organizational Behavior, 15*(4), 307–324.

DeFillippi, R., & Arthur, M. (1996). Boundaryless contexts and careers: A contempetency-based perspective. In M. Arthur, & D. Rousseau, *The boundaryless career* (pp. 116–131). New York, NY: Oxford University Press.

Deloitte. (2018). *2018 Deloitte Millennial Survey: Millennials disappointed in business, unprepared for Industry 4.0.* Retrieved from https://www2.deloitte.com/content/dam/Deloitte/global/Documents/About-Deloitte/gx-2018-millennial-survey-report.pdf

Dewey, J. (2004). *Democracy and education.* North Chelmsford, MA: Courier Corporation.

Dillard, C. W. (2017). *Chickering's seven vectors and student veteran development.* Retrieved from NACADA: https://www.nacada.ksu.edu/Resources/Academic-Advising-Today/View-Articles/Chickerings-Seven-Vectors-and-Student-Veteran-Development.aspx

Dittman, M. (2005, June 5). Generational differences at work. *Monitor on Psychology 36*(6), p. 54.

Drucker, P. F. (2005, January). *Managing oneself.* Retrieved from Harvard Business Review: https://hbr.org/2005/01/managing-oneself

Dumais, S. (2018, March 4). *Grand challenges.* Retrieved from UNH Today: https://www.unh.edu/unhtoday/2018/03/grand-challenges

Dweck, C. S. (2007). *Mindset: The new psychology of success.* New York, NY: Random House Publishing Group.

Eagan, K., Stolzenberg, E. B., Zimmerman, H. B., Aragon, M. C., Sayson, H. W., & Rios-Aguilar, C. (2017). *The American freshman: National norms fall 2016.* Los Angeles, CA: Higher Education Research Institute, UCLA.

Economist, The. (2018, June 7). *AI, radiology and the future of work.* Retrieved from https://www.economist.com/leaders/2018/06/07/ai-radiology-and-the-future-of-work

Eisner, E. (1992). The misunderstood role of the arts in human development. *Phi Delta Kappan 73*(8), 591.

Erhardt, N. L., Werbel, J., & Shrader, C. (2003). Board of director diversity and firm financial performance. *Corporate Governance: An international review 11*(2), 102–111.

Etzioni, A. (1988). *The moral dimension.* New York, NY: The Free Press.

Friedman, T. L. (2016). *Thank you for being late: An optimist's guide to thriving in the age of accelerations.* New York, NY: Farrar Straus and Girou.

Frier, S. (2018, October 11). *Facebook has removed more than 800 U.S. accounts spreading fake news.* Retrieved from Time: http://time.com/5422546/facebook-removes-800-fake-news-accounts/

Gallup. (n.d.). *How does the Strada-Gallup Alumni Survey work?* Retrieved from Gallup: https://www.gallup.com/185474/strada-gallup-alumni-survey.aspx

Gallup. (2017). *State of American well-being: The cost of diabetes in the U.S.: Economic and well-being impact.* Retrieved from https://wellbeingindex.sharecare.com/diabetes-us-economic-well-being-impact/

Gartner. (2017, December 13). *Gartner says by 2020, artificial intelligence will create more jobs than it eliminates.* Retrieved from Gartner | Newsroom Press Releases: https://www.gartner.com/en/newsroom/press-releases/2017-12-13-gartner-says-by-2020-artificial-intelligence-will-create-more-jobs-than-it-eliminates

Gooblar, D. (2018, July 24). *How to teach information literacy in an era of lies.* Retrieved from the Chronicle of Higher Education: https://www.chronicle.com/article/How-to-Teach-Information/243973

Gray, K., & Koncz, A. (2018, February 22). *Employers, students differ in perception of graduates' "Career Readiness."* Retrieved from NACE Center: https://www.naceweb.org/about-us/press/2018/employers-students-differ-in-perception-of-graduates-career-readiness/

Greene, M. (1995). *Releasing the imagination: Essays on education, the arts, and social change.* San Francisco, CA: Jossey-Bass.

Hagel, J., & Brown, J. S. (2017, August 15). *Help employees create knowledge—not just share it.* Retrieved from Harvard Business Review: https://hbr.org/2017/08/help-employees-create-knowledge-not-just-share-it

Hallett, R., & Hutt, R. (2016, June 7). *10 jobs that didn't exist 10 years ago.* Retrieved from World Economic Forum: https://www.weforum.org/agenda/2016/06/10-jobs-that-didn-t-exist-10-years-ago/

Head, A. J., Van Hoeck, M., Eschler, J., & Fullerton, S. (2013). What information competencies matter in today's workplace? *Library and Information Research, 37*(114), 74–104.

Hillygus, D. S. (2005). The missing link: Exploring the relationship between higher education and political engagement. *Political Behavior, 27*(1), 25–47.

Jacob, W. J. (2015, January 20). *Interdisciplinary trends in higher education.* Retrieved from Palgrave Communications, ResearchGate: www.researchgate.net/profile/W_Jacob/publication/273294632_Interdisciplinary_Trends_in_Higher_Education/links/5b3b3e5ba6fdcc8506eaa503/Interdisciplinary-Trends-in-Higher-Education.pdf

Kessler, G. (2018, June 25). *Rapidly expanding fact-checking movement faces growing pains.* Retrieved from The Washington Post: https://www.washingtonpost.com/news/fact-checker/wp/2018/06/25/rapidly-expanding-fact-checking-movement-faces-growing-pains/

Knight, H. (2014, July 29). *How humans respond to robots: Building public policy through good design.* Retrieved from Brookings: https://www.brookings.edu/research/how-humans-respond-to-robots-building-public-policy-through-good-design/

Knight, R. (2014, September 25). *Managing people from 5 generations.* Retrieved from Harvard Business Review: https://hbr.org/2014/09/managing-people-from-5-generations

Kobau, R., Sniezek, J., Zack, M. M., Lucas, R. E., & Burns, A. (2010, May 25). Well-being assessment: An evaluation of well-being scales for public health and population estimates of well-being among US adults. *Applied Psychology: Health and Well-Being 2*(3), 272–297.

Kolata, G., Wee, S.-L., & Belluck, P. (2018, November 26). *Chinese scientist claims to use Crispr to make first genetically edited babies.* Retrieved from

The New York Times: https://www.nytimes.com/2018/11/26/health/gene-editing-babies-china.html

Kubota, T. (2017, November 15). *Stanford algorithm can diagnose pneumonia better than radiologists* . Retrieved from Stanford News: https://news.stanford.edu/2017/11/15/algorithm-outperforms-radiologists-diagnosing-pneumonia/

Lin, J. (2011). Technological adaptation, cities, and new work. *Review of Economics and Statistics 93*(2), 554–574.

Linkedin Learning. (2018). *2018 Workplace Learning Report*. Retrieved from https://learning.linkedin.com/content/dam/me/learning/en-us/pdfs/linkedin-learning-workplace-learning-report-2018.pdf

Lipman, V. (2017, January 25). *How to manage generational differences in the workplace*. Retrieved from https://www.forbes.com/sites/victorlipman/2017/01/25/how-to-manage-generational-differences-in-the-workplace/#148e10b44cc4

Liu, M. (2016, November). *Verbal communication styles and culture*. Retrieved from Oxford Research Encyclopedias: https://oxfordre.com/communication/view/10.1093/acrefore/9780190228613.001.0001/acrefore-9780190228613-e-162

Mackey, T. P., & Jacobson, T. E. (2011). Reframing information literacy as a metaliteracy. *College & Research Libraries, 71*(1), 62–78.

Manyika, J., Chui, M., & Miremadi, M. (2017). *A future that works: Automation, employment and productivity*. San Francisco, CA: McKinsey Global Institute.

Manyika, J., Lund, S., Chui, M., Bughin, J., Woetzel, J., Batra, P., Sanghvi, S. (2017). *Jobs lost, jobs gained: Workforce transitions in a time of automation*. San Francisco, CA: McKinsey Global Institute.

Marr, B. (2018, May 21). *How much data do we create every day? The mind-blowing stats everyone should read*. Retrieved from Forbes: https://www.forbes.com/sites/bernardmarr/2018/05/21/how-much-data-do-we-create-every-day-the-mind-blowing-stats-everyone-should-read/#3639673a60ba

Matney, L. (2017). *Walmart is bringing VR instruction to all of its U.S. training centers*.RetrievedfromTechCrunch:https://techcrunch.com/2017/05/31/walmart-is-bringing-vr-instruction-to-all-of-its-u-s-training-centers/

141

Matre, M. (2017, July 21). *Millennials to traditionalists: How to manage five generations in the workplace*. Retrieved from Medix: http://www. medixteam.com/clients/millennials-traditionalists-manage-five-generations-workplace/

McBride, T. (2018, August 20). *The Mindset List: Class of 2022*. Retrieved from http://themindsetlist.com/2018/08/beloit-college-mindset-list-class-2022/

McDermott, B. (2018, January 22). *Machines can't dream*. Retrieved from Forbes: https://www.forbes.com/sites/sap/2018/01/22/machines-cant-dream/#56eb39a75b38

McGraw-Hill Education. (2018). *2018 Future Workforce Survey: Spring 2018*. Retrieved from https://s3.amazonaws.com/ecommerce-prod. mheducation.com/unitas/corporate/promotions/2018-future-workforce-survey-analysis.pdf

McKenzie, L. S. (2018, September 26). *Pushing the boundaries of learning with AI*. Retrieved from Inside Higher Ed: https://www.insidehighered. com/digital-learning/article/2018/09/26/academics-push-expand-use-ai-higher-ed-teaching-and-learning

McLeod, L. P., & Lobel, S. (1992). The effects of ethnic diversity on idea generation in small groups. *Academy of Management Proceedings* 1992 (1), (227–231). Briarcliff Manor, NY: Academy of Management.

Miller, T. (2009). Demographic diversity in the boardroom: Mediators of the board diversity-firm performance relationship. *Journal of Management Studies, 46*(5), 755–786.

Morgan, B. (2017, August 16). *10 things robots can't do better than humans*. Retrieved from Forbes: https://www.forbes.com/sites/ blakemorgan/2017/08/16/10-things-robots-cant-do-better-than-humans/#3c7a72adc83d

National Academy of Engineering. (2019). *Introduction to the grand challenges for engineering*. Retrieved from NAE Grand Challenges for Engineering: http://www.engineeringchallenges.org/challenges/16091.aspx

National Science Foundation. (2018, November 5). *NSF announces awards to shape the human-technology partnership for the well-being of workers and their productivity*. Retrieved from https://www.nsf.gov/news/news_ summ.jsp?cntn_id=297116

Noe, R. A., Clarke, A. D., & Klein, H. J. (2014). Learning in the twenty-first century workplace. *Annual Review of Organizational Psychology and Organizational Behavior, 1*, 245–275.

Noland, M., Tyler, M., & & Kotschwar, B. R. (2016, February). Is gender diversity profitable? Evidence from a global study. *Peterson Institute Economics Working Paper No. 16-3.*

Northeastern University. (n.d.). *Self authored integrated learning.* Retrieved from Northeastern Self-Authored Integrated Learning: https://sail. northeastern.edu/

Pascarella, E. T., & Terenzini, P. T. (2005). Theories and models of student change in college. In E. T. Pascarella, & P. T. Terenzini, *How college affects students: A third decade of research Volume 2.* Indianapolis, IN: Jossey-Bass.

Penn State University. (2012, June 22). *Land-grant universities celebrate Morrill Act sesquicentennial.* Retrieved from https://news.psu.edu/ story/148276/2012/06/22/land-grant-universities-celebrate-morrill-act-sesquicentennial

Pew Research Center. (2018, April 11). *The generations defined.* Retrieved from http://www.pewresearch.org/fact-tank/2018/04/11/millennials-largest-generation-us-labor-force/ft_18-04-02_generationsdefined 2017_working-age/

Piktialis, D., & Greenes, K. A. (2008). *Bridging the gaps: How to transfer knowledge in today's multigenerational workplace.* Retrieved from The Conference Board: https://www.conferenceboard.ca/e-library/abstract.aspx? did=2663&AspxAutoDetectCookieSupport=1

Popowitz, M. & Dorgelo, C. (2018). *Report on university-led grand challenges.* Retrieved from UCLA Grand Challenges: https://escholarship.org/ uc/item/46f121cr

Raish, V., & Rimland, E. (2016). Employer perceptions of critical information literacy skills and digital badges. *College & Research Libraries, 77*(1), 87–113.

Rasmussen, L. J., & Sieck, W. R. (2015, September). Culture-general competence: Evidence from a cognitive field study of professionals who work in many cultures. *International Journal of Intercultural Relations, 48*, 75–90.

Regalado, A. (2018, April 13). *Pet cloning is bringing human cloning a little bit closer*. Retrieved from MIT Technology Review: https://www.technologyreview.com/s/610681/human-cloning-just-got-a-little-bit-closer-heres-why/

Reints, R. (2018, October 24). *Yahoo agrees to $50 million settlement for those affected by the 2013 data breach*. Retrieved from Fortune: http://fortune.com/2018/10/24/yahoo-settlement-data-breach/

Richard, O. C. (2017). Racial diversity, business strategy on firm performance: A resource-based view. *Academy of Managment Journal, 43*(2), 164–177.

Rossi, F. (2015, November 5). *How do you teach a machine to be moral?* Retrieved from The Washington Post: https://www.washingtonpost.com/news/in-theory/wp/2015/11/05/how-do-you-teach-a-machine-to-be-moral/

Saa, P., Moscoso-Zea, O., & Lujan-Mora, S. (2018, January). Wearable technology, privacy issues. *International Conference on Information Theoretic Security* (pp. 518–527). Cham, Switzerland: Springer.

Saracevic, T. (2016). Are advances in information technology and advances in the information literacy in libraries in sync? Or out of sync? *Western Balkan Information Literacy Conference* (pp. 17–20). Limerick, Ireland: Institut Za Tehnologiju Limerik (IRSKA).

Scott, A., & Gratton, L. (2016). *The 100-year life: Living and working in an age of longevity*. New York, NY: Bloomsbury Publishing.

Shaffer, L. S., & Zalewski, J. M. (2011). Career advising in a VUCA environment. *NACADA Journal, 31*(1), 64–74.

Shirouzu, N., Taylor, E., & Carey, N. (2018, April 26). *The auto plants of the future may have a surprisingly human touch*. Retrieved from Reuters: https://www.reuters.com/article/us-autos-robotics/the-auto-plants-of-the-future-may-have-a-surprisingly-human-touch-idUSKBN1HY060

Singer, N. (2018, July 26). Amazon's facial recognition wrongly identifies 28 lawmakers, ACLU says. *The New York Times*, pp. B-4.

Sokoloff, J. (2012). Information literacy in the workplace: Employer expectations. *Journal of Business & Finance Librarianship, 17*(1), 1–17.

Solove, D. J. (2008). *Understanding privacy*. Cambridge, MA: Harvard University Press.

144

Spitzberg, B. H., & Changnon, G. (2009). Conceptualizing intercultural competence. In *D. Deardorff (Ed.),The SAGE handbook of intercultural competence (pp. 2–52)*. Thousand Oaks, CA: SAGE Publications, Inc.

Stevens, R. (2010, June). Managing human capital: How to use knowledge management to transfer knowledge in today's multi-generational workforce. *International Business Research, 3*(3), 77–83.

Stony Brook University School of Journalism. (2016). *Center for News Literacy*. Retrieved from https://www.centerfornewsliteracy.org/

Strada Education Network. (n.d.). *New survey reveals crisis of confidence in workforce readiness among college students*. Retrieved from http://www.stradaeducation.org/news/new-survey-reveals-crisis-of-confidence-in-workforce-readiness-among-college-students/

Teagle Foundation. (n.d.). *Integrating the liberal arts through the Grand Challenge Scholars Program Framework*. Retrieved from http://www.teaglefoundation.org/Grants-Initiatives/Grants-Database/Grants/Liberal-Arts-and-the-Professions/Integrating-the-Liberal-Arts-through-the-Grand-Cha

University at Albany State University of New York. (2018, October 18). Empowering yourself in a post-truth world. Retrieved from University at Albany News: https://www.albany.edu/news/88843.php

USAID. (2018, February 19). *Grand challenges for development*. Retrieved from https://www.usaid.gov/grandchallenges

U.S. Army Heritage & Education Center. (2018, February 16). *Q. Who first originated the term VUCA (Volatility, Uncertainty, Complexity and Ambiguity)?* Retrieved from https://usawc.libanswers.com/faq/84869

Van Fleet, J. (2015, April 23). *The engineering grand challenges at a liberal arts univeristy*. Retrieved from Union College | Engineering: https://muse.union.edu/ele-symposium/2015/04/23/vanfleet/

Von Bergen, C., Soper, B., & Parnell, J. A. (2005). Workforce diversity and organisational performance. *Equal Opportunities International, 24*(3/4), 1–16.

Wall Street Journal. (n.d.) *How to manage different generations*. Retrieved from http://guides.wsj.com/management/managing-your-people/how-to-manage-different-generations/

Wiggers, K. (2018, October 12). *Google AI claims 99% accuracy in meta-static breast cancer detection*. Retrieved from Venture Beat: https://venturebeat.com/2018/10/12/google-ai-claims-99-accuracy-in-metastatic-breast-cancer-detection/

Wilson, H. J., & Daugherty, P. R. (2018). *Collaborative intelligence: Humans and AI are joining forces*. Retrieved from Harvard Business Review: https://hbr.org/2018/07/collaborative-intelligence-humans-and-ai-are-joining-forces

Wineburg, S., & McGrew, S. (2017, October 9). *Lateral reading: Reading less and learning more when evaluating digital information*. Retrieved from https://papers.ssrn.com/sol3/papers.cfm?abstract_id=3048994

World Economic Forum. (2016, January). *The future of jobs: Employment skills and workforce strategy for the fourth industrial revolution*. Retrieved from http://www3.weforum.org/docs/WEF_Future_of_Jobs.pdf

World Economic Forum. (2018). *The future of jobs 2018*. Retrieved from http://reports.weforum.org/future-of-jobs-2018/

Youssef-Morgan, C. M., & Hardy, J. (2014). *A positive approach to multicul-turalism and diversity management in the workplace*. In J. Pedrotti, & Lisa Edwards (Eds.), *Perspectives on the intersection of multiculturalism and positive psychology* (pp. 219–233). New York, NY: Springer.

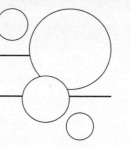

CHAPTER 3

Discovering Possibilities: Designing for the Future

This chapter focuses on a variety of ways colleges and universities can create educational experiences that respond to current and future needs. In order to do so, higher education must

Broaden Perspective by:
· Balancing intellectual exploration and discovery with job readiness
· Ensuring the broader context
· Validating both training and education
· Recognizing that learning happens everywhere

Leverage What We Know about How People Learn by understanding that:
· Learners' prior knowledge can help or hinder learning.
· How learners organize knowledge influences how they learn and apply what they know.
· Learners' motivation determines, directs, and sustains what they do to learn.
· To develop mastery, learners must acquire component skills, practice integrating them, and know when to apply them.
· Goal-directed practice coupled with targeted feedback enhances the quality of learning.

- Learners' current level of development interacts with social, emotional, and intellectual climate of the course to impact learning.
- To become self-directed learners, people must learn to monitor and adjust their approaches to learning.

Change Strategies and Seize Opportunities to:
- Design for mobility
- Design for learner agency
- Provide for maximum flexibility
- Design for integration
- Utilize experiential learning
- Design with specific learning outcomes articulated
- Develop partnerships

Align People, Processes, Structures, and Technology:
- Faculty
- Structures
- Administrators and professional staff
- Learners
- Processes
- Technology
- Administrative support structures

INTRODUCTION

Now that we have set the context (chapter 1) and discussed what different learners across the continuum will need throughout their lives and careers (chapter 2), we turn our attention to thinking about how higher education can respond. Our goal is to present and explore a variety of ideas that may stimulate the generation of new approaches for our readers to consider.

We are not suggesting that all institutions engage in everything we discuss in this chapter. In fact, we think future success, which depends on remaining relevant, necessitates that colleges and universities make strategic decisions about their foci so as not to attempt to "be all things to all people," thus spreading effort and resources too thin. Specifically, we do not believe that there is a single solution; this is not a "one size fits everyone" exercise. Rather, these decisions require that we broaden our perspective about learning and our unique role in it, leverage learning research, build meaningful partnerships, and align our strategies accordingly.

BROADEN PERSPECTIVE

In the minds of many educators, there are dichotomies that impact our decisions and behaviors. Some believe education should focus on exploration and discovery as opposed to job readiness, and vice versa; some believe breadth is more important than depth, and vice versa; others view education as more important and relevant than training, and vice versa; and many believe that learning happens mainly as a result of academic curricula as opposed to all the other experiences occurring simultaneously. In all of these cases, we need to embrace these different ways of thinking, create a convergence, and respond accordingly given our current context—for example, the state of the workplace, longevity of employees, and impact of technology.

Balancing Intellectual Exploration and Discovery with Job Readiness. The tension in academe between those who believe that the purpose of college is job readiness (i.e., employment preparation and practical skills) and those who believe that it is intellectual exploration and discovery has existed for quite some time. These debates are traceable even in the colonial days; Thomas Jefferson believed that access to a liberal education would strengthen democracy, whereas others were more focused on the

149

utilitarian nature of education. Some attribute the contemporary debate back to then Governor Ronald Reagan when, in 1967, he said that taxpayers should not be "subsidizing intellectual curiosity" (Berrett, 2015, para. 6). We, on the other hand, see intellectual exploration and discovery and job readiness as complementary goals. We do not want graduates who can think lofty thoughts and not actually do anything—"great blockheads" as Benjamin Franklin might have called them (Berrett, 2015, para. 16) nor do we want graduates who can only do what they are specifically educated or trained to do and nothing beyond. We should want all of our graduates to be both thinkers and doers, which means that colleges and universities need to balance and integrate these two perspectives. As Wendy Libby, the president of Stetson University, said, "Education should lead to a job, absolutely, but it should also lead to a fulfilling and personally satisfying life in a society we want to live in, fight for and improve" (Libby, 2017, para.12).

One could argue that the fundamental skills that feed intellectual exploration and discovery are both (a) the lifelong skills that graduates will need to continue to be successful in their work lives given the onslaught of change we are expecting, and (b) the very skills that employers cite in the skills gap surveys—for example, critical thinking; analytical reasoning; effective communication (oral and written) with people inside and outside the organization; and the ability to solve complex problems, deal with ambiguity and complexity, apply knowledge in real-world settings, and locate, organize, and evaluate information from multiple sources (Chronicle of Higher Education, 2012; Hart Research Associates, 2015). Arguably, these skills would also enable graduates to be creators, for example, of a new economy that explores new business models or any number of other new ways of evolving our economy, culture, and society. Given the knowledge explosion—including new information, protocols, procedures, ways of doing things, in engineering, science, medicine, architecture,

150

business, economics, the art world—the life span of much of the knowledge and many of the "practical" skills graduates possess will become obsolete during the course of their career. In fact, the need for updated and/or expanded knowledge and practical skills is exactly the reason that many employees will continue to upskill throughout their work lives, as noted in chapters 1 and 2.

This balancing and integration of thinking and doing are imperative for a number of reasons. As we discussed in chapter 1, the cost of higher education and student debt load demand that our graduates be able to secure jobs that allow them to live comfortably (pay rent, buy food, secure transportation to work, and so forth) and meet their loan obligations. Also, as noted in chapter 1, combining perspectives will enable this generation to better meet the social challenges they both need and want to address (such as poverty, clean water, equality), and continue to learn and grow in their careers and lives—goals they have explicitly noted are important to them in survey research.

Another way to think about this issue is described by James Ellis, an employer brand consultant, who believes that "the future of work is the growing gap between the artists and the cogs" (2018, para. 3). He defines cogs as workers "whose tasks, scope and impact will be pre-defined and delivered to the worker . . . their roles are pre-determined and structured before they walk in the door . . . they do the job that they are given" (Ellis, 2018, para. 5-6). He contrasts the cogs to artists, defining artists **not** as those who went to art school but rather those who have the ability to "find new challenges and problems to solve . . . they are expected to look beyond what's in front of them and find ways to add value . . . they invent their job every day"; their work grows and changes over time (Ellis, 2018, para. 13). Although we do not like the word "cog" to describe human beings, we appreciate the differentiation he is making because it supports the argument that a college education should prepare graduates for both job readiness and continual exploration and discovery. This thinking is consistent with Daniel Pink's notion that we are entering the "Conceptual Age," where professional success will rely on "six senses," which include design, storytelling, sympathy, empathy, play, and meaning. Through the development of these fundamental human attributes, people will be more inventive, entrepreneurial, and better able to solve the problems of the future (Pink, 2006). These goals are consistent with the convergent goals of higher education that we are proposing.

Ensuring the Broader Context. In undergraduate education in particular, integrating disciplinary content and the broader context is important so that, for example, engineering majors understand the social context in which they are designing, and history majors understand data analysis, manipulation, and application in their work because big data is a critical component of meaning-making. Both will enable graduates to better solve problems, design solutions, and address challenges, as well as appreciate the broader world around them and participate as citizens of the nation and the world.

This is not a new vision in higher education, but rather a long tradition that is continuously being revised given current societal challenges and workplace realities. Citing Bruce Kimball's 1995 book *Orators and Philosophers: A History of Liberal Education*, Bowen indicated that "general education" became widely adopted in the early 20th century to identify that part of the curriculum that was not the major (Bowen, 2004, para. 2) and thus enable and encourage breadth in a college education. Some colleges and universities refer to this as the "core," which "implies the centrality of this part of the undergraduate experience . . .," whereas others use terms like "liberal arts" or "liberal studies" to indicate the "values of breadth and integration of knowledge and . . . the development of fundamental intellectual skills" (Bowen, 2004, para. 10).

Despite the name associated with your institution's program, the common goal is that learners develop a perspective that is broader than their major(s), as a way of complementing their knowledge, skills, and perspectives.

This general education notion continues to be important in the workplace, as noted by the frequent discussion of the value of T-shaped graduates and employees. In the T-shape

> [T]he vertical stem of the T is the foundation: an in-depth specialized knowledge in one or two fields. The horizontal crossbar refers to the complementary skills of communication (including negotiation), creativity, the ability to apply knowledge across disciplines, empathy (including the ability to see from other perspectives), and an understanding of fields outside your area of expertise. (Brooks, 2012, para. 1)

Some report that the term "T-shape" originated at McKinsey & Company in internal discussions of potential hires (Boynton, 2011), whereas others attribute it to David Guest who, in the early 1990s, used it "to describe the technology savvy employee that would be needed in the immediate future" (Gardner & Estry, 2017, p. 1). Regardless of its origin, its meaning has broadened in the past 30 years. Phil Gardner, a researcher who directs the Collegiate Employment Research Center at Michigan State University, has described what employers are looking for: the "ideal job candidate as a liberal arts student with technical skills or a business/engineering student with humanities training" (Brooks, 2012, para. 4). This notion has been reinforced by many employers, including IDEO's CEO Tim Brown (n.d.) and corporate leaders at IBM, Cisco, and ISSIP (Gardner & Estry, 2017).

The T-shaped notion of individual employees has also been extended to organizations for the same reasons:

The disciplined, analytical approaches generally taught in engineering and business schools work well when dealing with well-defined products to be developed or concrete problems to be solved. But, they're less effective when dealing with highly complex, fast-changing problems, where it's often not clear what's going on in the present, let alone how things will evolve into the future. We need different principles and processes to address this class of problems. This is where we need a more holistic, collaborative approach to pull together everything that's known about the problem, and a more team-based approach to help come up with a creative, pragmatic solution. (Wladawsky-Berger, 2015, para. 12)

IDEO's CEO Tim Brown contrasts that reasoning with the current reality:

Most companies have lots of people with different skills. The problem is, when you bring people together to work on the same problem, if all they have are those individual skills—if they are I-shaped—it's very hard for them to collaborate. What tends to happen is that each individual discipline represents its own point of view. It basically becomes a negotiation at the table as to whose point of view wins, and that's when you get gray compromises where the best you can achieve is the lowest common denominator between all points of view. The results are never spectacular but at best average. (Wladawsky-Berger, 2015, para. 6)

When the quote above references that individuals tend to represent their own views, it notes that our prior knowledge and experience are the lens through which we view the world. If that lens is narrow because all the individual possesses is disciplinary knowledge, then it will be hard for the person to think broadly about the problem, issue, or challenge, potentially hindering innovation (Foley, n.d.).

Many in academe have embraced this T-perspective for years, as evidenced not only by the long tradition of general education, core curricula, and liberal arts/studies, but also by recent changes in disciplines like engineering, medicine, and business. In 2000, the engineering profession's accreditation body, the Accreditation Board for Engineering and Technology (ABET), created Engineering Criteria 2000—colloquially known as "A through K," which represented an original set of 11 criteria—"to ensure that each program provides graduates with the technical and professional skills employers demand" (ABET, n.d.). This initial set included such expected outcomes (that students needed to demonstrate) as the ability to (a) function on multidisciplinary teams, (b) communicate effectively, (c) acquire the broad education necessary to understand the impact of engineering solutions in a global and societal context, (d) recognize the need for and to engage in lifelong learning, and (e) obtain knowledge of contemporary issues. Although ABET recently condensed the criteria into 7 rather than 11 principles effective 2019–2020, they still preserved those outcomes that address context, self-directed learning and professional skills (ABET, 2018).

More recently, some in medicine have adopted this perspective as well. For example, Rita Charon founded Columbia University's Program in Narrative Medicine, a field that "aims to strengthen clinical practice through recognizing, absorbing, and interpreting patients' stories" (Kafka, 2018, para. 1). According to Charon, who is a physician as well as a literary scholar:

> You need the fundamental skills and habits of mind, the gifts of perception. How do you see what's in front of your eyes? How do you find interpretations—even if they might conflict with one another?
>
> If somebody is in my office talking about chest pain, I think, Does this sound like heart trouble, stomach trouble, or muscle trouble?, while also using my narratological brain.

155

What is she telling me? Why is she telling me this now? What is the beginning of this story? Where is it going? Even the metaphors she's using. And then alongside that is the affective or emotional stream. What is she really worried about? If she lets on, in a little dependent clause that her father died of a heart attack when he was her age, well then, I have to hear that.

How does a person do all of that if they're only trained in the logical, rational, calculable, measurable aspects of human biology? I certainly don't want an internist who forgets how the heart works. But we know the hazards—not just the emotional, but the diagnostic hazards—of someone using the internist brain without a very active narratological brain. It is not just, "Oh, my heart goes out to you" that I'm trying for. It's not sympathy. It's accuracy. (Kafka, 2018, para. 5–7)

The business world is also validating the importance of broader skills, in ways similar to medicine, noting that business is not all about the numbers, but "today, more than ever, it's about the story. And that makes storytelling a skill almost as critical in business as corporate accounting these days" (Fry, 2018, para. 1). This kind of broadening mindset was also, in part, a driver in the Massachusetts Institute of Technology's decision in fall 2018 to announce the opening of a new College of Computing dedicated to reshaping its programs around artificial intelligence (AI) "to educate the bilinguals of the future," defined as "people in fields like biology, chemistry, politics, history and linguistics who are also skilled in the techniques of modern computing that can be applied to them" (Lohr, 2018, para. 5).

Despite its importance and the validation that these examples provide, some believe that general education has become "weaker and unfocused, disrespected and eroded" (Powell, 2014, para. 1). Others see it as being in continuous danger of extinction, given the current focus on return on investment, which sometimes calls for getting rid of general education and thus slicing off a few semesters of time to degree completion. For example, in March 2018, the University of Wisconsin-Stevens Point proposed cutting 13 liberal arts majors (while expanding others), citing fiscal challenges (Flaherty, 2018). They revised their plan in November of the same year to cut only six majors in order to "offer more career-focused programs" (Crowe, 2018, para. 1). But the question is, at what cost to the graduate's future success and the changing world of work? In the case of Wisconsin, a group of emeritus faculty responded that "leaders can blame their budget problems on politicians while giving them exactly what they want: a version of the Wisconsin idea that focuses on short-term business interests, rather than the long-term needs of students, the economy and the state" (Bishop et al., 2018). This university is not the first (e.g., Goucher College, University of Akron, University of North Carolina, University of Vermont, and University of Montana), nor will it be the last, to make this type of decision, but again, at what cost? As we argue in this section and the previous one, the liberal arts provide a vital educational component to effectively address the needs of graduates, employers, society, and the world in this fast-paced, continually changing environment. In fact, a 2019 survey of provosts/chief academic officers showed great concern about these trends, indicating that low numbers of majors in departments are not enough reason to eliminate them because it ignores the fact that "liberal arts departments' contributions may extend well beyond those who major in a given field" (Jaschik, 2019a, para. 14). Institutions need to be intentional about closing down entire departments, because along with those departments go the knowledge, perspectives, and skills that are needed to provide context and balance in the more professionally oriented disciplines, as evidenced by the engineering, medicine, and business examples cited earlier in this section.

What does not help the argument for including the broader context in an undergraduate education is that many college students, as well as graduates, articulate that they do not see the value

157

of general education courses to their future success (Amato 2013; Pracz, 2011; Wandschneider, 2014). Provosts in the 2019 survey agree: many believe that "liberal arts education has become too divorced from the career needs of students and graduates" and they "question the commitment of faculty members to helping students with career preparation" (Jaschik, 2019a, para. 24). The lack of importance students place on the liberal arts is the fault of colleges and universities that do not effectively and intentionally convey the value and relevance of broadening one's knowledge to the learners' potential chosen profession as well as their ability to function effectively as a member of society. So, whatever its name—general education, core curriculum, liberal arts, T-shaped people—providing undergraduates with a broader context in which to think and work will be valuable to them in both the short and long term, professionally and personally.

Having just argued for the importance of a broader context, we need to remind the reader that this not a necessity across the board (i.e., for all learners at all ages and stages of their life and career). For example, there are adult learners who need a specific skill or set of skills, or a particular body of knowledge, to complement what they already know. Some of these learners, having earned previous degrees or through life experience, already possess the breadth that allows them to view the world and their work within a broader context. Also, these adult learners often have limited time and resources to gain the knowledge and skills they need; therefore, their learning experience might require a much more focused approach. Some people articulate this difference in what learners need as either training or education (discussed in the next section), and we believe that all future employees will need both at different points in time given the rapidly changing world of work.

Validating Both Training and Education. Is there really a difference between these two concepts? We often think of training as something that requires drill, practice, feedback, and more practice, as in athletic training, or we think of it as practical instruction, as in job training or career training, such as apprenticeships, which often combine theory and practice in real-world settings. In the online Business Dictionary (n.d.), training is defined as "organized activity aimed at improving information and/or instructions to improve the recipient's performance or to help him or her attain a required level of knowledge or skill" (para. 1). Corporate training company AllenComm (n.d.) defines training as "a program that helps employees learn specific knowledge or skills to improve performance at their current roles," and defines development as "more expansive and focuses on employee growth and future performance, rather than an immediate job role" (para. 1). We think of AllenComm's definition of development as education.

First, consider the similarities. Important commonalities exist between training and education or, as we like to call both, learning. They both (a) include disciplinary knowledge and discipline-specific skills as well as a focus on outcomes, (b) require a lot of practice, (c) involve timely and constructive feedback, and (d) connect theory with practice in some experiential way.

The differences, in our minds, are that training typically focuses on discrete skills and/or pieces of knowledge and centers on improving immediate performance, whereas education concentrates on not only gaining discrete skills and pieces of knowledge but also on the integration of that knowledge and those skills as well as the ability to know when to access and use them in new or novel contexts (often referred to as "transfer") (Ambrose, Bridges, DiPietro, Lovett, & Norman, 2010, pp. 108–112).

We just noted that we think of both training and education as learning, based on the following definition: "learning is a process that leads to change, which occurs as a result of experience and increases the potential for improved performance and future learning (adapted from Mayer, 2002)" (Ambrose et al., 2010, p. 3). In this definition, learning involves change in areas such as skills, knowledge, beliefs, behaviors, and/or attitudes, and this change must have a lasting impact on how the learner thinks and acts. That change can happen in both training and education—albeit, as we just noted, in different ways.

There is no doubt that the future will require some of us in higher education to accommodate learners with both ongoing education (e.g., career switchers) as well as training (e.g., career enhancers per upskilling). Furthermore, we need to think about training as potential building blocks toward education, which can eventually result in a more advanced credential that does, in fact, enable learners to integrate and transfer their knowledge and skills to new settings. This approach is often referred to as *stackable* educational experiences or curricula, which allows those who either do not need a degree initially or who are upskilling to gain "bite-sized" chunks of knowledge and/or skills with a micro-credential that can, eventually, lead to a "bigger" credential, such as a certification, license, or degree (discussed in more detail later in this chapter). As noted by the founder of Human Capital LLC, Michael Echols: "Training is most often necessary but not sufficient to gain the full value of the human capital investment" (2018, para. 10).

From this point on, we will refer to both training and education as learning.

Recognizing That Learning Happens Everywhere. Learning is a holistic process because learners are intellectual, social, and emotional beings who engage their environment in an integrated way. The recent emergence of co-curricular transcripts and comprehensive learning records (CLRs) in undergraduate education suggests a growing recognition that postsecondary education is more than the accumulation of course credits. One significant development in this area was the funding of a $1.6 million project by the Lumina Foundation in 2015 for the American Association of Collegiate Registrars and Admissions Officers (AACRAO) and NASPA – Student Affairs Administrators in Higher Education to

160

work with 12 diverse representative institutional types (e.g., community colleges, private, public, Historically Black Colleges and Universities [HBCUs], online competency-based programs) to develop model comprehensive learner records that would "capture, record, and communicate learning when and where it happens in a student's higher education experience" (American Association of Collegiate Registrars and Admissions Officers, 2019, para. 3). By design, the CLR was to include learning outcomes that resulted from students' experiences in class and "outside of class that contribute to students' career-ready skills and abilities" (American Association of Collegiate Registrars and Admissions Officers, 2019, para. 3). In 2017, the Lumina Foundation funded a second project with $1.2 million focused on building on the first project, to scale and expand the adoption of a comprehensive learning record. This second project is also being administered through AACRAO and NASPA in partnership with the National Institute for Learning Outcomes Assessment (American Association of Collegiate Registrars and Admissions Officers, 2019).

Lumina's initiatives recognize that learners do not interface with the university consistent with an organizational chart that neatly compartmentalizes their learning experiences. Consequently, we need to leverage the full resources of both our educational ecosystem as well as the workplace (for those returning adults, for example), adopting an inclusive view of the co-curriculum (e.g., clubs, organizations, study abroad, service, co-op, athletics, student employment, leadership programs) and learning that takes place "on the job," to create pathways to competency development that are engaging, intentional, empowering, and transformative for learners. We need to work toward ensuring that learners understand that learning is ubiquitous and enhanced by making it explicit in every interaction and in every environment. The artificial boundaries of in-class (formal and structured) and out-of-class (informal and unstructured) learning—and of in-college (formal and structured) and out-of-college (informal and unstructured) learning—should be reframed to better acknowledge and embrace the fact that learning knows no boundaries and that people's learning experience is an integrated one rather, than one traveling along parallel or separate and unequal paths (Kuh, 1994).

Taking such a comprehensive approach to learning is particularly timely as we engage a generation of undergraduate students who are even more socially conscious (Eagan, 2017). To effectively navigate the accelerating changing environments, individuals will need to be more conscious of their knowledge, skills, and competencies; be able to articulate and adapt them to potential work and life situations; and be more self-directed in their own continual growth and development. Given these realities, it is increasingly important for learners to develop skills that will enable them to (a) routinely self-assess their strengths and growth needs, (b) be more intentional and self-directed in choosing their next learning experiences, and (c) draw connections between their learning and the real-world contexts they face.

Besides broadening our perspective and rethinking some of our basic assumptions about education, learning, and our role in it, we need to take advantage of the research that can promote the broader agenda to continually educate our current learners and graduates across their life and career span.

LEVERAGE WHAT WE KNOW ABOUT HOW PEOPLE LEARN

We are in an enviable place in higher education at this point in time because the research on learning has become robust enough that it can truly impact the way we design and deliver educational opportunities and experiences. Ambrose et al., (2010) identify seven fundamental principles that represent how people learn across contexts,

162

cultures, disciplines, and stages of development that are useful as we adapt what we do to the various learner populations discussed in chapter 1 and their respective goals and needs (Ambrose et al., 2010). The following is a brief synopsis of each of those principles:

1. **Learners' prior knowledge can help or hinder learning.** Prior knowledge facilitates learning when learners are able to connect to and build upon what they already know. In other words, it is the lens through which we take in all new information. However, if that knowledge is inaccurate, inappropriate, inactive, or insufficient, it will hinder learning. Effective educational experiences work to identify and fill in gaps, correct misconceptions, address when learners are applying what they know inappropriately, and activate what they do not recognize as relevant. Obviously, post-traditional and adult learners who are upskilling or changing careers bring a lot of knowledge, skills, and experience into further education, which does not necessarily mean that all of the knowledge is accurate, activated, sufficient, and/or used appropriately. We need to routinely create prior learning assessment(s) (discussed later in the chapter) to identify, and then address, those shortcomings, as well as build on the valuable knowledge and skills post-traditional and lifelong learners possess, given their previous learning through both formal (academic curricula) and informal (work and life experience) mechanisms. For all of our learner populations, prior learning assessment is vitally important to both their future learning and to how we design effective educational experiences, because these are the building blocks for future learning.

2. **How learners organize knowledge influences how they learn and apply what they know.** Organization of knowledge influences one's ability to retrieve and use it flexibly and fluently in new contexts. Experts unconsciously create and maintain rich and complex networks organized around meaningful features

163

and abstract principles, connecting important concepts, procedures, facts, and other elements within the domain. Conversely, novices (those new to a discipline or body of knowledge) often create superficial knowledge structures that can potentially hinder their ability to retrieve and use the knowledge they possess. Effective instruction helps learners at all ages and stages develop their own connected and meaningful knowledge organizations that better support their learning and performance. Surfacing current organizational structures and aiding their continual development (e.g., via visualizations like concept maps) will help tremendously in the learners' ability to use appropriate knowledge when necessary. Post-traditional and lifelong learners will most likely have both more knowledge and more robust organizational structures than traditional-age undergraduates, but they may not recognize this phenomenon; thus, explicitly drawing attention to this aspect of learning could improve their learning experience as much as that of the traditional-age undergraduate.

3. **Learners' motivation determines, directs, and sustains what they do to learn.** Motivation influences the direction, intensity, persistence, and quality of learning behaviors in which learners engage. If learners see the value and relevance of what they are learning (either short or long term) and believe they can be successful in learning the content or skill, they will engage in the behaviors that will result in learning. Effective educational experiences explicitly provide value and relevancy by articulating the various ways in which the current knowledge and skills learners are gaining might be used in future contexts and build expectations for success through activities in which the learner participates. Post-traditional learners' goals and confidence levels (for those who have been out of school for a while or who never attended) may vary from traditional-age learners', so the design of educational experiences needs to align with the respective learner audiences.

4. **To develop mastery, learners must acquire component skills, practice integrating them, and know when to apply them.** To achieve mastery, learners need to develop a set of key component skills, practice combining and integrating them to develop greater fluency and automaticity, and recognize the conditions of appropriate application. Effective educational experiences require experts to regain consciousness of aspects of expert practice that they often have lost conscious awareness of, in order to explicitly model and describe those elements of mastery. Research clearly shows, for example, that experts will often (a) overestimate what novices know and can do and underestimate how long novices will take to complete a task, (b) skip or combine steps that have become "second nature" to them, (c) inaccurately predict where novices will have difficulty, and (d) presume novices will do things the way we, as experts, do them. Some refer to this as an "expert blind spot" (Hinds, 1999; Nathan & Koedinger, 2000; Nickerson, 1999). Because we all work toward helping learners gain mastery of some body of knowledge and/or skill, we need to ensure that we design experiences that provide practice and feedback on the acquisition of component skills and pieces of knowledge as well as the integration of the knowledge and skills and the ability to know when to apply what they have learned.

5. **Goal-directed practice coupled with targeted feedback enhances the quality of learning.** Practice is any activity in which learners engage their knowledge and/or skills, and feedback is information given to learners about their performance that guides future behavior. The two must be effectively combined if learning is to occur, because people learn what they practice and only what they practice. Effective educational experiences provide frequent, deliberate, and goal-directed practice along with timely, constructive, and actionable feedback. Technology can be used to provide

real-time, constructive feedback as learners engage in online learning activities that offer practice (Carnegie Learning, n.d.; Shuster, 2013), and the flipped classroom allows practice to occur in a place where educators can provide real-time, constructive feedback. No matter the level of sophistication of the learner or the knowledge or skills to be gained, practice and feedback are vital to the process.

6. **Learners' current level of development interacts with the social, emotional, and intellectual climate of the course to impact learning.** Learning does not happen in a vacuum, but rather in a context where intellectual pursuits interface with socioemotional issues, because learners are complex beings. Effective educational experiences create productive learning environments that view people holistically, addressing some of those socioemotional needs, which can vary based on the learners' age and stage of life and career. For example, there is a lot going on in the lives of traditional-age undergraduates beyond learning physics, history, engineering, economics, and so forth; at the same time, they are developing and maturing in a number of ways, such as (a) managing new emotions as they become both aware of new or intensified emotions and learning how to control them, (b) developing autonomy as they learn to make decisions and take responsibility for the outcomes, (c) establishing mature interpersonal relationships, (d) establishing a sense of identity as they move into adulthood, and (e) developing purpose in terms of what fulfills them and integrity to guide their decisions and behavior (Chickering, 1969; Chickering & Reisser, 1993). While identity development and student development theories have become more complex, moving away from the somewhat linear view of early theorists to incorporate various dimensions of identity (e.g., race, ethnicity, sexual orientation) and the interplay of contexts and environments on development, these theories

continue to acknowledge the power and complexity of psycho-social dynamics on students during these college years (Torres, Jones, & Renn, 2009).The critical point in all of the research is that undergraduates do not leave the social-emotional part of themselves outside of our classrooms, labs, and studios, and the climate we create can enhance or hinder learning. The same is true for post-traditional and lifelong learners, because we continue to grow and develop throughout our lives, and most adult learners are also balancing significant family and work obligations. Adult learners might harbor doubts about their learning capabilities if it has been a while since they were in a formal learning situation, and they often care deeply about the relevance of what they are learning given limited time and resources to devote to this endeavor (Wlodkowski, 2008). Recognizing our learners as holistic human beings who continue to develop can go a long way!

7. **To become self-directed learners, people must learn to monitor and adjust their approaches to learning.** Metacognition is the process of reflecting on and directing one's own thinking, which enables learners to become self-directed (i.e., to gain the lifelong learning skills they will need as they advance in their jobs or change occupations over the course of their lives). Effective educational experiences help learners develop skills to assess the demands of a task, evaluate their own knowledge and skills, plan their approach, monitor their progress, and adjust their strategies as needed. The good news is that many post-traditional and lifelong learners have developed these skills through the course of their personal and professional lives (Wlodkowski, 2008). The situation is different for traditional-age undergraduates who do not naturally engage in self-directed learning strategies, although as educators we can easily help them develop these important skills by the way we design educational activities.

167

It is important that educators understand how learning works in order to create the conditions that prompt learners to engage in the behaviors that lead to learning. Focusing on teaching rather than learning is a common misstep among educators. One of the best depictions of this is a cartoon wherein a child explains to his friend that he taught the dog how to whistle; puzzled, the friend remarks that he does not hear the dog whistling, to which the first child responds, "I said I *taught* the dog, I didn't say he *learned* how" (Blake, 1974). In the end, however, we must remember, as Nobel laureate Herbert Simon reminds us, that "Learning results from what the student does and thinks and only from what the student does and thinks. The teacher can advance learning only by influencing what the student does to learn" (Ambrose et al., 2010, p. 1). So how do we create the conditions to influence learner behavior, especially given the diversity of learners and their goals? That is what we discuss in the next section.

CHANGE STRATEGIES AND SEIZE OPPORTUNITIES

We now move from a discussion of thinking (i.e., broadening our perspectives and understanding how people learn) to a discussion of actions (i.e., designing higher education institutions to remain relevant in the 21st century). This will require that all institutions strategically determine how to redesign their respective learning environments to meet the needs of the learners they decide to focus on. Naturally, any strategy is impacted by its translation and adoption across the many roles (e.g., faculty, staff, administrators) and functions on any campus.

Design for Mobility. Mobility in higher education is focused on providing learners, at all ages and stages of life and career, with the ability to easily move in and out and among

168

various learning opportunities given their goals, needs, and constraints (e.g., time, financial resources, geography). We should consider mobility from all angles and consider the traditional-age, post-traditional, and lifelong learners' perspectives, because their respective life situations are unique and potentially call for different solutions.

Traditional-age learners. Mobility for traditional-age learners will become increasingly important for not only those who begin their careers at community colleges, but also for those who are not able to or interested in committing to 2 or 4 consecutive years, and for those who transfer between or among 4-year institutions because their initial decision of institution did not work out for any number of reasons (e.g., financial, geography, shifting interests, medical or unexpected change in life situations).

One of community colleges' traditional roles in higher education has been to prepare learners (i.e., students who have already earned a high school diploma) to transfer to 4-year institutions, although current data indicate that relatively few of those learners actually attain a bachelor's degree: "Of the nearly two million students who enter higher education through community colleges each year, 80 percent indicate that they intend to transfer and earn a bachelor's degree . . . , but only about a quarter transfer to a four-year institution, with about one in six completing a bachelor's degree within six years of starting at a community college . . ." (Xu, Ran, Fink, Jenkins, & Dundar, 2017, p. 1). These numbers are staggering given that community colleges enroll nearly half of the nation's undergraduates (Xu et al. 2017, p. 1). Furthermore, 42 percent of those who start their postsecondary education at a community college come from low-income families (Shapiro et al., 2017).

Four-year institutions are increasingly working with community colleges to create more transfer partnerships, improve on the ones already in existence, and try to better understand

and address the student experience and institutional structures. However, research continues to show that "politics and divergent academic cultures lead to curricular and cultural gaps ... and environmental differences and disparities in student academic preparedness continue to impact student success" (Shapiro et al., 2017, p. 6). And once again, this research validates that the effect is more pronounced for lower-income students, further indicating the systemic disadvantages faced by low-income individuals in accessing educational opportunity and achieving success. Having said that, research also provides some essential and highly effective transfer practices. For example, Fink and Jenkins (2017, p. 303) studied six pairs of high-performing partnerships and found such practices as (a) institutions collaborating to create transfer program maps that clarified pathways for students, (b) faculty at the community colleges teaching courses "at a level of rigor sufficient to prepare students to meet the expectations of 4-year college-level instruction," (c) faculty at the 4-year colleges advising students before they matriculated from the community college, as well as during and after, and (d) institutions creating transfer student orientations to welcome students and create a sense of belonging. We can enhance mobility for these learners by leveraging what we already know works.

Community colleges have also focused on adult basic education (ABE) to help those in this group upgrade their skills and earn a postsecondary credential "in order to raise their standard of living by qualifying for higher wage jobs" (Jacobs & Tolbert-Bynum, 2008, p. 1.) The federal definition of ABE is "adults who are 16 years of age or older and currently functioning below the 8th grade level ... out of school, without having obtained a secondary diploma or its equivalent" (Jacobs & Tolbert-Bynum, 2008, p. 2). ABE programs include, for example, General Education Diploma (GED), English as a Second Language (ESL), continuing education, basic literacy, and apprenticeships, and they work toward helping these learners pursue a postsecondary credential, which as we discussed in chapter 1, is vital to their financial well-being and social mobility.

Another group for whom mobility has been problematic is the 35 percent of college students who transfer at least once during their college career (this number is exclusive of the community college to 4-year institution transfers) (United States Government Accountability Office, 2017; Selingo, 2018). The biggest issue facing these students is the lost number of credits or credits applied to electives rather than degree requirements, which can impact both their time to degree and financial situation; almost half of these students receive Pell Grants (based on financial need). While articulation and degree pathway agreements exist, including agreements that facilitate transfer across state lines, there are still many barriers to both access and smooth and easy transitions (United States Government Accountability Office, 2017). In fact, some draw important distinctions between articulation and degree pathway agreements, asserting that articulation agreements are designed to serve the needs of registrars, whereas degree pathway agreements are more focused and designed for students.

Post-traditional and lifelong learners. Higher education also needs to provide flexible, accessible pathways for postgraduates to continually come in and out of our institutions as they upskill and/or prepare to switch jobs or careers. We already established that many of these learners will need to gain knowledge or a specific skill or set of skills to continue to function effectively in their current position, possibly multiple times throughout their work life, whereas others may need to be educated in a new field to move up in their career (e.g., an engineer getting an MBA; an accountant gaining cultural competence to work abroad; an artist developing business management skills to launch a web design company) or enter a new career. We have also discussed the life situations (e.g., family responsibilities, limited time and resources) unique to this group. For these learners, we will need to provide more modularized opportunities for learning, provide credit for prior knowledge and skills, keep track of their competencies, and design alternative credentials, among other things (all of which are discussed later in the chapter).

Design for Learner Agency. Agency is important for traditional-age, post-traditional, and lifelong learners because people like to "play a part in their self-development, adaptation, and self-renewal with changing times" (Bandura, 2001, p. 2). In other words, human beings want the ability "to make choices and to act on these choices in ways that make a difference in their lives" (Martin, 2004, p. 135). Bandura (2001) identifies the four core features of human agency: intentionality, forethought, self-reactiveness, and self-reflectiveness:

> An agent has to be not only a planner and forethinker, but a motivator and self-regulator as well. Having adopted an intention and an action plan, one cannot simply sit back and wait for the appropriate performances to appear. Agency thus involves not only the deliberative ability to make choices and action plans, but the ability to give shape to appropriate courses of action and to motivate and regulate their execution. This multifaceted self-directedness operates through self-regulatory processes that link thought to action . . . . People are not only agents of action but self-examiners of their own functioning. The metacognitive capability to reflect upon oneself and the adequacy of one's thoughts and actions is another distinctly core human feature of agency. Through reflective self-consciousness, people evaluate their motivation, values, and the meaning of their life pursuits. It is at this higher level of self-reflectiveness that individuals address conflicts in motivational inducements and choose to act in favor of one over another. (Bandura, 2001, pp. 8, 10)

172

For those of us developing educational opportunities and experiences for a variety of learners, we need to design education that addresses learners' intentionality, forethought, self-reactiveness, and self-reflectiveness. For example, since learners' needs will undoubtedly be impacted by many things (e.g., their life and career goals, personal time constraints associated with family and work obligations, available financial resources), they will need personalized and customized pathways designed to meet them where they are. This might, for example, involve shorter time frames of focused material or alternative venues to on-site experiences. Learners may also be at the stage where they can easily engage in self-directed learning because they have developed those skills elsewhere (e.g., in previous educational settings, in the workplace), which enables us to provide more self-paced, competency-based opportunities. In both cases, learners will take the initiative to design their own learning experience, mimicking the expectation in the workplace, summed up by Mark Allen (2018): "each employee is the owner and architect of their own careers, and their career development is directly related to the knowledge, skills and learning they acquire along the way"(para. 50). In the end, agency will prepare our graduates for the continually changing workplace by helping them identify their learning needs, choose appropriate learning experiences to meet those needs, and learn to assess and reflect on their learning—all components of becoming an autonomous, self-directed learner (Ambrose et al., 2010).

In the business, marketing, and manufacturing worlds, some may refer to learner agency as customization. Customization gives control to users so that they can achieve their preferred experience. This assumes that users know what their goals and needs are, which is true for many of the learners who will be upskilling or reskilling. Customization has been successful in many venues, such as fast-food places where you put together your meal by choosing your carb, protein, vegetable, dressing, and so forth, or the online clothing sites where you choose the template, the material, the color, and so forth. The result is an experience or product specifically tailored to what the user wants or needs. For traditional-age students, especially the iGens, we know that "Most critically, they expect to be treated as individuals. Students raised amid the tailored analytics of online retailers . . . presume that anything put in front of them is customized for them" (Pappano, 2018, para. 9).

This customized approach enables learners to choose the what, when, where, and how when they engage in the educational experience and employ a "just-for-me" approach that feeds, for some, the "just-in-time" learning need. This allows learners to be agents of their own learning.

Provide Maximum Flexibility. Flexibility is key to the mobility and learner agency discussed in the two previous sections, as learners identify their needs and goals and choose among educational opportunities and experiences to meet them, whether their goal is to gain a defined skill or set of skills (e.g., cultural competence, the ability to perform a set of statistical analyses, a computer language, supply chain skills) or a second baccalaureate or master's degree. This flexibility can be enhanced not only through customization but also through personalization that tailors an experience based on users' previous behavior, using data and predictive technology. As opposed to customization, which gives control to the learner, it is the "system" that personalizes the experience for learners. Think about the recommendations that Netflix and Amazon provide based on your previous choices and purchases; that is personalization. In the educational realm, this would mean that we offer a number of different pathways that align with various learner audiences' needs, and learners then choose which one(s) meet those needs.

In both cases (customization and personalization), flexibility will only lead to learning if, among other things, we design learning opportunities that (a) build on what learners already know and can do (especially as they come in and out of educational opportunities), (b) clearly identify competencies and assessments to assure mastery, and (c) allow modularity and stackability so that learners can engage in just-in-time and just-for-me learning continuously throughout their lives. Some in the business world are thinking the same way. For example, Patty Woolcock, executive director of the California Strategic HR Partnership, says, "The future of learning is three 'justs': just enough, just-in-time, and just-for-me. It means that training is going to have to be just as agile as the workforce—where speed, flexibility, and innovation are key. It means that more learning will happen in teams, and on platforms where training can be delivered any time, any place, at the user's convenience" (Younger, 2016, para. 3).

Prior Learning Assessments (PLA). In order for mobility, agency, and flexibility to become a reality, we need to become much better at assessing what learners already know and can do given that the vast majority of learners in the future will be post-traditional and lifelong learners, including those with previous credentials of varying kinds, as well as those with little or no formal higher education. Both groups have life and job/career experience that have resulted in knowledge and skills on which they can build, and for which they do not need to sit in a traditional course in order to simply "gain the credits." These assessments would both help learners to make the appropriate decisions and help institutions to coach them more effectively, as well as save time and money, accelerating progress toward learners' goals. A study conducted by the Council for Adult and Experiential Learning (CAEL) of more than 62,000 students enrolled at 48 institutions, spanning a 7-year period, found that persistence and graduation rates across all ethnicities and genders were significantly improved for those students who earned credit for prior learning (Klein-Collins, 2011). Another study looking at the different types of prior learning assessments (e.g., portfolios, College Level Examination Program [CLEP], American Council on Education [ACE], or a combination) at four community colleges similarly found that persistence and graduation rates are improved for students who receive credit for prior learning, most especially for those who received CLEP credit (Hayward & Williams, 2015).

Colleges and universities do not need to start from scratch in this area. Institutions like Western Governors University (WGU), Thomas Edison State University, Prescott College, and SUNY Empire State, among others, have successfully engaged in this work for quite some time. WGU describes the process as follows: "Students take formal pre-assessments at the beginning of each module (or course segment) to determine the material they've already mastered (if any) and where they need to focus their learning. Students that pass the assessment can move on to the next module" (Western Governors University, n.d. para. 14). Thomas Edison takes a different approach toward the same goal: they work with learners to create a portfolio that demonstrates learning that they may have acquired through alternative means (i.e., work, training programs, the military, volunteer service, creative or artistic pursuits etc.); the portfolio includes a narrative and supporting documentation. SUNY Empire State College reminds us that prior learning assessments grant credit for *verifiable learning,* not the experience itself. Despite the fact that many colleges and universities are very different from and do not aspire to be like these institutions, we still can learn from them.

The state of Tennessee took a bold step in tying their K–12 and postsecondary education systems to their workforce development plans for 2025 and included prior learning assessment as a component of the plan. Their plan "Drive to 55" calls for 55 percent of Tennesseans to possess a postsecondary credential, and it recognized that in order to move the needle from approximately 38 percent of adults with credentials, new approaches would be needed, and barriers identified and removed. A number of working task forces were appointed, including one for prior learning assessment. Their work culminated in the launching of the "Time-wise TN" website (Tennessee Higher Education Commission & Student Assistance Corporation, n.d.), which outlines the prior learning assessment options of examination, past training, and/or portfolio review, among other information (Boyle, Gotcher, & Otts, 2018).

According to data presented in December 2017 on the website of the Education Commission of the States, 24 states have statewide PLA policies that require or allow each public institution to award credit for prior learning. Further, 9 states also provide guidance and information to students regarding the fees associated with PLA options, and 11 states set limits on the number of credits that could be acquired through PLA programs (Education Commission of the States, 2019).

Accepting this whole notion of prior learning assessments requires a shift on the part of faculty to understanding and embracing that knowledge and skills can be learned/gained in settings other than traditional ones—settings such as classrooms, studios, and labs, as discussed earlier. It also requires changing many of the federal financial aid programs that were based on assumptions of "seat time" within specific time frames (e.g., trimesters, semesters) rather than evidence of actual learning. In an effort to explore these issues, the National Association of Student Financial Aid Administrators (NASFAA) appointed a task force in November 2014, with the specific goal of developing recommendations for changes in Title IV regulations that might accommodate and support these emerging new learning models. The report identified a number of recommendations designed to break away from the use of "time" as a fundamental construct. The summary states

Within innovative learning models, Title IV requirements need to be separated from the construct of time, which creates several opportunities to revise time-based rules like SAP, R2T4, attendance and the like. The rules, systems and processes that work for traditional, term based, brick and mortar programs do not always work to advance the innovation that currently exists within higher education, and the recommendations in this paper are the first step to help ensure barriers are eliminated that stifle this innovation. ED, accreditors, States, system vendors and schools need to work together to ensure high-quality education is delivered to students, while reducing administrative burden, encouraging innovation and safeguarding taxpayer dollars. (National Association of Student Financial Aid Adminstrators, 2015)

Although the Department of Education has started to experiment with providing Title IV aid for competency-based education and/or prior learning assessment, there continues to be a focus on "seat time" and instruction, rather than demonstrated outcomes in the distribution and access to federal financial aid programs. Additionally, students are required to be degree-seeking and enrolled at least half-time in order to be eligible for a Pell Grant and Title IV loan programs. Many of the lowest-earning members of our population are often seeking "just enough" training and leave after their goals have been met, often without a completed degree. In such circumstances, one could certainly argue that degree completion is not the only beneficial outcome for a learner worthy of assistance. While there is advocacy calling for change from many corners (e.g., NASFAA, CAEL, institutions) and experimentation by the Department of Education is under way, these financial aid constraints provide obstacles to millions of learners in acquiring the credentials they need and the workforce the nation needs (Phillips, 2018). These policies need to become better synchronized with emerging and innovative learning models to facilitate greater access and completion for students.

Competency-Based Education (CBE). As educators, we know that people learn more when goals are clear and explicit, because this allows learners to engage in approaches and strategies to move them toward meeting those goals. This type of education moves us away from "seat time" as the measure of learning, to proof that competency has been developed at whatever level of performance the learner is focusing on (e.g., a skill, a set of skills, integrated knowledge). As some point out, CBE is not a new concept, but rather a reworking of the 1990s' outcome-based education (OBE) for secondary schools, which promoted the shifting of educational institutions from "time to mastery," where "the amount of learning was fixed and the time spent in school was supposed to be variable" as opposed to "the amount of time is fixed and the learning is a variable . . ." (Greene, 2018, para. 3). OBE experienced a number of problems (e.g., appropriate outcomes, aligned assessments, abandonment of letter grades, inclusion of noncognitive objectives, concern that education was viewed as a set of tasks to be performed), which should not take away from CBE, given all the lessons learned from OBE. As we have argued above, competencies can be focused at all levels of mastery, from a single skill to a set of skills to an ability to integrate across knowledge and skills to create and innovate solutions to current challenges.

Whether we call them outcomes or competencies, we should clearly articulate to our learners, in whatever type of educational experience they are involved, what we believe they will know and be able to do if they fully engage in practice and receive timely and constructive feedback. In the end, their success (and ours) will be based on their ability to demonstrate what they have learned. As one educator noted, we need to "make the transition from a traditional teaching-driven model to a learning-driven model anchored in well-defined learning objectives" (Johnson, 2017, para. 5).

179

And, as noted in the section above, if learners can demonstrate through a prior learning assessment that they already have mastered some of the objectives or competencies, they can progress more quickly, not wasting valuable time and money. Perhaps one of the best-known institutions to provide competency-based degrees at scale is WGU, which, as just discussed, has developed robust prior learning assessments because they go hand in hand with competency-based education. Another is Brandman University, for whom flexibility is a keystone because their target learners are working adults. Brandman offers competency-based programs that are self-paced and nonterm. Finally, organizations like the Competency-Based Education Network (C-BEN) exist to facilitate the development of such programs at other institutions by sharing their knowledge, expertise, and experiences. Colleges and universities can learn from and build on these programs and organizations.

Modularization and Stackability. As we have mentioned several times, the diversity of learners' goals and the need for continual learning in the workplace begs for us to design educational experiences for flexibility, such as shorter chunks, variety of time frames, and different modes of delivery. This means that learners will not necessarily need to gain a credential at one institution in a set amount of time, but rather they can (a) gain knowledge and skills in a variety of different ways and venues (e.g., work-related, online, community college, other universities, boot camps, volunteer experiences, military service), (b) demonstrate their proficiency and competence through prior learning assessments, (c) fill in the gaps given their current and future needs with other educational experiences (e.g., modules, courses, programs), and (d) eventually stack all of those toward some kind of credential (discussed later in this chapter).

Examples of this approach do exist. Purdue University Global has built ExcelTrack, "a competency-based program where courses are built in a modular format allowing students to earn one credit towards completion of a class in pieces . . . a five-credit course may have five one-credit outcomes . . ." (Chatlani, 2018, para. 5). If learners already know the content or have demonstrated the skill, based on an assessment, they skip that module and move to the next. This has worked well for people who have attended multiple colleges (with credits from them) in advance of finding Purdue, as they work to earn a credential. Of course, colleges and universities may want to design their own programs in modular and stackable forms, thus enabling learners to continue to learn over their lifetime at an institution they know and trust.

A flexible approach to learning (e.g., PLA, CBE, and modularization and stackability) allows learners to engage with either or both customization and personalization, depending on their needs and interests, and is enhanced through prior learning assessments, competency-based educational experiences, and modularity and stackability. As discussed previously, today's learners include 40 percent who are 25 or older, 62 percent who are working, (and of that, 26 percent who are working full-time), 28 percent who have children, and 33 percent whose families earn $20,000 or less per year (Bill & Melinda Gates Foundation, n.d.-c). To align with who our learners are and what they need, we must rethink it all—content, delivery modes, class scheduling, financial aid, and how we advise and mentor learners. The Maricopa Community Colleges system has always had a diverse student body, and they offer such flexibility as 48 potential start dates per year, training programs where students get credit while getting paid, and credit for prior learning and life experience (Bill & Melinda Gates Foundation, n.d.-b). Again, we can learn from those institutions despite how different they may be from our own.

<u>Expand Types of Credentials to Meet Learners' Needs.</u> By this point, we hope that readers clearly see the necessity for higher education to expand our work to address the needs of the increasing

number of lifelong learners (e.g., career enhancers, career switchers, 31 million with some credits toward a degree but no degree) as well as those whose life situation does not enable a 4-year degree, while continuing to serve the shrinking traditional-age college population. As discussed earlier in the chapter, this will require that some colleges and universities become more flexible, provide learners with more agency, and foster mobility by creating more modular and stackable educational experiences, among other things—which will entail rethinking credentials to capture competencies in a way that allows learners to continue to expand and build their knowledge and skills throughout their lives and careers.

When people talk about alternative, or nondegree credentials, the typical set (as of this writing) includes certificates, industry certification, digital badges, micro-credentials, and licenses. These credentials are gained in shorter periods of time, are more affordable, are often competency-based, and usually focus on just-in-time and/or job-relevant skills and competencies. In the best of all worlds, they would also serve as pathways to traditional degrees for those who seek that option. These nondegree credentials can be an attractive alternative for working individuals and professionals who might be looking to upskill, reskill, or develop new competencies. Additionally, underserved populations who do not possess a degree, and who are not likely to pursue a degree, may see these credentials as a viable route to improving their employment options. For this group, this could be an affordable start to a college education (Fain, 2018). As Sean Gallagher (2016) reminds us in his book *The Future of University Credentials: New Developments at the Intersection of Higher Education and Hiring*, we need different options at different price points for learners with different goals. This means that credentials are not in competition with traditional college degrees but can stack toward the degree (see the discussion of stackability earlier in this chapter). Rachel Carlson, CEO and co-founder of Guild Education, sums it up nicely:

> Employers see the value in the right credentials, whether they're short-term or long-term .... Get rid of the false choice. Let employees earn short-term credentials that are relevant to their jobs today, while also working toward a bachelor's degree, which remains by far the best investment to reach the middle class. (Fain, 2018, p. 29)

Many universities are already exploring this landscape of alternative credentials. The University of Washington's Continuum College has recently begun to offer noncredit certificates in data analytics, data science, machine learning, and project management "in four formats: self-paced and online; accelerated and blended with online and classroom components that can be completed in less than two months; group-based and online with an expected length of five to nine months; and a part-time, classroom-based evening version" (Fain, 2018, p. 2). Clearly, the design of this program was meant to meet learners where they are (e.g., amount of time, venue, cost) and was developed in collaboration with "local" employers, including Boeing, Microsoft, and Amazon. Wichita State University began offering an online, self-paced badge program in 2015 for working professionals, with the option of badges stacking toward a degree. These badges "are tied to credit hours, and are subject to all Higher Learning Commission regional accreditation standards" (Mazzullo, 2018, para. 6).

California's new online community college will not offer degrees; rather, it will offer short-term credentials that will be stackable and map to college credits. This means they will meet the needs of what they call "stranded workers" who need to upskill as well as serve as on-ramps to degree programs for those who want to eventually do that (Fain, 2018). To accomplish this, faculty

183

members "are working closely with employers, industry associations and unions to develop and map required competencies for the credential programs. Those competencies will include core technical skills as well as foundational ones in literacy, numeracy and digital and soft skills" (Fain, 2018, p. 30).

According to Fain (2018),

> Many of the alternative credential programs that experts are watching most closely were created through a kind of reverse engineering, where faculty members and college administrators work with employers to first understand the skills needed on the job—both the specific (hard) and less tangible (soft) variety. Broken into competencies, those skills are then used to create course context and curricula, often featuring modularized, short-term lessons and assignments. Without employer involvement in creating them, however, competencies fail the test of being workplace relevant. (p. 37)

We would be remiss if we did not point out that a large part of the process Fain described above should be familiar to faculty members designing and revising degree programs. We should all begin by (1) understanding what the world needs in our graduates, (2) agreeing on what we can do in the specified amount of time we have with our learners, (3) defining program outcomes to align with those needs, and then (4) designing courses and other educational experiences as well as assessments to help learners achieve those outcomes. In certain circles in higher education, we call this approach "backward design" (Wiggins & McTighe, 2005).

There are multiple and well-founded concerns about the integrity and quality of credentials that people are currently working to address. Quality control is among one of the most prominent, especially given the for-profit college scandal a few years ago. No one wants to see learners end up with debt and questionable credentials that are not accepted or valued by employers. In fact, for those working in this realm, one of the most important aspects of creating alternative credentials is ensuring that it is done with job-market data to identify workforce needs and, in best-case scenarios, in collaboration with industry partners.

Another concern connected to the quality of programs resulting in credentials is the current "wild, wild west" environment, where there are many options offered by different entities, which can be confusing to potential learners. Thankfully, progress has been made on this front as well. George Washington University's Institute of Public Policy, Workcred, and Southern Illinois University Carbondale's Center for Workforce Development have jointly begun to create a centralized registry of credential information, a project funded by the Lumina Foundation in 2013 (Credential Engine, n.d.-a). The result of this work is Credential Engine, a nonprofit founded in 2016 whose mission is "to bring transparency to all credentials, reveal the marketplace of credentials, increase credential literacy, and allow students, workers, employers, educators, and policy makers to make more informed decisions about credentials and their value" (Credential Engine, n.d.-a, para. 1). This is a tall order for the more than 300,000 credentials they have already identified, a number that they believe is conservative given their research, which is still progressing. Their numbers include, among other things, degree programs and certificate programs offered by postsecondary institutions, which account for the lion's share of credentials—64.2 percent degrees and 20.1 percent certificates. Credential Engine is also documenting high school diplomas, registered apprenticeships, state-issued occupational licenses, certifications, boot camp certificates, MicroMasters, and Nanodegrees, and will continue to focus on the nondegree credentials in the future. If successful, potential learners will be able to "find and compare credential options; have access to data to determine if the opportunity meets their needs; determine how credentials connect to each other and the larger credential marketplace; and understand the credential process, including quality assurance for the experience leading to the credential" (Samson, 2018, para. 1; Credential Engine, n.d.-b, para. 4). Perhaps among their most important work is creating a set of definitions for credentials, what they are calling Credential Transparency Description Language. All of this work is in its infancy, and the most recent report from the group outlines a series of recommendations to a number of organizations who can partner with Credential Engine to help them assist current and future learners (American Council on Education, 2018b; Credential Engine n.d.-b).

Others are also working on data collection about alternative credentials. The National Student Clearinghouse wants to tie student-level information to wage data to be able to create a more holistic view of the various learning pathways and understand "the use of the noncredit channels, perhaps in concert with the for-credit ones" (Fain, 2018, p. 23). Connecting Credentials, another initiative begun by the Lumina Foundation in collaboration with the Corporation for a Skilled Workforce, is focused on better understanding the landscape and has resulted in a beta credential framework as well as a commitment from Lumina to continue to support the credential work through both its grant-making and convening work (Lumina Foundation, 2015). Skillful (a nonprofit initiative of the Markle Foundation, Microsoft, LinkedIn, and the state of Colorado) has created a toolkit that will provide historical data about graduates of training programs (e.g., employment outcomes, wages), thus enabling, among other things, potential learners to make more informed decisions and trainers to continually revise offerings to meet workforce need (Markle Foundation, n.d.). And The T3 Innovation Network, a collaboration between the U.S. Chamber of Commerce Foundation and Lumina, "is exploring the emerging technologies and standards in the talent marketplace to better align student, workforce, and credentialing data with the needs of the new economy" (U.S. Chamber of Commerce Foundation, n.d., para. 5).

The Workforce Data Quality Campaign, a project from the National Skills Coalition, recently published two reports focused on how states are working—and can work—to meet their goals on the number of residents with a postsecondary credential (Leventoff, 2018). One of the campaign's goals was to survey states to determine who is collecting data on nondegree credentials and identifying "credentials of value" (Leventoff, 2018, p. 2). Unfortunately, their survey revealed that everyone is struggling to collect these data, but the good news is that at least 30 states are trying to identify credentials of value (using labor-market data and employment and wage outcomes) in order to support workforce development and allocate financial aid (Fain, 2018, p. 24).

One of these reports has identified some best practices. For example, the Virginia Community College System keeps track of certification and licensing programs that meet the following criteria: "(1) be based on skills standards developed or endorsed by employers; (2) be recognized by multiple employers and educational institutions, as well as across geographic areas, where appropriate; (3) involve a test or other demonstration that the student has acquired the required skills; and (4) be validated by a third party, such as the American Welding Society, the National Healthcareer Association, or the Virginia Department of Health Professions" (Leventoff, 2018, pp. 7–8).

Similarly, the Tennessee Department of Education maintains a list that requires certifications to meet these criteria: "(1) industry recognized and valued; (2) aligned to a career and technical education course and/or program of study; (3) accepted for credit or hours by post-secondary institutions; and (4) lead to high-quality employment" (Leventoff, 2018, p. 7). And Montana is the only state identified by the Workforce Data Quality Campaign identified that is leveraging data "on labor market outcomes—both results for graduates from specific programs as well as supply and demand analysis—for its colleges to make informed and targeted decisions about educational offerings" (Fain, 2018, p. 24).

Interestingly, this credential work goes back a few decades. In 1945, the American Council on Education (ACE) began a relationship with the military to evaluate the Joint Service Transcripts (JSTs) for the Department of Defense in an effort to provide veterans with college credit for the training they received while serving in any branch of the military (American Council on Education, n.d.-b). ACE has also offered its College Credit Recommendation Service since 1974, which provides recommendations for academic credit from training that takes place outside of degree programs. In fact, according to ACE, in December 2019 the CREDIT transcript (the $1.5 million Lumina-funded project between ACE and Credly mentioned earlier in this chapter) "will be transformed into a modular, digital profile that includes workplace competencies in addition to credit recommendations, allowing students to use their training to seek new employment opportunities as well as apply to college" (American Council on Education, n.d.-a).

Here are some examples of how the CREDIT transcript works. The American Society for Healthcare Risk Management offers a 3-day/10-hour educational experience for risk management professionals with 1–5 years of experience, which ACE recommends is the equivalent to 1 semester hour in risk management or health-care administration, for those students who can pass the final exam. Delta Air Lines offers a 3-week/120-hour course on avionics systems, which ACE recommends as equivalent to 6 semester hours in avionics. Fidelity Investments offers a 36-hour experience focusing on loan mechanics, which ACE recommends is equivalent to 1 semester hour in financial planning, retirement planning, or benefits management. And IBM Corporation offers a 4-day/32-hour experience on complex project and program

188

management that ACE recommends is equivalent to 2 semester undergraduate hours in project management, business administration, or management, and 1 semester hour in a graduate degree.

Finally, the question of how learners will keep track of credentials arises when we discuss the notion that learners will continue to upskill and reskill throughout their careers. In response, a group of institutions has been piloting what they call "a modern transcript" using blockchain; this transcript would be "digital, portable, owned by the student, and can be verified using the encrypted assets" (Fain, 2018, p. 45).

In the end, colleges and universities will have to make decisions about whether to offer a wider set of credentials. Make no mistake, however, that noncollege providers are stepping up in this realm, often partnering with foundations, employers, professional organizations, and others. As of this writing, it appears that community colleges are the predominant institutions engaged in alternative credentials, as well as online graduate programs at 4-year universities; they are paving the way and we can learn much from them. Inside Higher Ed's report titled *On-Ramps and Off-Ramps: Alternative Credentials and Emerging Pathways Between Education and Work* has many interesting examples of current credentialing work (Fain, 2018), as does Gallagher's (2016) *The Future of University Credentials*.

Design for Integration. Because learning happens everywhere (as discussed earlier), it is important that all of our learners have the ability to extract meaning from both everyday moments in their professional and personal lives as well as from structured learning opportunities, *and* integrate the knowledge, skills, perspectives, and wisdom gained in a way that creates a coherent and unified view of their work, the world, and their place in it. We want learners to integrate within their own identities, and integrate across venues and experiences. So, we are talking about integration on at least two levels.

Let's begin with integration within the learner. Whether we are talking about our learners as intellectual, social, or emotional beings (typically faculty focus more on intellectual, and student affairs folks more on social-emotional), those aspects of who we are do not live separately from each other. In other words, this is an inaccurate and artificial division. For example, learners do not bring their intellectual selves only into learning situations and leave their identity and emotions outside the classroom, lab, online environment, community service, or work. Rather, they experience learning holistically given who they are and where they are developmentally, as young college-age adults or mature and experienced adult returning professionals. Conversely, learners do not leave their intellectual selves behind when they engage in conversations with roommates or coworkers, join a team, or volunteer at a food bank. This means that, as a learner, our view of ourselves (e.g., our abilities, limitations, motivations, confidence), our beliefs (e.g., about intelligence, the nature of learning), and our goals interact with the learning experience to influence learning and performance (as discussed in principle 6 in the section "Leverage What We Know about How People Learn").

A second form of integration is across learning experiences. For example, an adult who has learned to mediate conflict among their children or siblings or by coaching or refereeing Little League baseball, and/or those who have negotiated to buy a house or a car, can bring that knowledge and skill to both their workplace and a business course. At the same time, mediation and negotiation learned in a formal course setting can be used in a variety of nonacademic and nonwork settings.

Northeastern University in Boston recently launched an initiative that both authors of this book created called Self-Authored Integrated Learning (SAIL), which for Northeastern is the next generation of experiential learning. This initiative is focused in part on bridging the perceived skills gap (discussed in chapter 1) by helping learners (1) become more intentional, self-directed, and aware of the intellectual and professional skills they are developing as a result of various learning experiences; (2) integrate the knowledge and skills across those experiences; (3) transfer the knowledge and skills across contexts; and (4) better articulate what they know and can do (Northeastern University, n.d.). Additionally, the initiative acknowledges that learning has no boundaries and embraces the concept that learning happens everywhere, not exclusively within the confines of the academic setting (as previously discussed). This mindset leverages more completely not only the full offerings and benefits of the university learning ecosystem but also of learning that happens on the job, through one's personal life, service, in the military, and so forth, enabling the inclusion and recognition of the many places that learners develop critical intellectual and professional skills.

In the area of integration for traditional-age undergraduate learners, SAIL brings to the forefront knowledge and skills that may be developed in one area that should be integrated and transferred to others. For example, when a member of the hockey team reviews the recording of a game with her coaches and team, she receives feedback about both her personal performance as well as her contribution to the team's performance. She practices in areas where she underperforms, clearly using the constructive feedback in her practice and future games. This scenario is no different from the feedback she gets on her design project—the question is, does she recognize the need for and value of taking that feedback and incorporating it into her next project? Or a resident assistant spends endless hours over the course of 2 years mediating conflict between several sets of roommates— hearing each perspective, promoting active listening to each party, prompting for underlying assumptions and perspectives, identifying common goals, and discussing options and a mutually agreeable solution. Does that student use this skill set in a policy course where his dysfunctional

191

team is working toward addressing the problem of food deserts in U.S. cities? Facilitating the recognition, integration, and transference of skills and knowledge across artificial boundaries is critically important in developing self-directed, lifelong learners capable of achieving personal and professional success and well-being.

Utilize experiential learning. Experiential learning is often referred to as "learning by doing," but that is too simplistic a definition. At Northeastern University in Boston, our institution, where experiential learning has more than a hundred-year history, we developed the following definition of experiential learning:

> the practice of **mindful reflection** on the **integration of theory and practice** through **authentic settings** (e.g., professional work experience, research, community involvement, co-curricular activities, and industry challenges) with **real-world opportunities, responsibilities and consequences** that enhance the students' abilities to **transfer** knowledge and skills to new contexts and prepare them for a **lifetime of learning and growth**.

We view experiential learning as extremely important because "theory lacks meaning outside of practice" (Eyler, 2009). Although experiential learning can and does take place in limited ways in classroom, lab, and studio situations, it is much more powerful and robust when learners have opportunities to use their knowledge and practice their skills in authentic, real-world situations with real parameters, constraints, and consequences for their decisions and behavior. And to ensure deep learning, reflection prompts learners to think about their learning—what they have gained, how, what it connects to, and how they might use it in the future in different contexts. This process of experience combined with intentional reflection will help learners expand their ability to use their knowledge and skills in different, unique, and unfamiliar situations and contexts.

Research has long recognized and documented that undergraduate student learning, growth, and development occur well beyond formal instructional offerings (Astin, 1985, 1993; Brown & Adler, 2008; Pascarella & Terenzini, 1991; Tinto, 1987, 1993). Scholars have worked to understand what experiences correlate to the most powerful learning outcomes (Kuh, 2008) and have used these data to call for, among other things, more "fluidity and connection between the formal curriculum and the experiential co-curriculum" (Bass, 2012, p. 26). In fact, some have suggested that the optimal way to learn is "reciprocally or spirally between practice and content," (Bass, 2012, p. 28) a reverse of typical curricula that are built from content, and eventually engage students in practice. The best-case scenario, according to Bass (2012), is an educational environment that weaves the connections back and forth across the formal and experiential curriculum.

As we said above, aspects of experiential learning occur in many traditional settings and pedagogies. Figure 3.1 shows the continuum from course-based pedagogies that approximate the real world to program-based experiences immersed in the real world. Many disciplines have long used effective pedagogies like case studies, simulations, or labs to connect theory to practice, an important initial component of experiential learning (Bolkan, 2013; Li, 2010; O'Neil, 2014; Scientist, 2013). But as you move along the continuum to what we are calling real-world immersion, learners connect theory to practice with all of the constraints, parameters, and consequences that exist in the world of work. As we evolve higher education, we should be thinking about how to move across the continuum as learners progress through programs of study.

Many universities around the world embrace experiential education (often using different nomenclature), with one of the

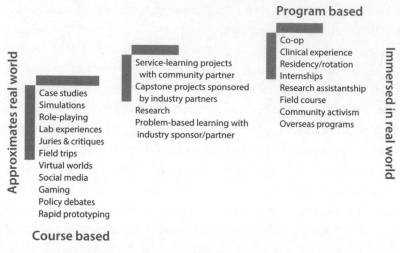

Figure 3.1 Continuum of experiential learning examples

most prominent models being cooperative education, known colloquially in the United States and Canada as "co-op." Northeastern University is one of them and is the second oldest in the country. As of this writing, 95 percent of the graduating class engaged in at least one 6-month co-op, 78 percent do two, and 33 percent do three (Northeastern University Decision Support Office, 2018). In most cases, they are paid co-ops in which students are treated as full-time employees, with job responsibilities that mimic full-time work. Co-ops are different from internships in that internships are often a summer or semester commitment, can be either part-time or full-time, can be paid or unpaid, and typically do not interfere with the regular flow of the academic year. Co-ops, on the other hand, alternate with semesters, quarters, or trimesters; are typically paid and full-time; and most often are 6-month commitments.

To align with the definition of experiential learning presented a few paragraphs ago, Northeastern University prepares learners, before they go out on their first co-op, to think about their learning goals and to understand the type of learning in which they will engage in the work-based environment. Students are asked to embrace a growth mindset (Dweck, 2006), which tells us that intelligence is not fixed and that we can "get smarter" through time, effort, practice, and feedback. During their 6-month co-op, learners are asked to reflect (in writing at several different times) on the learning that is taking place, and after their experience they engage in both a self-assessment and a debriefing as well as receive a final evaluation from their work supervisor. This reflection allows learners to analyze their own performance and identify ways to enhance it in the future, despite how successful they may have been.

Although such co-op opportunities allow learners to "try out" their chosen profession, more importantly, there is a full range of intellectual advantages that do not exist within "traditional" educational models. For example, experiential learning that is immersed in the real world (right side of Figure 3.1) does the following:

· Motivates students because they see the relevance and value of what they are learning (Ambrose et al., 2010, pp. 66–90);
· Moves them toward mastery of their knowledge and skills as they use that mastery in a variety of authentic and new contexts, thus deepening and cementing the knowledge and skills and ensuring transfer to even more contexts over time (Ambrose et al., 2010, pp. 91–120);
· Provides the ultimate practice and feedback cycle essential to learning, as learners use their knowledge and skills to complete their job tasks and responsibilities, receiving feedback on their performance that has real consequences (Ambrose et al., 2010, pp. 121–152);

195

- Helps them develop skills that one cannot develop in a classroom, studio, lab, such as learning how to deal with the unexpected, learning how to improvise, and learning how to adapt to changing conditions—in other words, learning how to be agile, as we discussed in chapter 2; and
- Teaches them how to learn in a work-based environment (including learning from peers), thus promoting self-directed learning (Ambrose et al., 2010, pp. 188–224).

Because not all learners have the time, authorization to work due to their immigration status (i.e., international students), or ability to physically engage with co-ops (given their life circumstances), another form of experiential learning that adapts to learners' needs are micro-internships. Northeastern University has developed XN (Experience Network) for their online master's and professional degree programs, which enable students to virtually work on real projects from employers. These experiences are not paid but rather count toward course requirements. Engaging in several of these projects during the course of their program provides many of the same benefits described above.

High school educators are increasingly seeing the value of experiential learning as well. For example, the Center for Advanced Professional Studies (CAPS) was created by the Blue Valley School District in Kansas to develop relationships with business and industry to provide profession-based learning (CAPS Network, n.d.). In this program, students "are fully immersed in a professional culture, solving real world problems, using industry standard tools and are mentored by actual employers, all while receiving high school and college credit" (CAPS Network, n.d.). High school students spend half of their day in traditional classrooms and the other half in another building that is dedicated to CAPS, which includes a variety of labs and simulation rooms, as well as spaces for presentations to industry partners that have provided a project or challenge to the students. Included in the CAPS guiding principles of the program are self-discovery and exploration, professional skills development, and entrepreneurial mindset. CAPS has been developing a network of school districts across the country, from Montvale, New Jersey to Ridgefield, Washington, and from Shakopee, Minnesota, to Dallas, Texas.

Individual high schools are also embarking on experiential learning. Five years ago, teacher Stephen Plum and colleagues reached out to community partners in research labs, hospitals, and a fire station, among others, to develop field experiences to complement their high school curriculum by showing students the relevance of what they were learning; the added bonus was the students' self-awareness and sense of belonging that developed (Plum, 2018). The website for Hamilton Southeastern (HSE) Schools in Fishers, Indiana, boldly includes experiential learning as part of its academic program, stating, "Deep learning is active and relational. HSE is committed to providing students with many opportunities to learn through interaction with the broader community, both inside and outside traditional classroom walls" (Hamilton Southeastern Schools, 2019, para. 1). HSE provides a number of types of experiential learning ranging from apprenticeships to student development of a project for a client, internships, project and service-based learning, among other opportunities available to promote real-world experiences (Hamilton Southeastern Schools, 2019).

Another example of public support for experiential learning can be found in the Bellmore-Merrick Central School district on Long Island in New York, where in 2013 voters passed a $50 million bond issue, enabling the district to build a state-of the-art-broadcast studio (BMB Broadcasting) and a professional kitchen in two of its high school buildings. Assistant Principal Marie Netto stated, "The skills [students are] gaining in the program are going to transcend the four walls of Mepham High School and help them to experience real-world problems and work toward a solution" (Brinton, 2017). Beyond these examples, there are a number of others that speak to the growing trend and recognition of the value in creating experiential learning opportunities for students at all levels of the educational continuum. This growth in experiential learning opportunities in K–12 education suggests that learners will have greater expectations for similar experiential learning opportunities in postsecondary education.

New businesses are also cropping up to capitalize on the power of experiential learning. For example, Pole Star Experiential Learning is a company whose vision is to "guide the future workforce toward professional excellence by creating personalized experiential learning opportunities through virtual internships and proprietary innovation to develop, measure, and improve career performance" (Pole Star Experiential Learning, n.d., para. 2). Like other experiential learning opportunities, they bridge the gap between theory and practice through virtual internships in real-world settings. Parker Dewey is an organization that offers short-term, project-based learning (some call them micro-internships) to undergraduates or recent graduates through digital projects posted by employers. These employers post a project with a due date and fixed fee along with questions about the applicant's approach or process for screening purposes. The company then selects the individual(s) to complete the project. It is a win-win because learners gain experience and employers receive a product and potentially identify talent to expand their applicant pool. Higher education needs to take note of these entities because this opens a field of opportunity for third-party providers, creating undesired competition (Fain, 2018).

We are also seeing a resurgence of apprenticeships that provide integration of on-the-job and classroom learning, work experience, access to professional mentors and networks, and even postsecondary credits and credentials (Parton, 2017). The U.S.

Department of Labor definition of a registered apprenticeship includes four criteria: "Paid, on the job learning under the supervision of skilled employees, related classroom-based instruction, ongoing assessment against skills standards, and culmination in a portable, industry-recognized credential" (Parton, 2017, p. 3). And though there is no agreed-upon definition for youth apprenticeship in the United States, there is an evolving interest and "states are leading a new wave of efforts to expand" them (Parton, 2017, p. 5). For example, the Rhode Island Department of Education received a $500,000 grant in 2018 from the U.S. Department of Education to launch the Rhode Island Youth Apprenticeship Program focusing on cybersecurity and data analysis (Warwick Beacon, 2018, para. 1). Paul Quinn College in Texas received a $1 million grant from Strada Education Network to expand its work-college program, where students attend class 3 days a week and work the other 2 days with local employers like PepsiCo, FedEx, and Toyota (Patterson, 2018).

Design with Specific Learning Outcomes Articulated. Whether designing a module, a course, a program, a boot camp, or any other educational activity, educators need to explicitly identify the expected end state—that is, what the learner should be able to do at the end of the activity or experience, whether you call that a learning objective, goal, outcome, or competency (people often use these words interchangeably). This approach allows learners to work toward something concrete, direct their effort by choosing appropriate strategies to get there, monitor their understanding and progress along the way, ask for help if needed, and determine their level of success. We briefly discussed this notion earlier in the chapter in the section on competency-based education (CBE), because the key to CBE is articulating the competencies that learners will demonstrate to show success.

The National Institute for Learning Outcomes Assessment (NILOA) and the Association of American Colleges and

Universities (AAC&U) have developed numerous resources to support institutions in advancing the development of learning outcomes and related assessment practices. NILOA also provides coaches, at no cost to selected institutions, to assist in their assessment activities. Additionally, as many of us know, both regional and disciplinary accreditation agencies also promote program outcomes in order to help programs determine their success in the educational realm as well as areas in need of improvement. For example, the New England Association of Schools and Colleges' (NEASC) Commission on Institutions of Higher Education (CIHE) standard 4.2 states

> The institution publishes the learning goals and requirements for each program. Such goals include the knowledge, intellectual and academic skills, competencies, and methods of inquiry to be acquired. In addition, if relevant to the program, goals include creative abilities and values to be developed and specific career-preparation practices to be mastered. (New England Commission of Higher Education, 2016, para. 48)

CIHE does not identify what those learning goals should be, but rather expects that they are established by each program. This is true of other regional accreditation bodies, and even some of the disciplinary bodies as well. For example, the Association to Advance Collegiate Schools of Business (AACSB) requires that business programs

> state the educational expectations for each degree program. They specify the intellectual and behavioral competencies a program is intended to instill. In defining these goals, the faculty members clarify how they intend for graduates to be competent and effective as a result of completing the program. (Association to Advance Collegiate Schools of Business, 2018, p. 2)

They also provide a list of expectations of the "general skills areas and general business and management skill areas" (p. 35), but do not designate a definitive set of learning outcomes.

On the other hand, ABET, the accreditation body for engineering and engineering technology, applied and natural sciences, and computing, defines a set of foundational outcomes for all undergraduate engineering programs, with the understanding that programs will add their own to this list. Their set includes

1. an ability to identify, formulate, and solve complex engineering problems by applying principles of engineering, science, and mathematics;
2. an ability to apply engineering design to produce solutions that meet specified needs with consideration of public health, safety, and welfare, as well as global, cultural, social, environmental, and economic factors;
3. an ability to communicate effectively with a range of audiences;
4. an ability to recognize ethical and professional responsibilities in engineering situations and make informed judgments, which must consider the impact of engineering solutions in global, economic, environmental, and societal contexts;
5. an ability to function effectively on a team whose members together provide leadership, create a collaborative and inclusive environment, establish goals, plan tasks, and meet objectives;
6. an ability to develop and conduct appropriate experimentation, analyze and interpret data, and use engineering judgment to draw conclusions; and
7. an ability to acquire and apply new knowledge as needed, using appropriate learning strategies.

The business world is also moving toward learning goals. According to Gino (2018, para. 41), "A body of research demonstrates that framing work around learning goals (developing competence, acquiring skills, mastering new situations, and so on) rather than performance goals (hitting targets, proving our competence, impressing others) boosts motivation." We already discussed, earlier in this section (learning principle #3 in the section "Leverage What We Know about How People Learn"), the connection between motivation and learning, with which clearly the world of work agrees.

Develop Partnerships. Partnerships will become increasingly important given the context discussed in chapter 1 and the array of educational needs from various learner audiences discussed in chapter 2. These partnerships will take many forms and will minimally involve industry, nonprofits, community colleges, 4-year institutions, K–12, communities, other academic institutions, foundations, and local, state, and federal governments that rally around a shared goal or goals, to both promote and enhance the academic and professional success of all learners.

<u>Partnerships with Industry.</u> Recognizing the need for industry and educational partnerships is not a new idea. The Business-Higher Education Forum (BHEF), a nonprofit organization that was founded in 1978, is made up of

> Fortune 500 CEOs, college and university presidents, and other leaders dedicated to the creation of a highly skilled future workforce. BHEF members collaborate and form strategic partnerships to build new undergraduate pathways; improve alignment between higher education and the workforce; and produce a diverse, highly skilled talent pool to meet demand in emerging fields. (Business-Higher Education Forum, n.d., para. 1)

They work to identify trends, launch initiatives, and forge partnerships to address talent needs. These activities are often funded through member foundations and have resulted in partnerships and undergraduate programs in emerging fields such as data science, analytics, and cybersecurity (Business-Higher Education Forum, n.d.). This collaboration is just one example of how these partnerships can play an important role in aligning education with workforce needs.

In the early years of product design, a product was conceived by industrial designers, then handed off to engineers to manufacture, and then to the marketing division to sell—an obvious sequential process. Needless to say, many products went through the entire process only to fail because, for example, there was no market for the product or the cost so exceeded the value that no one bought it. Industry finally realized this sequential process was flawed and redesigned their processes so that the marketing professionals and engineers became part of the design team from the beginning. This change resulted in universities like Carnegie Mellon (one of the first) creating courses and then entire programs focused on integrated product design so that graduates would possess the knowledge, skills, and experience to work on multidisciplinary teams (Cagan & Vogel, 2002).

We mention this story because it serves as an appropriate analogy—it no longer makes sense for us to educate students and send them into the workplace only to find out later, through alumni surveys and/or employer complaints, that our graduates are underprepared. At a minimum, we need continual input from employers to help shape our programs, and we need partnerships that allow us to leverage the best of both worlds.

Many colleges and universities today (particularly in certain disciplines like engineering and business) have departments and programs with advisory boards that include employers to help shape curricular revisions. This, along with data collected from a variety of entities (e.g., Burning Glass, employer surveys, Department of Labor), can inform the direction we need to take as we evolve how we prepare graduates for the world of work. However, that is not enough.

As we discussed earlier in this chapter, both the current and future world of work demand continual education at different stages and levels of sophistication, designed in a way that (a) is flexible and customized, (b) provides learner agency, and (c) leverages the experiential nature of learning while also meeting employer needs. Fortunately for higher education, there are a variety of types of partnerships that have been created over the past few years. For example, Northeastern University has partnered with IBM to enable badges earned at the company to count toward a graduate degree—initially in data analytics, project management, and portfolio management—validating the notion that adult learners have gained knowledge and skills through work experience that should count toward a credential. Northeastern has also joined with GE to provide an accelerated bachelor of science degree in advanced manufacturing systems to GE employees—delivered by Northeastern faculty at GE facilities—which can be completed within 1.5 to 3 years depending on prior academic credits and on-the-job training and experience. It is important to acknowledge that this program was one of eight pilot programs selected in 2016 by the federal government through the Department of Education's Educational Quality Through Innovative Partnerships (EQUIP) initiative. The EQUIP initiative was intended to expand access to high-quality educational programs, particularly for students from low-income backgrounds, to open pathways to credentials that would lead to meaningful employment. The programs were intended to partner traditional postsecondary institutions with nontraditional providers (e.g., MOOCs, boot camps, employers), offering 50 percent or more of the educational program, and quality assurance entities (QAEs) that were expected to ensure quality and protect against fraud and, once approved, open the way for student participants to receive Title IV funds. As of this writing, only five of the pilot programs remain active, and only one (Dallas County Community College District) has received final approval.

While this type of innovative thinking is critical, and this three-way partnership has potential for many others like it, a number of issues need to be worked out to move it forward (McKenzie, 2018).

East Mississippi Community College partnered with local officials a few years ago to train workers for manufacturing jobs coming to the Golden Triangle in Mississippi. This initiative and investment have ballooned into a Center for Manufacturing Technology Excellence 2.0, financially supported by six counties, the state, and the federal government, and soon to be housed in a state-of-the-art building to offer training in new and existing fields (Meridian Star, 2018). Tarrant County College in Texas recently partnered with Delta Air Lines to help them meet their need for aircraft maintenance technicians, given the impending retirement of more than half of their current maintenance technicians who are eligible for retirement (Campbell, 2018).

These partnerships are, in part, the future of higher education. If we do not accept this challenge, higher education could lose out to both the companies and for-profit entities who will fill the gap. For example, Ernst & Young (EY) announced a program in August 2017 that would enable employees to gain skills and earn digital credentials in areas such as data visualization, AI, data transformation, and information strategy. There are multiple goals for this initiative, according to Nancy Altobello, EY Global Vice Chair of Talent:

> By using badges to recognize our peoples' skills, we are increasing their career value and professional visibility, as well as equipping them with the right skills and experience to respond to the changing needs of our clients and to deliver our purpose of building a better working world. (Ernst & Young, 2017, para. 2)

Clearly, EY is not relying on universities to help their employees/learners gain knowledge and skills in a just-in-time, just-for-me manner.

Google, too, has created its own educational solution: an online IT Support Professional Certificate that takes some 8 months to complete (8–10 hours/week), costs $49 per month (Google provides need-based scholarships), and can lead to a job where the average median annual wage is $52,000 at such employers as Bank of America, Cognizant, GE Digital, H&R Block, Hulu, Infosys, Intel, Kforce, MCPc, PNC Bank, Ricoh USA, Smucker's, Sprint, TEKSystems, UPMC, Veterans United Home Loans, and Walmart (Brittany, 2018).

Memphis-based CodeCrew is also not relying on secondary schools or higher education to foster the skills involved in mobile app development, web app development, game development, robotics, and drone programming. They provide in-school electives, after-school and weekend programs, summer programs, internships, and a 6-month coding school to meet these needs, "all while teaching fundamental computer science concepts that apply long term to all levels of the field" (CodeCrew, n.d., para. 4). The code school focuses on students with at least a high school diploma or GED, and it has no upfront costs:

> Upon graduation and landing employment, these students will enter into an income sharing agreement (often referred to as ISAs) where CodeCrew receives a small percentage of their salary for three years, and only if that salary exceeds a monthly rate equivalent to $35,000 annually. (CodeCrew, n.d., para. 13)

Other programs offer ISAs as well (Lambda, Venmo, Upstart, Lumni, and Better Future Forward, among others), some successful and others less so (Unglesbee, 2019). Either way, ISAs are yet another example of a new educational model outside the traditional educational realm, although recently some traditional

206

institutions are considering the concept as well. For example, the University of Utah announced in January 2019 that it would experiment with ISAs for some students, following the lead of Purdue University (Fain, 2019). It will be important for all of us to follow these pilot programs, since some critics believe ISAs may not always be in the best interest of students (Newton, 2019).

Companies have long provided learning and development opportunities to help their employees upskill, and this continues given the current and future state of work. For example, Walmart University has created a training program and incentivizes its entry-level employees by raising their hourly rate by $1 for completing the program. As Bolden-Barrett (2017, para. 7) notes, however, "A training program that only prepares workers to be better Walmart employees may be good for the company but could fall short of truly helping workers." Although this may be acceptable to some employees, others may want to broaden their knowledge base and enhance their skills to move their careers forward, not necessarily at Walmart. Some colleges and universities have already begun to partner with employers to broaden and enhance learning and development programs; for example, College for America has partnered with McDonald's, Comcast, Dunkin Donuts, and Aetna Insurance, among others. These collaborations are better than competition by companies and/or for-profit third-party entities.

Colleges and universities could also eventually lose out to apprenticeship programs. For many years, according to Top, apprenticeships in the United States were "often thought of as Plan B to college," and high schools did not promote apprenticeship programs because "states base their high school ratings on the number of graduates that go to college afterwards" (Top, 2017, para. 12). This is not the case in other countries like France, Switzerland, Canada, Germany, and the United Kingdom; in fact, according to Sarah Ayres Steinberg, a policy analyst at the Center for American Progress, in Washington D.C., "Apprenticeship programs in the U.K. are promoted as cost-effective alternatives to university-based education" (Leonard, 2015, para. 6). Given some of the challenges we face in higher education (e.g., cost, graduation rates), it is not inconceivable that apprenticeship programs could move beyond traditional occupations like building and construction trades (Steinberg, 2014), much like the migration of the T-shaped employee moving from the tech industry to other sectors of the economy, as noted earlier in this chapter.

The Wall Street Journal reported in September 2018 that some tech and finance companies in New York have begun to institute apprenticeship programs (King, 2018). IBM is using apprenticeships to train employees in areas like software engineering, cybersecurity, and data analytics. IBM launched an apprenticeship program registered with the Department of Labor in 2018 with a goal of 100 apprentices; as of this writing, the first group, according to Joanna Daly (2017), VP of Talent, "are on their way to becoming software developers in our Cloud business and mainframe administrators for technologies like Blockchain" (para. 4). Stack Overflow hired apprentices with no computer science degree but who had participated in a boot camp. Microsoft, Amazon.com, and JPMorgan Chase, among others, are hiring apprentices from Apprenti, a company that provides "education and on-the-job training for tech jobs to non-traditional recruits," including veterans, women, and underrepresented minorities (Pinsker, 2019). The program is a collaboration between the Department of Labor and the Washington Technology Industry Association. The starting salary for the Apprenti program is $45,000 during training, rising to $51,000 after 6 months of on-the-job training, ending with at least $75,000 when hired, and Apprenti boasts that most of the students do get hired.

This model could become a more attractive one than a traditional college education. A 2017 study by the Harvard Business

School and Burning Glass explored "new frontiers for apprenticeships," identifying occupations ripe for this type of program, which include, for example, insurance underwriters, human resource specialists, graphic designers, database administrators, claims adjusters, examiners and investigators (Fuller & Sigelman, 2017). The UK is taking apprenticeship one step further through "Go Pro Early," a program that enables students to go to work for a company directly out of high school and earn their college degree while working. According to Brandon Busteed (2019), president of Kaplan University Partners and former executive director of Education & Workforce Development at Gallup: "It's simply a matter of time before the new world of 'going to a job to get a college degree' disrupts the linear education pathway as we know it" (para. 3). PricewaterhouseCoopers (PWC) and others are currently piloting such approaches (Busteed, 2019).

Apprenticeship programs also provide an opportunity for partnerships with colleges and universities. For example, Harper College's partnership with a Swiss-based insurance company has enabled a group of students to work 3 days a week and attend classes the other 2, for 2 years, after which they will receive both an associate's degree and a job with a starting salary of $30,000 (Preston, 2018), without incurring any debt. The hospitality industry has also embraced apprenticeships given the 600,000 or so entry-level job openings (Fain, 2018), with participation from Hilton, Hyatt Hotels Corporation, and Wyndham Hotels and Resorts. Along with an apprenticeship program for food service workers from the National Restaurant Association Educational Foundation, these opportunities are 2-year paid experiences, tied to industry certifications, with clear pathways to online degree programs at some 300 institutions around the world through a partnership with Pearson Education (Fain, 2018).

The federal government has resources for building registered apprenticeship programs on the Department of Labor website,

"A Quick-Start Toolkit" (Department of Labor, n.d.). They define the components of an apprenticeship program as (a) business involvement (because employers are the foundation of the program), (b) structured on-the-job training, (c) related instruction, (d) rewards for skills gained, typically an increase in wages, and (e) a nationally recognized occupational credential. Programs can be customized to meet the needs of the employers and apprentices, so there is flexibility in program design (e.g., time-based, competency-based, hybrid), the related instruction (e.g., on site, online, at a school), and the training model (e.g., concurrent instruction and on-the-job training, front-loaded with instruction, segmented alternating between instruction and on-the-job training). Companies with such programs include Mercedes, Harley-Davidson, Northrop Grumman, Walgreens, the U.S. Mint, and GE, to name a few (Department of Labor, n.d.).

<u>Partnerships with Community Colleges</u>. If we revisit the analogy to product development described at the beginning of this section, then again we should ask ourselves whether it is enough to create articulation agreements with community colleges or if we should be more collaborative in coordinating with them in sharing information about the content of their and our courses, the pedagogies we both use, the expectation of each academic culture, the misconceptions about transfer students' abilities, and the success rate of transfer students. Researchers at the Community College Research Center at Columbia University have been exploring, among other topics, the question of the role of receiving institutions in facilitating an effective transfer process and providing the right type and level of support to enable students' academic success (Xu, Ran, Fink, Jenkins, & Dundar, 2017). These researchers have developed a "framework for identifying partnerships between two- and four-year institutions that are more effective than expected in enabling community college entrants to transfer to a four-year institution and earn a bachelor's degree in

210

a timely fashion" (Xu et al., 2017, p. 3). Their research has been expanded by Wyner, Deane, Jenkins, & Fink (2016), who distilled a set of essential transfer practices that include prioritizing transfer, creating clear programmatic pathways with aligned high-quality instruction, and providing tailored transfer student advising. Their resulting document, *The Transfer Playbook*, also identifies high-performing community college-university partnerships in six different states (Wyner et al., 2016).

For example, faculty, staff, and academic leaders from Florida International University (FIU) and Broward College meet annually for dialogue, and the two have "jointly established an off-campus building where faculty and staff from each institution collaborate on programs and courses" (Wyner et al., 2016, p. 9). FIU and its community college partners also meet each year to review transfer students' experience and success, with the goal of "collectively identifying strengths and gaps in existing program maps . . . and discuss[ing] curricula, teaching methods, and course learning outcomes" (Wyner et al., 2016, p. 25). Holyoke Community College (HCC) Honors Program has forged a partnership with the University of Massachusetts-Amherst Commonwealth Honors College to support those transfer students. HCC also includes UMass faculty colleagues on their program review committees to provide honest feedback "about gaps in two-year program offerings from the four-year perspective" (Wyner et al., 2016, p. 25). Broward College (BC) and Florida Atlantic University (FAU) have created the BC-FAU Link Program, "which intentionally connects prospective FAU transfer students to a range of transfer-related services earlier in their studies at BC" (Wyner et al., 2016, p. 9). Front Range Community College and Colorado State University faculty jointly secured a National Institutes of Health (NIH) grant to

> create a clearly articulated pathway for students to transfer
> with full junior status in biochemistry, biomedical sciences,

211

or psychology. The grant also provided students with supplemental instruction, research training workshops, and the opportunity to apply to participate in summer undergraduate research at CSU. (Wyner et al., 2016, p. 10)

Most of these successful partnerships also have either central transfer advisers who work across the university (Colorado State University has a transfer center in their admissions office), specific transfer advisers in the colleges, or both.

These and other colleges and universities continue to think outside the box to support partnerships that will enhance the academic success of transfer students. Miami Dade College (MDC) and Florida International University (FIU) are discussing "the possibility of giving FIU-bound students who plan to major in STEM fields the opportunity to participate in research activities through the college's School of Science research program while still enrolled in MDC" (Wyner et al., 2016, p. 24). Universities in states like Colorado, Connecticut, and Massachusetts are exploring moving from transfer requirements focused on credits earned to those focused on demonstrating competencies.

Unfortunately, however, recent research indicates that "the more competitive colleges are in admissions, the less likely they are to admit transfer students from community colleges," which means that "the most elite colleges are missing out on many talented students" (Jaschik, 2019b, para. 3, 5). According to Janet L. Marling, Executive Director of the National Institute for the Study of Transfer Students:

Many of them [students] could succeed academically but do not see themselves attending the most competitive institutions, where many students enroll straight from high school and come from wealthy backgrounds. And even though

212

these colleges offer generous financial aid, including to low-income transfer students, which is not something that these students know. (Jaschik, 2019b, para. 19)

This is an area ripe for exploration for many colleges and universities.

Partnerships with K–12. The same product development analogy from the beginning of the section holds true here as well. In chapter 1 we discussed the lack of college readiness for many who graduate from high school. Instead of providing remedial courses, or worse, watching young people drop out of college, we should be coordinating more effectively with K–12. These partnerships can and do exist in the areas of research, professional development for teachers and school leaders, and curricular and co-curricular programs and innovations.

For example, researchers at the University of Chicago partnered with Chicago Public Schools

on a data-driven initiative to keep students on track to graduate. Every six weeks, the Institute gives school principals a "freshmen-on-track" metric for each student, and individual schools and teachers then use that information to determine the best academic intervention. (Gimbel, 2018, para. 5)

At least 20 other university-partnerships have adopted this model. This research comes out of the Urban Education Institute at the University of Chicago, which focuses on equity and excellence in public schools across the country through applied research, training teachers and school leaders, operating a pre-K–12 public school, and providing research-based tools and resources (University of Chicago, n.d.). This is one example of a powerful and impactful partnership.

Another partnership model focuses on professional development and curricular enhancements, as evidenced by a project North Dakota State University engaged in with local school districts (Tomanek, 2005). In this partnership, middle and high school science and math teachers identified units of instruction that needed to be upgraded, and/or areas or units in which they were not fully confident, and worked with graduate students to address these challenges (overseen by university faculty members). An external evaluator on the project noted that part of the success of this partnership was that it did "not begin with what university faculty members believed must be changed in K–12 classrooms. Rather, . . . in response to needs identified by practicing teachers for their specific classrooms and curricula" (Tomanek, 2005, p. 29). In other words, successful partnerships cannot be one-sided.

Montour School District and Carnegie Mellon University (CMU) have been partnering since 2015; their initial collaboration began with the LearnLab, whose goal was, in part, to "create technology-enhanced experiments that would be situated in real classrooms and that will be associated with day-to-day learning of various parts of the curriculum primarily in science, mathematics and second language acquisition" (LearnLab Carnegie Mellon University, n.d., para. 1). The lab was created in the high school permitting "CMU researchers to work side by side with school staff members to identify instructional conditions that maximize student learning" (Reis, 2015, para 3). The partnership expanded in 2018 to include a program in artificial intelligence (AI) in the district, which will teach and expose students to data literacy, autonomous robotics, AI (including speech recognition and computer vision), and STEM inquiry skills (Aglio, 2018).

Finally, we would be remiss if we did not acknowledge one of the most prominent ways that higher education institutions partner with secondary education: through dual and concurrent

214

enrollment programs. These programs allow students to earn college credit while in high school through approved college courses taught by college-approved high school instructors. In the 2010–2011 school year, the U.S. Department of Education reported that more than 1.4 million high school students earned credits this way (U.S. Department of Education, 2016). According to the Institute of Education Science, these programs help students achieve college success in three ways:

> First, allowing high school students to experience college-level courses helps them prepare for the social and academic requirements of college while having the additional supports available to high school students; this may reduce the need for developmental coursework. Second, students who accumulate college credits early and consistently are more likely to attain a college degree. Third, many *dual enrollment programs* offer discounted or free tuition, which reduces the overall cost of college and may increase the number of low socioeconomic status students who can attend and complete college. (U.S. Department of Education, Institute of Education Sciences, 2017, para. 1)

Lest readers worry about the quality and rigor of such programs, there is an accrediting body for concurrent enrollment partnerships. The purpose of the National Alliance of Concurrent Enrollment Partnerships (NACEP) is to "ensure that college courses offered by high school teachers are as rigorous as courses offered on the sponsoring college campus" (National Alliance of Concurrent Enrollment Partnerships, n.d.). In May 2016, the Department of Education signaled its support of these programs by inviting 44 institutions to participate in offering dual-enrollment programs and providing access to Title IV funds for up to 10,000 students (U.S. Department of Education, 2016).

    <u>Partnerships with Communities.</u> Colleges and universities exist within physical as well as intellectual communities, and partnering with these communities can be a win-win for all involved. One of the most prominent ways in which this currently happens is through the increasing number of service learning programs at colleges and universities, a form of experiential education. Essentially, service learning enables learners to connect what they are learning in a particular course to a community challenge or need; in other words, it meets both course and community goals. This differentiates it from volunteerism. For example, (a) students in a design course might design logos and an online presence for a nonprofit organization, (b) students in a computer science course might help a start-up to create and maintain a database, (c) students in a history course might help a community to compile a town history, and (d) students in a statistics or economic course might perform some analyses to determine the viability of road repair.

    Beyond those course-specific community partnerships, however, are larger university-community partnerships. For example, the University of Pennsylvania's Netter Center for Community Partnerships' core mission is

> bringing to bear the broad range of human knowledge needed to solve the complex, comprehensive, and interconnected problems of the American city so that the local community of West Philadelphia, Philadelphia, the University itself, and society benefit. This includes both local programs in West Philadelphia, as well as regional, national, and international efforts to build partnerships between higher education, communities, and schools . . . . A major component of the Netter Center's work is mobilizing the vast resources of the University to help transform traditional public schools into innovative University-Assisted Community Schools (UACS). University-Assisted

Community Schools educate, engage, empower, and serve not only students, but also all other members of the community in which the school is located. (Netter Center for Community Partnerships, n.d., para. 1–2)

The Seattle University Youth Initiative gives back to the community in which it is located by working with numerous partners to provide families with access to high-quality health care, affordable housing, healthy and affordable food, safe neighborhoods, and economic opportunities (Netter Center for Community Partnerships, n.d.).

The Center for Community Engagement at Seattle University has created safety plans and crime reports to help community leaders advocate for services and new policies, has provided free help with preparing tax returns for neighborhood residents, and has supported neighborhood health clinics through the College of Nursing (Seattle University, n.d.). The University of Buffalo's Center for Urban Studies, among other things, partners with community-based organizations and local institutions "on neighborhood redevelopment projects, including the development of neighborhood plans, commercial corridor and retail plaza development, food security, community needs assessment, community outreach initiatives and discrete research studies on varied neighborhood revitalization and community economic development" (University of Buffalo Center for Urban Studies, n.d., para. 5).

Quite a few institutions have programs to support community schools. For example, the program at the University of Tennessee-Knoxville leverages its students, faculty, and staff to "provide school children academic support services, physical education, music, and art programs after regular school hours . . . to enhance the interpersonal skills, critical-thinking skills, and academic success of participating children" (University-Assisted Community Schools, n.d.).

It is important to note that many of these partnerships also come in the form of three- or four-way partnerships, pushing collaboration to another level. For example, funded by the U.S. Department of Education, California State East Bay's Hayward Promise Neighborhood (HPN) received additional funding of $29.8 million in January 2018 to expand its work in the Hayward Jackson Triangle neighborhood (Cal State East Bay, 2018). This program provides support and service in a variety of areas, including mentors and tutors in local high schools, which has resulted in marked increases of students from those schools to Cal State East Bay and Chabot College. HPN has also coordinated with others to provide prenatal care and job training, among other things. A number of Promise Neighborhood programs have been funded through the HPN, whose vision is that "all children and youth growing up in Promise Neighborhoods have access to great schools and strong systems of family and community support that will prepare them to attain an excellent education and successfully transition to college and a career" (U.S. Department of Education, n.d.). This funding began in 2010 and is available to nonprofit organizations as well as institutions of higher education. Other colleges and universities that have received this funding include Berea College, Drexel University, Rutgers, Texas Tech, University of Maryland-Baltimore, Mercer University, Ohio University, and the University of Arkansas at Middle Rock. These programs are clearly three-way partnerships among the federal government, institutions of higher education, and communities.

The Higher Ed Forum of Oklahoma is another example of a three-way partnership. Its mission is to develop

collaborative and innovative strategies to coordinate, integrate and support the educational pipeline. As an anchor institution consortium, the Forum links high schools to colleges through academic service learning projects, internships, career exploration, and facilitates experiential learning opportunities to improve student achievement. (n.d., para. 1)

This consortium brings together higher education institutions, school districts, and community agencies to "enhance pathways for student achievement focused on college readiness and college completion and support innovation, diversity and the scholarship of our anchor institution consortium" (The Higher Ed Forum of Oklahoma, n.d., para. 5), among other goals.

There are many models and much expertise to facilitate further partnerships for those colleges and universities that are interested. The Lumina Foundation has teamed up with the Kresge Foundation and have designated and supported many communities in their work as "Talent Hubs." They have encouraged a number of partnerships that support collaborative efforts in support of people of multiple backgrounds receiving educational opportunities post–high school (Lumina Foundation, n.d.-b).

Partnerships with Foundations. These types of partnerships are probably among the most prevalent and long-standing collaborations with higher education. Foundations such as the Bill & Melinda Gates Foundation, Carnegie Corporation of New York, Ford Foundation, John D. & Catherine T. MacArthur Foundation, Lumina Foundation for Education, W. K. Kellogg Foundation, and the William and Flora Hewlett Foundation, among others, have partnered with colleges and universities for years on both research and education. As many of our readers know, these foundations each designate foci (which can change every few years for some foundations) and provide funding in those areas. For example, currently the Gates Foundation grant-making focuses on global development, global growth and opportunities, and global health, among other areas. Recent grants (2018) include University of Maryland research to "establish procedures for high-throughput genome editing for application in precision breeding to improve productivity, health, heat tolerance, and reproductive performance of tropical livestock" (Bill & Melinda Gates Foundation, n.d.-d, para. 2) and the work of the University of Washington to "demonstrate the efficacy of a single-dose HPV Vaccine to prevent infection among girls and women in Kenya" (Bill & Melinda Gates Foundation, n.d.-a, para. 2).

The Hewlett Foundation provides grants to

> advance education for all, preserve the environment, improve lives and livelihoods in developing countries, promote the health and economic well-being of women, support vibrant performing arts, strengthen Bay Area communities and make the philanthropy sector more effective. (Hewlett Foundation, n.d.-a, para. 2)

In 2018, for example, they funded Johns Hopkins University for a program that will "support advocacy for favorable family planning policies in sub-Saharan Africa and other regions" (William & Flora Hewlett Foundation, n.d.-b).

Beyond funding research, many of these foundations also fund educational initiatives. For example, in 2018 the Hewlett Foundation supported (a) Michigan State University for an evaluation of competency-based education pilots in seven school districts, (b) Columbia University's Teachers College to create a documentary about educational inequality in the United States, and (c) California State University to scale their open online library, which will impact affordability by promoting and providing greater use of open textbooks and other instructional materials. The Gates Foundation funded some $5 million (in 2015) to the Association of Public and Land-Grant Universities to "accelerate the production of credentials of value, especially for low-income, first generation students, while documenting increasing and sharing new knowledge about the institutional change process" (Bill & Melinda Gates Foundation, 2018).

220

The Lumina Foundation, whose overarching goal is to increase the higher educational attainment rate to 60 percent by 2025, has provided funding to Georgetown University "to strengthen the alignment of post-secondary education and workforce through research and technical assistance" (Lumina Foundation, n.d.-a, para. 1–2). They have funded the development of the comprehensive learning record (CLR) discussed earlier in this chapter, a collaborative project between the American Council on Education's (ACE) College Credit Recommendation Service (CREDIT) and Credly, a digital credential platform to facilitate the translation of employer training programs to academic credit that will be placed on a transcript (American Council on Education, 2018a). Lumina has also supported the Global Attainment and Inclusion Network (GAIN), a global alliance across eight countries charged with identifying promising practices that are flexible and student-centered and that enable diverse student populations to navigate the postsecondary system throughout their lifetimes to obtain knowledge, skills, and credentials. They also are expected to explore innovative modes of delivery, credentialing, credit recognition, and degree pathways among the participating countries (American Council on Education, 2017).

As with other partnerships we have seen, foundations also engage in three-way partnerships as well. For example, in 2010 12 large foundations committed to a collective $500 million to

> leverage the U.S. Department of Education's $650 million in Investing in Innovation (i3) Fund aimed at similarly aligned investments, making more than $1 billion available to expand promising innovations in education that support teachers, administrators, technology tools, and school design across all K–12 schools—public, private and public charter. (Bill & Melinda Gates Foundation, 2010, para. 1)

Finally, many academics partner with government agencies—for example, the National Institutes of Health, National Science Foundation, Department of Defense, Department of Education, Department of Energy, and the National Endowment for the Humanities—to fund their research. These may be the most prevalent and well-known partnerships in higher education, although these partnerships predominantly focus on funding research.

ALIGN PEOPLE, PROCESSES, STRUCTURES, AND TECHNOLOGY

We began this chapter by noting that those of us in higher education need to think differently if we are to adapt to the fast pace of change in the world of work, provide learners with what they need to be successful throughout their careers, and stay relevant. Doing so requires changes in not only our beliefs, values, and attitudes, but also in the way we carry out our work. Because of the multitude of institutional cultures and the fact that adaptation will depend on the decisions institutions make regarding the previous discussions in this chapter, there are some fundamental issues that could help colleges and universities as they work through aligning the decisions they make with people, processes, structures, and technology. We provide some examples of decisions and their implications, although this set is not all inclusive because there are many different choices that institutions will need to grapple with specific to their own context and mission. That said, it is critical that institutions carefully and thoughtfully construct a vision and mission that is unique and realistic because all other choices will flow from it.

Faculty

The future faculty will no doubt look different at some colleges and universities based on a number of decisions an institution makes, including, for example, the audience of learners targeted, use of technology, focus on personalization and/or customization, competency-based learning, stackable options, and/or alternative credentials. If a university decides to expand their focus beyond traditional-age undergraduates to include more educational opportunities for post-traditional or lifelong learners, accomplishing this will necessitate thinking about the type of faculty who will teach these very different audiences in very different time frames and venues, resulting in different credentials. It may be that the traditional faculty model works well for undergraduates and Ph.D. students but that a new set of faculty who are working professionals in the field are more effective for post-traditional and/or lifelong learners. In such a case, universities will need to create multiple faculty tracks with potentially different criteria, qualifications, career ladders, incentives, and reward structures. This will require rethinking the contingent faculty role and involvement for those professionals and practitioners with expertise, experience, and perspectives different from the full-time faculty who do not necessarily want a full-time faculty position. It is not a secret that often these contingent faculty do not have a full understanding of the curriculum because they do not attend faculty meetings or interact with the full-time faculty who define the curriculum. Obviously, there are models of this in particular disciplines, such as architecture, business, any discipline with clinical faculty, as well as models at universities that include teaching track faculty, clinical faculty, and professors of the practice as well as the traditional tenure track faculty. Whatever the decisions, recognition that the work could be very different among the faculty is the first step in aligning people with institutional goals. As the American Academy of Arts and Sciences reminds us, "universities should make a clear, ongoing commitment to improving how all faculty are selected, trained, evaluated, and supported" (Commission on the Future of America, 2017, p. 18).

The daily work of faculty may also change depending on an institution's chosen path. Faculty may find themselves designing and teaching more modular and short-term "courses," or providing content expertise to others who design the online experience and coach students through it, or meeting frequently with employers to collaborate on hybrid programs. The faculty may find themselves in more of a coaching role if engaging with adult returning professionals or spending time at a local manufacturing plant if co-teaching with an engineer from the company. They may not be physically located on campus, and the majority of their interactions with learners may be virtual. Aligning educator roles and responsibilities with learner needs will need to be thoughtfully and flexibly sculpted to meet the changing demands of the organization and its learners.

Along with different roles and work, the reward structure should adapt to accommodate changes. Obviously, institutions will need to think about criteria for reappointment and promotion based on the programmatic choices they make. If they are creating different faculty tracks, for example, with one track focused on building self-paced, modular, and stackable programs; another focused on undergraduate teaching; and a third focused on research, their career ladders, reward structures, and compensation may look different.

Finally, faculty will need to be supported as they learn to design new types of educational experiences and align with different types of learners. Teaching and learning centers will become even more important as faculty have to learn to develop (a) competency-based programs, (b) modular and stackable experiences, (c) prior learning assessments, (d) experiential learning opportunities, (e) online learning that provides immediate and constructive feedback, (f) education that allows learners to customize their experience, and (g) personalized educational designs that tailor an experience to certain target audiences. These centers are often staffed by professionals with expertise that faculty members simply do not have. Institutions will also need to allocate time for faculty to gain the knowledge and skills they need to design education for the future and resources for those with the expertise to support faculty development.

Administrators and Professional Staff

A number of individuals across our campuses play critical roles in facilitating student learning and success beyond the faculty. A glance at any university directory easily provides insight into the wide variety of administrative and professional roles that exist at our institutions, ranging from deans, directors, department chairs, to advisers, counselors of various types (i.e., personal, academic, career, financial), student life professionals, and so forth. Frequently, the value and significant contributions that are made by these individuals is overlooked and not always coordinated with strategic institutional and/or learner goals. Each individual is part of the overall educational ecosystem and must be aligned with the institutional mission and goals. We urge thoughtful consideration for the potential value-added these roles can play, if properly leveraged and aligned, in expanding learning opportunities, as well as student and institutional success. Thoughtful integration and connection of these many functions, roles, and professionals will enrich learner experiences, potentially build important communities of practice that transcend typical siloes, and result in the achievement of important institutional and learner outcomes. They all need to be engaged in the conversation about the future of each of our institutions.

Learners

There are many implications for institutions depending on the population of learners on which they choose to focus. If institutions expand their programming and credentials to attract more first-generation students, they will need to help some of them learn college-going behavior.

Many successful students engage in behaviors that lead to their success, such as taking advantage of seeing faculty during their office hours, joining study groups, and using supplemental online materials when struggling. They learn to engage in these practices from their college-educated parents, siblings, friends, teachers, and school counselors. But for those who are not privy to such advice, we will need to find ways to encourage this behavior when these learners arrive on our campuses. There are institutions that successfully support first-generation students, and learning from them will be essential. Also, the Center for First-Generation Student Success, a collaboration between NASPA and the Suder Foundation, provides a plethora of research, data, and strategies as well as programs and services to help institutions realize success among this group. The 2016 book *Becoming a Student Ready College*, by McNair et al., shifts the paradigm from students not being "college ready" and places the focus on the college becoming "student ready." Essentially, they call for educators to reflect on the simple question of "What do I need to do to help my students succeed?" Too often educators spend time identifying and complaining about students' deficiencies and lack of preparedness rather than approaching learners with a holistic mindset, empathy, and consideration for what is needed to ensure that they achieve the desired outcomes; this is a central focus to this paradigm shift (McNair et al., 2016).

If institutions decide to focus more heavily on returning adult learners, they will need to address the lack of confidence, autonomy, and control that this population sometimes experiences. Many adult learners will either be coming back into the education realm after having been out for a while or experiencing it for the first time if they never went to college. These working adults, who have families and full-time jobs, are often "in control" of those aspects of their lives. Coming into a situation where they are not in control can raise levels of anxiety, especially if their job depends on upskilling. Further, balancing the many demands on their time and attention can add stress and anxiety to an already overwhelming schedule. Institutions should design toward and interact with these human emotions and constraints to help post-traditional and other adult learners be successful.

There are both research and successful practices that can provide insight into this issue. For example, wraparound services such as the Accelerated Study in Associates Program (ASAP), launched by City University of New York (CUNY) in 2007, is now being successfully adopted by community colleges in Ohio, California, and the state of New York. The program provides a robust set of support services, including enhanced advising, block and cohort course scheduling, tutoring, career advising, waivers to cover the gap between financial aid and tuition and fees, textbook assistance, and support for transportation (e.g., Metro Card in New York City, gift cards in Ohio for gas and food). CUNY initially started with 1,132 students and scaled to 25,000. A finding by MDRC, a nonpartisan, nonprofit education and social policy research organization, indicated that the results from the Ohio schools were very positive and promising; persistence rates improved, the number of credits earned increased, and most notably, the graduation rates were more than double (19 percent vs. 7.9 percent) between the ASAP group and the control group (MDRC, 2018). These approaches represent exactly the strategic, holistic, pragmatic, and ecological approach to create student success advocated by the authors of *Becoming a Student-Ready College* (McNair et al., 2016).

Finally, we may need to advise all of these learners differently given the fast-paced change in the workplace. As we noted earlier in the chapter, we hear from many employers who value a liberal arts degree, for example, noting that these learners who also gain some experience (e.g., a course or two, a certificate, a boot camp) in analytics or computing have an advantage, and for those in engineering or science programs, liberal arts courses help to round out the perspectives, knowledge, and skills needed and valued in the workplace. We will need to ensure that we are advising learners appropriately so that they can make informed choices. Achieving this goal may require that some institutions rethink their advising model; for example, moving to a coaching/mentoring or team-based model for some learners may be best. This will also require that those advising, coaching, and/or mentoring learners have access to information from employers about the knowledge and skills they expect, as well as labor market data that projects jobs of the future.

Structures

It is not only people who may need to change, but also some of the structures that we have held near and dear in academe. For example, we might rethink the department and/or college structure in order to truly accommodate the type of preparation that learners need. For many years in the academy, we have discussed the fact that global challenges are not going to be solved by one discipline (e.g., global warming, clean water, poverty, human trafficking, and clean energy sources), which has resulted in more and more interdisciplinary research. Unfortunately, this interdisciplinarity has not become the norm in our educational practices. Departments still exist, often with different cultures, policies, and practices that can lead to territoriality and work against interdisciplinarity—for example, what "counts" as course load if team teaching, what comprises effective teaching, what constitutes robust evidence in a discipline, what represents acceptable assessment in a discipline, and how creativity is defined in a discipline. Institutions may need to question whether this departmental structure works *both* for the populations they will serve and the education they want to provide.

Institutions will also need to address how to ensure that traditional siloed entities at colleges and universities work more closely together toward shared goals. Greater collaboration and new partnerships should emerge as enrollment management strategies become increasingly more important to institutional success. Adopting a strategic enrollment management (SEM) approach—which by its very definition is data driven and calls for the comprehensive coordination of all university planning, practices, programs, and policies to achieve an institution's desired enrollment—requires new partnerships (Hossler & Bontrager, 2014). For those institutions that decide to focus more heavily or primarily on lifelong learning, academic units may want to partner more closely with alumni relations to effectively engage alumni to return when they need to upskill or reskill. For those institutions that want to include more experiential learning in their curriculum, academic units may need to leverage the knowledge, expertise, and relationships of colleagues in career centers and employer engagement offices. For institutions that want to work toward coherence across curricular and co-curricular opportunities, partnering with student affairs professionals will be key. These are only a few of the many internal partnerships we need to engage in, because many of the changes discussed in this chapter will require that we work across all of these boundaries. Essentially, we need to move away from organization-centric thinking to learner-centered development.

It will also be necessary to coordinate more effective employer engagement in our institutions to ensure effective use of time and resources to both gather information and make connections. If an institution becomes more interested in experiential learning that places learners in real employment situations (e.g., co-ops, apprenticeships, micro-internships, short-term projects), leveraging the expertise and relationships of those on your campus who engage with employers is vital. If an institution wants to prepare professionals to meet employer needs, building in continual employer interaction can add value and complement data drawn from other sources (e.g., Department of Labor, National Association of Colleges and Employers [NACE], Burning Glass). Our colleagues with relationships with those who employ our students are key to helping align our education with industry, nonprofit, and government needs.

Processes

Along with people and structures, we will need to reexamine many of our processes. For example, faculty governance may need to evolve to accommodate the fast pace of change we are experiencing in the world of work. For those institutions that decide to focus on meeting market demands for graduates with certain knowledge and skill sets and create shorter-term credential programs, time often becomes a constraint so as not to lose the window of opportunity. And because many of us still believe that the curriculum should stay in the hands of the faculty, we need to ensure that our governance structures and processes for approving new programs, for example, are efficient and effective, and that they incorporate appropriate environmental inputs (e.g., populations served, workforce and industry needs, new technologies). Faculty governance will also play a role in expanding faculty models just discussed, as well as criteria and reward structures for those new and different types of faculty. The American Academy of Arts and Sciences envisions an evolution of shared governance:

> In practice, shared governance has often meant "divided authority," with faculty controlling the curriculum, administrators controlling the budget, and regents or trustees attending to the institution's long-run financial viability. The Commission foresees a future in which these interdependent elements of curriculum, budget, and long-run finances will need to be managed through deep collaboration among all parties. (Commission on the Future of America, 2017, p. 67)

Many of us may also need to think about how prior learning will "count" in gaining credentials at our institutions. As we discussed earlier in this and previous chapters, learners who come to us to reskill or upskill will be bringing a lot of knowledge and skills gained on the job and in life (as well as in previous coursework and degrees for those who have them). We will need to acknowledge this (through prior learning assessments) and enable learners to build from it (through customized and/or personalized programs). Each institution will have to decide how they will treat this prior learning.

Finally, to make evidence-based decisions, we need to ensure that administrators, faculty, and staff have access to data on such things as workforce needs, characteristics of the learners being served, and alumni satisfaction, among other information, that will impact their work (e.g., in designing learning experiences and programs, supporting students, and redesigning systems and processes). There are many sources of information about workforce needs and how well colleges and universities are faring (e.g., surveys, third-party entities like Burning Glass, the Department of Labor), and yet a lot of data is not effectively shared with those in the institution who are "on the front line" and making decisions

231

(e.g., curriculum committees, department chairs, deans), designing the education (e.g., faculty), and supporting students (e.g., advisers, admissions personnel, student affairs practitioners of all kinds, and career counselors). Some of those data live in career centers, some with institutional research offices, some with government relations professionals on campus, and some with disciplinary associations. We need to create processes that routinely collect and provide data to those who need it, when they need it, with the expectation that it will be used to shape their work. This is evidence-based decision making at its best.

Technology

Success in the areas discussed in this chapter requires that technology support the decisions we make. For example, online and hybrid experiences will need to (a) include the ability for learners to engage in prior learning assessments, choose among personalized opportunities, and/or customize the experience according to their needs, (b) enable self-paced timing, (c) provide constructive and timely feedback to promote mastery, and (d) keep track of credentials as learners continually come in and out of our institutions to upskill or reskill. Interoperability will become even more important both within institutions as well as across institutions for those learners who will access learning experiences across multiple colleges and universities. Every institution has legacy systems that do not talk to one another, so this area will require a lot of thought as well as resources, and yet we cannot move forward if we do not leverage the technology appropriately and effectively.

Administrative Support Structures

Colleges and universities will not be successful in implementing change unless our administrative support structures (e.g., human

232

resources, financial aid, admissions, registrar, student accounts, budget, and accounts payable) are nimble enough to accommodate the flexibility of programming and diversity of educator and learner types we discussed in this chapter. Currently, many organizations are tethered to practices and procedures that are deeply rooted in legacy systems, compliance, and "we've always done it this way" approaches. Often these are not learner centered and somewhat inflexible. These situations create unnecessary barriers to learners and constraints on educational innovation. Aligning these support structures with the decisions institutions make will require changes in both attitudes and beliefs as well as processes and technology.

In other words, we need to leverage the full ecosystem of the university. There are many examples one could use here, but perhaps one of the most important—and yet not obvious to many—is that faculty members need to recognize student affairs and other student-facing professionals as student culture specialists and collaborate with them to design offerings that align with the student populations being served. These professionals typically fully understand the growth and development trajectories of traditional-aged undergraduates and adult learners, because a lot of research is available on both populations. Further, student success and persistence are possible only when barriers are removed, and a comprehensive learner-centric design of institutional support services is in place. These services, many of which have been described above, require attention to detail and the shifting realities across student communities (e.g., food insecurity, transportation, housing, scheduling) and can flexibly respond to the changing spectrum of needs across a diverse mixture of students.

In the end, it all comes down to this: we need to create a culture of educational innovation in our institutions—and battle the culture of status quo that is often the dominant institutional culture because it has served us well in the past. Culture consists of shared beliefs, values, and attitudes that are manifested in such things as expectations, goals, reward structures, processes, roles, and language. How the leadership of an organization signals value for innovation and flexibility—or for maintaining the status quo—will impact whether and how the organization will evolve and change. In colleges and universities, achieving this goal will require leadership at all levels, from the president of the university to the leadership of the faculty governance body as well as the provost, deans, chairs/heads, vice presidents, and faculty leaders. As Schein (2010) reminds us, culture is a two-way street: leaders are often the principal architects of culture, and an established culture influences what kind of leadership is possible. Culture will clearly shape the decisions institutions make, and given the traditional nature of many colleges and universities, staying relevant will require evolving and changing culture. It may also require a new type of leadership.

CONCLUSION

There is a lot to think about as colleges and universities respond to the present and prepare for the future. Each institution needs to revisit their respective vision and mission to determine whether and how that might change. Interestingly enough, even for those institutions whose mission and vision remain the same, external changes will require adaptation in the way they educate their learners (e.g., changing demographics, continued technological advancements, evolving world of work, economics, competition for students, diversity, and globalization).

In this book's introduction, we discussed the demise of Kodak and the railroads, resulting from executives viewing their businesses too narrowly and simply not asking the right questions. Higher education is at a similar crossroad and must avoid a myopic and

234

narrow view of its potential role and place in the future. Intentionality in designing an organization's plan to move forward is critical, along with consideration for diversification of revenue streams. This is the time to remember that we are in the education business and need to identify new products, approaches, and partnerships to achieve positive results. Relevance based on deference to higher education's presumed expertise may have worked in the past but cannot be assumed into the future. There are too many demands, competitors, shifting sands, expectations, and economic factors involved—complacency, isolation, and inertia will no longer suffice.

We are optimistic that higher education can respond effectively given the talent within our colleges and universities, the compelling nature of the agenda, the growing interest in partnerships with industry, and foundation investment, along with growing social public policy advocacy. There are pioneering institutions, programs, and people already exploring new ways to respond to the plethora of changing conditions, as evidenced by the many examples in this book. They can both inspire and educate the rest of us as we all work to navigate the complexity of the present and ensure our relevance into the future.

REFERENCES

ABET. (n.d.). *History*. Retrieved from https://www.abet.org/about-abet/history/

ABET. (2018, October 8). *FAQs for EAC C3 & C5 criteria changes*. Retrieved from https://www.abet.org/wp-content/uploads/2018/10/FAQs-for-EAC-C3-C5-10-11-2018.pdf

Aglio, J. (2018, July 19). *An inside look: America's first public school AI program*. Retrieved from Getting Smart: https://www.gettingsmart.com/2019/01/an-inside-look-americas-first-public-school-ai-program/

Allen, M. (2018, January 30). *The future of workplace learning.* Retrieved from Talent Economy: https://quarterly.talenteconomy.io/issue/winter-2018/the-future-of-workplace-learning/

AllenComm. (n.d.). *What is employee training and development?* Retrieved from https://www.allencomm.com/what-is-employee-training-development/

Amato, M. (2013, February 18). *An argument against gen eds.* Retrieved from the College Voice: https://thecollegevoice.org/2013/02/18/an-argument-against-gen-eds/

Ambrose, S. A., Bridges, M. W., DiPietro, M., Lovett, M. C., & Norman, M. K. (2010). *How learning works.* San Francisco: Jossey-Bass.

American Association of Collegiate Registrars and Admissions Officers. (2019). *AACRAO signature initiatives.* Retrieved from https://www.aacrao.org/signature-initiatives

American Council on Education. (n.d.-a). *Credit.* Retrieved from https://www.acenet.edu/news-room/Pages/College-Credit-Recommendation-Service-CREDIT.aspx

American Council on Education. (n.d.-b). *Military evaluations.* Retrieved from https://www.acenet.edu/higher-education/topics/Pages/Military-Evaluations.aspx

American Council on Education. (2017, July 10). ACE, Lumina Foundation to establish alliance for global innovation in tertiary education. Retrieved from https://www.acenet.edu/news-room/Pages/ACE-Lumina-Foundation-to-Establish-Alliance-for-Global-Innovation-in-Tertiary-Education.aspx

American Council on Education. (2018a). ACE, Credly announce new initiative to translate on-the-job training experiences into skills, college credit. Retrieved from https://www.acenet.edu/news-room/Pages/ACE-Credly-Announce-New-Initiative-to-Translate-On-the-job-Training-Experiences-into-Skills-College-Credit.aspx

American Council on Education. (2018b). *New focus on transparency in credentials helps validate learning experiences.* Retrieved from https://www.acenet.edu/news-room/Pages/New-Focus-on-Transparency-in-Credentials-Helps-Validate-Learning-Experiences.aspx

Association to Advance Collegiate Schools of Business. (2018, July 1). *2013 eligibility procedures and accreditation standards for business accreditation.* Tampa, FL: Author.

Astin, A. W. (1985). *Achieving educational excellence: A critical assessment of priorities and practices in higher education.* San Francisco, CA: Jossey Bass.

Astin, A. W. (1993). *What matters in college? Four critical years revisited.* San Francisco, CA: Jossey-Bass.

Bandura, A. (2001). Social cognitive theory: An agentic perspective. *Annual Review of Psychology, 52,* 1–26.

Bass, R. (2012, March 21). *Disrupting ourselves: The problem of learning in higher education.* Retrieved from EDUCAUSE Review: https://er.educause.edu/articles/2012/3/disrupting-ourselves-the-problem-of-learning-in-higher-education

Berrett, D. (2015, January 26). The day the purpose of college changed. *The Chronicle of Higher Education, 61*(20), A18–A21.

Bill & Melinda Gates Foundation. (n.d.-a) University of Washington Foundation. Retrieved from https://www.gatesfoundation.org/How-We-Work/Quick-Links/Grants-Database/Grants/2018/06/OPP1188693

Bill & Melinda Gates Foundation. (n.d.-b). *Today's college students have diverse needs. These two schools get it.* Retrieved from The Washington Post: https://www.washingtonpost.com/sf/brand-connect/gates/todays-college-students-have-diverse-needs/

Bill & Melinda Gates Foundation. (n.d.-c). *Today's college students.* Retrieved from https://postsecondary.gatesfoundation.org/what-were-learning/todays-college-students/

Bill & Melinda Gates Foundation. (n.d.-d). *University of Maryland.* Retrieved from https://www.gatesfoundation.org/How-We-Work/Quick-Links/Grants-Database/Grants/2018/05/OPP1189771

Bill & Melinda Gates Foundation. (2010, April 12). *Major foundations commit $500 million to education innovation in concert with U.S. Department of Education's $650 million "Investing in Innovation" fund.* Retrieved from https://www.gatesfoundation.org/Media-Center/Press-Releases/2010/04/12-Foundations-Commit-to-Education-Innovation-with-US-Department-of-Education

237

Bill & Melinda Gates Foundation. (2018, October). *How we work: Grant*. Retrieved from https://www.gatesfoundation.org/How-We-Work/Quick-Links/Grants-Database/Grants/2015/10/OPP1134374

Bishop, E. S., Bowen, B., Dixon, B., Enright, R., Hekmat, H., Lawlor, W., Wolensky, R. (2018, April 27). *Emeritus faculty: University of Wisconsin-Stevens Point has lost its compass*. Retrieved from Stevens Point Journal: https://www.stevenspointjournal.com/story/opinion/columnists/2018/04/27/uw-stevens-point-major-cuts-university-lost-compass-emeritus-faculty/558612002/

Blake, B. (1974, May 6). *Tiger Comic by Bud Blake*. Retrieved from Life of an Educator – Dr. Justin Tarte: http://www.justintarte.com/2013/09/its-not-teaching-if-theres-no-learning.html

Bolden-Barrett, V. (2017, August 10). *Walmart Academy raises questions over who benefits from training programs*. Retrieved from HRDive: https://www.hrdive.com/news/walmart-academy-raises-questions-over-who-benefits-from-training-programs/449038/

Bolkan, J. (2013, December 17). *Stanford prof unveils scalable virtual labs*. Retrieved from Campus Technology: https://campustechnology.com/articles/2013/12/17/stanford-prof-unveils-scalable-virtual-labs.aspx

Bowen, S. H. (2004). *Reality check: What's in a name? The persistence of "General Education."* Retrieved from Association of American Colleges & Universities: https://www.aacu.org/publications-research/periodicals/reality-check-whats-name-persistence-general-education

Boyle, M., Gotcher, D., & Otts, D. (2018). One state's use of prior learning assessment to augment its workforce development agenda. *The Journal of Continuing Higher Education, 66*(1), 54–58.

Boynton, A. (2011, October 18). *Are you an "I" or a "T"?* Retrieved from Forbes: https://www.forbes.com/sites/andyboynton/2011/10/18/are-you-an-i-or-a-t/#1e18b0196e88

Brinton, S. (2017, December 22). *Experiential learning, vocational education making a comeback*. Retrieved from LI Herald.com | Glen Head: http://www.liherald.com/glenhead/stories/experiential-learning-vocational-education-making-a-comeback,98695?

Brittany, R. (2018, January 17). *Google offers free IT support certification, but there's a catch*. Retrieved from Slash Gear: https://www.slashgear.

com/google-offers-free-it-support-certification-but-theres-a-catch-17516222/

Brooks, K. (2012, April 19). *Career success starts with a "T"* Retrieved from Psychology Today: https://www.psychologytoday.com/us/blog/career-transitions/201204/career-success-starts-t

Brown, J., & Adler, R. (2008). Minds on fire: Open education, the long tail, and learning 2.0. *EDUCAUSE Review*, *43*(1), 16–32.

Brown, T. (n.d.). IDEO CEO Tim Brown: T-shaped stars: The backbone of IDEO's collaborative culture. (M. T. Hansen, Interviewer). Retrieved from http://web.archive.org/web/20110329003842/http://www.chiefexecutive.net/ME2/dirmod.asp?sid=&nm=&type=Publishing&mod=Publications::Article&mid=8F3A7027 421841978F18BE895F87F791&tier=4&id=F42A23CB49174C5E 9426C43CB0A0BC46

Business Dictionary. (n.d.). *Training*. Retrieved from http://www. businessdictionary.com/definition/training.html

Business-Higher Education Forum. (n.d.). *About BHEF*. Retrieved from http://www.bhef.com/about

Busteed, B. (2019, April 30). *This will be the biggest disruption in higher education*. Retrieved from Forbes: https://www.forbes.com/sites/brandonbusteed/2019/04/30/this-will-be-the-biggest-disruption-in-higher-education/#6b1906fd608a

Cagan, J., & Vogel, C. M. (2002). *Creating breakthrough products: Innovation from product planning to program appeal*. Upper Saddle River, NJ: Prentice Hall, Inc.

Cal State East Bay. (2018, January 2). *Cal State East Bay's Hayward Promise neighborhood receives nearly $30M*. Retrieved from Cal State East Bay Today: https://www.ebtoday.com/stories/cal-state-east-bay-s-hayward-promise-neighborhood-receives-nearly-30m

Campbell, E. (2018, October 31). Training Delta Airlines and Tarrant County College partner for maintenance. *Fort Worth Star Telegraph*.

CAPS Network. (n.d.). *What Is CAPS?* Retrieved from https://yourcapsnetwork.org/

Carnegie Learning. (n.d.). *Carnegie Learning*. Retrieved from https://www.carnegielearning.com/

Chatlani, S. (2018, August 1). *The challenge of a universal transcript.* Retrieved from Education Dive: https://www.educationdive.com/news/the-challenge-of-a-universal-transcript/529005/

Chickering, A. (1969). *Education and identity.* San Francisco, CA: Jossey-Bass.

Chickering, A., & Reisser, L. (1993). *Education and identity (2nd ed.).* San Francisco, CA: Jossey-Bass.

Chronicle of Higher Education. (2012, December). *The role of higher education in career development: Employer perceptions.* Retrieved from Chronicle-assets: https://chronicle-assets.s3.amazonaws.com/5/items/biz/pdf/Employers%20Survey.pdf

CodeCrew. (n.d.). *Our program.* Retrieved from https://www.code-crew.org/about

Commission on the Future of America. (2017). *The future of undergraduate education, the future of America.* Cambridge: American Academy of Arts and Sciences. Retrieved from https://www.amacad.org/publication/future-undergraduate-education

Credential Engine. (n.d.-a). *About Us.* Retrieved from https://credentialengine.org/about/

Credential Engine. (n.d.-b). *Why is credential transparency valuable?* Retrieved from https://credentialengine.org/understand-credentials

Crowe, C. (2018, November 12). *How one university went from proposing to cut 13 liberal-arts programs to eliminating only 6.* Retrieved from the Chronicle of Higher Education: https://www.chronicle.com/article/this-university-proposed/245070

Daly, J. (2017, November 10). *Apprenticeships are a new and old solution to job growth, here's why.* Retrieved from The Hill: https://thehill.com/opinion/education/359835-apprenticeships-are-a-new-and-old-solution-to-job-growth-heres-why

Dan, A. (2012, January 23). Kodak failed by asking the wrong marketing question. Retrieved from Forbes: https://www.forbes.com/sites/avidan/2012/01/23/kodak-failed-by-asking-the-wrong-marketing-question/#5f64233a3d47

Department of Labor. (n.d.). *A quick-start toolkit: Building registered apprenticeship programs.* Retrieved from https://www.doleta.gov/oa/employers/apprenticeship_toolkit.pdf

240

Dweck, C. S. (2006). *Mindset: The new psychology of success*. New York, NY: Ballantine Books.

Eagan, M. K.-A. (2017). *The American freshman: National norms fall 2016*. Los Angeles, CA: Higher Education Research Institute, University of California, Los Angeles.

Echols, M. (2018, September 26). *Is a college degree obsolete?* Retrieved from Chief Learning Officer: https://www.clomedia.com/2018/09/26/is-a-college-degree-obsolete/?utm_campaign=ED_CLO_CLO%20Today_Q3_2018&utm_source=hs_email&utm_medium=email&utm_content=66232420&_hsenc=p2ANqtz-_JnbcnXFJQ2MUVm-TxlEH9KUyMDe7XXUOeFHHn9-pH7BAT4e4JdkNDvpqQE7YCHrJsnZ-XEK6RAx

Education Commission of the States. (2019). *50-state comparison: Prior learning assessment policies*. Retrieved from https://www.ecs.org/50-state-comparison-prior-learning-assessment-policies/

Ellis, J. (2018, October 2). *The future of work isn't tech and AI. It's artists and cogs*. Retrieved from ERE: https://www.ere.net/the-future-of-work-isnt-tech-and-ai-its-artists-and-cogs/?utm_source=linkedIn&utm_medium=social&utm_campaign=SocialWarfare

Ernst & Young. (2017, August 14). New program will allow EY people to earn credentials in future-focused skills. Retrieved from EY News: https://www.ey.com/gl/en/newsroom/news-releases/news-ey-new-program-will-allow-ey-people-to-earn-credentials-in-future-focused-skills

Eyler, J. (2009). The power of experiential education. *Liberal Education (95)4*, 24–31.

Fain, P. (2018). *On-ramps and off-ramps: Alternative credentials and emerging pathways between education and work*. Washington, DC: Inside Higher Ed.

Fain, P. (2019, January 23). *University of Utah introduces income-share experiment*. Retrieved from Inside Higher Ed: https://www.insidehighered.com/quicktakes/2019/01/23/university-utah-introduces-income-share-experiment

Fink, J., & Jenkins, D. (2017). Takes two to tango: Essential practices of highly effective transfer partnerships. *Community College Review*, 45(4), 294–310.

241

Flaherty, C. (2018, March 6). *U Wisconsin-Stevens Point to eliminate 13 majors*. Retrieved from Inside Higher Ed: https://www.insidehighered.com/quicktakes/2018/03/06/u-wisconsin-stevens-point-eliminate-13-majors

Foley, P. (n.d.). *Why we need T-shaped innovators*. Retrieved from Innovation Excellence: https://www.innovationexcellence.com/blog/2017/03/23/why-we-need-t-shaped-innovators/

Fry, E. (2018, October 2). *Why storytelling became the hot new skill in business*. Retrieved from Fortune: http://amp.timeinc.net/fortune/2018/10/01/storytelling-skill-business

Fuller, J. B., & Sigelman, M. (2017, November). *Room to grow: Identifying new frontiers for apprenticeships*. Retrieved from Harvard Business School: https://www.hbs.edu/managing-the-future-of-work/Documents/room-to-grow.pdf

Gallagher, S. R. (2016). *The future of university credentials: New developments at the intersection of higher education hiring*. Cambridge, MA: Harvard Education Press.

Gardner, P., & Estry, D. (2017). *A primer on the T-professional*. East Lansing, MI: Collegiate Employment Research Institute.

Gimbel, E. (2018, May 15). *Higher education and K–12 form partnerships to help educators and learners*. Retrieved from EdTech: https://edtechmagazine.com/k12/article/2018/05/higher-education-and-k-12-form-partnerships-help-educators-and-learners

Gino, F. (2018). *Why curiosity matters*. Retrieved from Harvard Business Review: https://hbr.org/2018/09/curiosity

Greene, P. (2018, October 8). *Is competency-based education just a recycled failed policy?* Retrieved from Forbes: https://www.forbes.com/sites/petergreene/2018/10/08/is-competency-based-education-a-recycled-failed-policy/#1f78130adfc5

Hamilton Southeastern Schools. (2019). *Hamilton Southeastern Schools*. Retrieved from https://www.hseschools.org/academics/experiential

Hart Research Associates. (2015, January 20). *Falling short? College learning and career success*. Retrieved from Association of American Colleges & Universities: https://www.aacu.org/sites/default/files/files/LEAP/2015employerstudentsurvey.pdf

Hayward, M. S., & Williams, M. R. (2015). Adult learner graduation rates at four US community colleges by prior learning assessment status and method. *Community College Journal of Research and Practice, 39*(1), 44–54.

Higher Ed Forum of Oklahoma. (n.d.). *Vision*. Retrieved from http://www.thehigheredforum.org/

Hinds, P. J. (1999). The curse of expertise: The effects of expertise and debiasing methods on prediction of novice performance. *Journal of Experimental Psychology: Applied 5*(2), 205–221.

Hossler, D., & Bontrager, B. (2014). *Handbook of strategic enrollment management*. San Francisco, CA: John Wiley & Sons.

Jacobs, J., & Tolbert-Bynum, P. (2008). *Shifting gears: Community colleges and adult basic education*. New York, NY: Community College Research Center.

Jaschik, S. (2019a). *For provosts, more pressure on tough issues*. Retrieved from Inside Higher Ed: https://www.insidehighered.com/news/survey/2019-inside-higher-ed-survey-chief-academic-officers

Jaschik, S. (2019b). *The (missed) potential of transfer students at elite colleges*. Retrieved from Inside Higher Ed: https://www.insidehighered.com/admissions/article/2019/01/22/study-finds-elite-institutions-admit-few-transfer-students-community

Johnson, D. (2017, October 3). *What's keeping competency-based education out of higher education's mainstream?* Retrieved from The Evolllution: https://evolllution.com/revenue-streams/market_opportunities/whats-keeping-competency-based-education-out-of-higher-educations-mainstream/

Kafka, A. C. (2018, October 4). *Why storytelling matters in fields beyond the humanities*. Retrieved from the Chronicle of Higher Education: https://www.chronicle.com/article/Why-Storytelling-Matters-in/244729

King, K. (2018, September 23). *Apprenticeships on the rise at New York tech and finance firms*. Retrieved from *The Wall Street Journal*: https://www.wsj.com/articles/apprenticeships-on-the-rise-at-new-york-tech-and-finance-firms-1537707601

Klein-Collins, R. (2011). *Underserved students who earn credit through prior learning assessment (PLA) have higher degree completion rates and shorter time-to-degree research brief.* Chicago, IL: Council for Adult and Experiential Learning.

Kuh, G. D. (1994). *Student learning outside the classroom: Transcending artificial boundaries. ASHE-ERIC Higher Education Report No. 8.* Washington, DC: ASHE-ERIC.

Kuh, G. D. (2008). *High-impact educational practices: What they are, who has access to them, and why they matter.* Washington, DC: Association of American Colleges and Universities.

LearnLab Carnegie Mellon University. (n.d.). *What did LearnLab set out to do?* Retrieved from https://learnlab.org/index.php/mission/

Leonard, B. (2015, January 30). *Are apprenticeship programs set to take off in the U.S.?* Retrieved from Society for Human Resource Management: https://www.shrm.org/resourcesandtools/hr-topics/organizational-and-employee-development/pages/apprenticeships-programs.aspx

Leventoff, J. (2018). *Measuring non-degree credential attainment: A 101 guide for states.* Retrieved from National Skills Coalition: https://www.nationalskillscoalition.org/resources/webinars/measuring-non-degree-credential-attainment

Li, S. (2010, June 20). *"Augmented reality" on smartphones brings teaching down to earth.* Retrieved from the Chronicle of Higher Education: https://www.chronicle.com/article/augmented-reality-on/65991

Libby, W. B. (2017, December 14). *The value of a liberal arts education.* Retrieved from Huffington Post: https://www.huffingtonpost.com/entry/the-value-of-a-liberal-arts-education_us_5a32d5a1e4b0e7f1200cf94c

Lohr, S. (2018, October 15). *M.I.T. plans College for Artificial Intelligence, backed by $1 billion.* Retrieved from The New York Times: https://www.nytimes.com/2018/10/15/technology/mit-college-artificial-intelligence.html

Lumina Foundation. (n.d.-a). *Grant database.* Retrieved from https://www.luminafoundation.org/grants-database/search/?q=Georgetown

Lumina Foundation. (n.d.-b). *Talent hubs.* Retrieved from https://www.luminafoundation.org/talent-hubs

Lumina Foundation. (2015, June 11). *Connecting credentials: A beta credentials framework.* Retrieved from https://www.luminafoundation.org/resources/connecting-credentials

Markle Foundation. (n.d.). *About Skillful*. Retrieved from https://www.markle.org/rework-america/skillful/#skillful

Martin, J. (2004). Self-regulated learning, social cognitive theory, and agency. *Educational Psychologist, 39*(2), 135–145.

Mazzullo, L. (2018, August 6). *Badges offer more courses for working professionals*. Retrieved from WSU News: https://www.wichita.edu/about/wsunews/news/2018/08-aug/badges_continuous_education.php

McKenzie, L. (2018, April 18). *A federal experiment flounders*. Retrieved from Inside Higher Ed: https://www.insidehighered.com/news/2018/04/18/federal-experiment-nontraditional-providers-stumbles-out-gate

McNair, T. B., Albertine, S., Cooper, M. A., Major Jr, T., McDonald, N., & Major, T. (2016). *Becoming a student-ready college: A new culture of leadership for student success*. San Francisco, CA: John Wiley & Sons.

MDRC. (2018, December 20). Ohio programs based on CUNY's accelerated study in associate programs (ASAP) more than double graduation rates. Retrieved from https://www.mdrc.org/news/press-release/ohio-programs-based-cuny-s-accelerated-study-associate-programs-asap-more-double

Meridian Star. (2018, July 27). *Counties tout EMCC's Center for Manufacturing Technology excellence role as economic driver*. Retrieved from https://www.meridianstar.com/news/business/counties-tout-emcc-s-center-for-manufacturing-technology-excellence-role/article_2ec4c5da-c07e-56e4-80b5-f85a8f55d259.html

Nathan, M. J., & Koedinger, K. R. (2000). An investigation of teachers' beliefs of students' algebra development. *Cognition and Instruction 18*(2), 209–237.

National Alliance of Concurrent Enrollment Partnerships. (n.d.). *About NACEP*. Retrieved from http://www.nacep.org/?s=ensure+that+college+courses+offered+by+high+school+teachers+are+as+rigorous+as+courses+offered+on+the+sponsoring+college+campus

National Association of Student Financial Aid Adminstrators. (2015). *Expanding educational opportunities for students*. Washington, DC: Author.

Netter Center for Community Partnerships. (n.d.). *Programs*. Retrieved from https://www.nettercenter.upenn.edu/what-we-do/programs

New England Commission of Higher Education. (2016, July 1). *NECHE Standards for Accreditation*. Retrieved from https://www.neche.org/resources/standards-for-accreditation/#standard_four

Newton, D. (2019, January 19). Investors bet $30M more on Lambda School's income-share tuition mode. Retrieved from Forbes: https://www.educationdive.com/news/investors-bet-30m-more-on-lambda-schools-income-share-tuition-model/545680/

Nickerson, R. S. (1999). How we know—and sometimes misjudge—what others know: Imputing one's own knowledge to others. *Psychological Bulletin, 125*(6), 737–759.

Northeastern University. (n.d.). *The next generation of experiential learning at Northeastern*. Retrieved from https://sail.northeastern.edu/

Northeastern University Decision Support Office. (2018). *Fact Book 2017-2018*. Boston, MA: Northeastern University.

O'Neil, M. (2014, January 10). *Nurse program reimagines diagnostic training for online students*. Retrieved from the Chronicle of Higher Education: https://www.chronicle.com/blogs/wiredcampus/nurse-program-reimagines-diagnostic-training-for-online-students/49227

Pappano, L. (2018, August 2). *The iGen shift: Colleges are changing to reach the next generation*. Retrieved from The New York Times: https://www.nytimes.com/2018/08/02/education/learning/generationz-igen-students-colleges.html

Parton, B. (2017). *Youth apprenticeship in America today*. Retrieved from https://na-production.s3.amazonaws.com/documents/Youth-Apprenticeship-Today.pdf.

Pascarella, E. T., & Terenzini, P. T. (1991). *How college affects students: A third decade of research*. San Francisco, CA: Jossey-Bass.

Patterson, J. (2018, October 29). *Brief Dallas-based work college Paul Quinn gets $1M to expand*. Retrieved from Education Dive: https://www.educationdive.com/news/dallas-based-work-college-paul-quinn-gets-1m-to-expand/540683/

Phillips, S. (2018). Policy implications of the intersection between prior learning assessment and competency-based education. *PLA Inside Out:*

An International Journal on Theory, Research and Practice in Prior Learning Assessment, 6: 1–5.

Pink, D. H. (2006). *A whole new mind: Why right-brainers will rule the future*. New York, NY: Penguin.

Pinsker, B. (2019, January 15). *Living the tech dream, thanks to a novel apprenticeship program*. Retrieved from US News and World Report: https://money.usnews.com/investing/news/articles/2019-01-15/living-the-tech-dream-thanks-to-a-novel-apprenticeship-program

Plum, S. (2018, October 5). *An authentic connection to learning*. Retrieved from Edutopia: https://www.edutopia.org/article/authentic-connection-learning

Pole Star Experiential Learning. (n.d.). *We are Pole Star Experiential Learning*. Retrieved from https://www.polestarel.com/About2/

Powell, J. (2014, January 24). *The tyranny of the college major*. Retrieved from The Atlantic: https://www.theatlantic.com/education/archive/2014/01/the-tyranny-of-the-college-major/283247/

Pracz, A. (2011, April 13). *General education courses are a waste of time and money*. Retrieved from Northern Star: https://northernstar.info/opinion/columnists/general-education-courses-are-a-waste-of-time-and-money/article_9c52826c-6639-11e0-8c12-0019bb30f31a.html

Preston, C. (2018, April 15). *Are apprenticeships the new on-ramp to good jobs?* Retrieved from Hechinger Report: https://hechingerreport.org/are-apprenticeships-the-new-on-ramp-to-middle-class-jobs/

Reis, S. (2015, August 21). *Montour partners with CMU Research Center*. Retrieved from the Pittsburgh Post-Gazette: https://www.post-gazette.com/news/education/2015/08/21/Montour-partners-with-CMU-for-research-center/stories/201508210073

Samson, C. (2018, April 5). *Counting U.S. secondary and postsecondary credentials. A credential engine report*. Retrieved from Credential Engine: https://credentialengine.org/2018/04/05/counting-u-s-secondary-and-postsecondary-credentials-april-2018-report/

Schein, E. H. (2010). *Organizational culture and leadership*. San Francisco, CA: Jossey-Bass.

Scientist, The (2013, January 1). *Games for science*. Retrieved from https://www.the-scientist.com/cover-story/games-for-science-39997

Seattle University. (n.d.). *Thriving neighborhoods.* Retrieved from https://www.seattleu.edu/cce/suyi/thriving-neighborhoods/

Selingo, J. (2018, July 29). *What do top colleges have against transfer students?* Retrieved from The Washington Post: https://www.washingtonpost.com/news/grade-point/wp/2018/07/29/what-do-top-colleges-have-against-transfer-students/?utm_term=.d4d0a4c17ed6

Shapiro, D., Dundar, A., Huie, F., Wakhungu, P. K., Yuan, X., Nathan, A., & Hwang, Y. (2017). *Tracking transfer: Measures of effectiveness in helping community college students to complete bachelor's degrees.* Bloomington: Indiana University, National Student Clearinghouse Research Center.

Shuster, B. (2013, December 13). *Online learning boasts bright future thanks to virtual reality platforms.* Retrieved from Education News: https://www.educationnews.org/online-schools/online-learning-boasts-bright-future-thanks-to-virtual-reality-platforms/

Steinberg, S. (2014). *Innovations in apprenticeship: 5 case studies that illustrate the promise of apprenticeship in the United States.* Washington, DC: Center for American Progress.

Tinto, V. (1987). *Leaving college: Rethinking the causes and cures of student attrition.* Chicago, IL: University of Chicago Press.

Tinto, V. (1993). *Leaving college: Rethinking the causes and cures of student attrition, 2nd edition.* Chicago, IL: University of Chicago Press.

Tomanek, D. (2005). Building successful partnerships between K–12 and universities. *Cell Biology Education, 4*(1), 28–29.

Top, E. (2017, November 16). *American apprenticeships on the rise.* Retrieved from E21: https://economics21.org/html/american-apprenticeships-rise-2696.html

Torres, V., Jones, S. R., & Renn, K. A. (2009). Identity development theories in student affairs: Origins, current status, and new approaches. *Journal of College Student Development 50*(6), 577–596.

Unglesbee, B. (2019, January 10). *Investors bet $30M more on Lambda School's income-share tuition model.* Retrieved from EducationDive: https://www.educationdive.com/news/investors-bet-30m-more-on-lambda-schools-income-share-tuition-model/545680/

United States Government Accountability Office. (2017). *Students need more information to help reduce challenges in transferring college credits.* Washington, DC: Author.

University of Buffalo Center for Urban Studies. (n.d.). *Who we are*. Retrieved from http://centerforurbanstudies.ap.buffalo.edu

University of Chicago. (n.d.). *The Urban Education Institute bridges education research and practice to foster greater equity and excellence in public schooling.* *Retrieved from* https://uei.uchicago.edu/

University-Assisted Community Schools. (n.d.). *About University Assisted Community Schools, College of Education, Health & Human Services.* Retrieved from University of Tennessee, Knoxville: https://uacs.utk.edu/home/

U.S. Chamber of Commerce Foundation. (n.d.). *T3-Innovation Network*. Retrieved from https://www.uschamberfoundation.org/t3-innovation

U.S. Department of Education. (n.d.). *Program description Promise neighborhoods*. Retrieved from https://www2.ed.gov/programs/promiseneighborhoods/index.html

U.S. Department of Education. (2016, May 16). Expanding college access through the dual enrollment Pell experiment: https://www.ed.gov/news/press-releases/fact-sheet-expanding-college-access-through-dual-enrollment-pell-experiment

U.S. Department of Education, Institute of Education Sciences. (2017, February n.d.). *WWC intervention report: Dual enrollment programs.* Retrieved from https://ies.ed.gov/ncee/wwc/Docs/InterventionReports/wwc_dual_enrollment_022817.pdf

Wandschneider, J. (2014, January 29). *Wandschneider: General education requirements waste students' time.* Retrieved from Iowa State Daily: http://www.iowastatedaily.com/opinion/wandschneider-general-education-requirements-waste-students-time/article_0f2b155a-8875-11e3-add2-001a4bcf887a.html

Warwick Beacon. 2018. *Youth apprenticeship program accepting applications.* Retrieved from http://warwickonline.com/

Wiggins, G., & McTighe, J. (2005). *Understanding by design.* Alexandria, VA: Association for Supervision and Curriculum Development.

William and Flora Hewlett Foundation. (n.d.-a). *About Us. William and Flora Hewlett Foundation.* Retrieved from https://hewlett.org/about-us/

William and Flora Hewlett Foundation (n.d.-b). Johns Hopkins University for support of the advance family planning project. Retrieved from https://hewlett.org/grants/johns-hopkins-university-for-support-of-the-advance-family-planning-project-1/

Wladawsky-Berger, I. (2015, December 18). *The rise of the T-shaped organization*. Retrieved from The Wall Street Journal: https://blogs.wsj.com/cio/2015/12/18/the-rise-of-the-t-shaped-organization/

Wlodkowski, R. J. (2008). *Enhancing adult motivation to learn: A comprenhensive guide for teaching all adults (3rd ed.)*. San Francisco, CA: Jossey-Bass.

Wyner, J., Deane, K. C., Jenkins, D., & Fink, J. (2016). *The transfer playbook: Essential practices for two-and four-year colleges*. Washington, DC: Aspen Institute.

Xu, D., Ran, F. X., Fink, J., Jenkins, D., & Dundar, A. (2017). *Strengthening transfer paths to a bachelor's degree: Identifying effective two-year to four-year college partnerships. CCRC Working Paper No. 93*. New York: Community College Research Center, Teachers College.

Younger, J. (2016, October 11). *How learning and development are becoming more agile*. Retrieved from Harvard Business Review: https://hbr.org/2016/10/how-learning-and-development-are-becoming-more-agile?autocomplete=true

Western Governors University (n.d.). *A guide to implementing a CBE program*. Retrieved from https://www.wgu.edu/competency-based-education/implementation.html

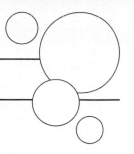

CHAPTER 4

Charting a Path Forward: Getting Us from Here to There

In this final chapter, we suggest an approach for beginning the process of navigating the complexities of our day in order to pave the road to relevance for higher education. We discuss the need to

- Embrace Disruption with an Innovative Mindset
- Employ Systems Thinking
- Engage Design Thinking
- Create Skunk Works: An Organizational Approach to Innovation
- Break the Cycle That Perpetuates Socio-Economic Gaps of Access and Success
- Reduce Administrative Redundancies
- Lessen Noise to Enhance Mobility
- Nurture Transformational Leadership

INTRODUCTION

In a seminal piece first published in the *Harvard Business Review* in 1990 (reprinted in the same journal in 2001), John P. Kotter differentiates between management and leadership: "Management is about coping with complexity. Leadership, by contrast, is about coping with change" (Kotter, 2001, para. 10). Kotter stresses that faster technological change, greater competition, deregulation, and the changing demographics of the workforce, among other factors, contribute to the net result that "doing what was done yesterday, or doing it 5% better, is no longer a formula for success. Major changes are more and more necessary to survive and compete effectively in this new environment" (Kotter, 2001 para. 11). While he was talking about the business world of almost 30 years ago, he might as well have been describing the current situation in higher education. Status quo for most colleges and universities is simply not an option if they are going to remain relevant, and today's environment requires both strong leadership and management to effectively respond with transformational change.

It is evident now that Kotter was right; these changes impacted the business world and many were not ready or handled the changes poorly. For example, in studying corporate transformations, many of which fail miserably, Anand and Barsoux (2017, para. 2) point out that although flawed implementation is often blamed, it is actually more so that "organizations pursue the wrong changes—especially in complex and fast-moving environments, where decisions about what to transform in order to remain competitive can be hasty or misguided." Again, this rings true for higher education, and it is why, in part, we have implored our readers throughout this book to be thoughtful and intentional in making informed decisions about the future foci of their respective institutions. Choices about what audience(s) to target, with what programs, in what modalities, resulting in what credentials, and so forth are key to future success. Once these decisions are made, leaders at all levels of the institution can then work to create the right culture, climate, and conditions to evolve or transform their institutions to meet the demands of 21st century learners and employers. These institutional leaders will need to

(a) create a shared vision that motivates and inspires, (b) communicate a robust narrative that touches the hearts and minds of faculty, staff, learners, parents, and funders so that everyone is aligned toward reaching the same goals, (c) use data to inform decision making, (d) provide structures, resources, and change incentives that align with the vision and strategy, and (e) coordinate leadership activities across typically siloed divisions within the institution. The key question, then, is how can institutions create an effective process that will achieve their desired goals while responding to the fast pace of change, given that what got us to where we are today will not take us to where we need to go?

EMBRACE DISRUPTION WITH AN INNOVATIVE MINDSET

Much has been written about disruption since Christensen and colleagues began talking about it some 25 years ago (Bower & Christensen, 1995), more recent literature focuses specifically on higher education. We have identified some of the major drivers of disruptions throughout the book—for example, changing learner demographics, continuing need for upskilling, third-party competition, diminished state funding, rising operational expenses— which demand new approaches to meeting the current and future needs of learners, employers, and society. As John Maynard Keynes said, "The difficulty lies not in the new ideas, but in escaping from the old ones, which ramify, for those brought up as most of us have been, into every corner of our minds" (Keynes, 1936, p. vi). For this reason, embracing an innovative mindset is a requirement to move beyond the way we have always operated in higher education, to ensure that we challenge our own beliefs, assumptions, and misconceptions to effectively address current and future challenges.

253

The concept of "disruption" basically describes a circumstance where existing organizations delivering a product or service are focused on the high end of the market and on continuing to develop their product and/or service for those who consume their product or service and ignore the needs of other potential consumers. Other providers enter the market and successfully focus on the "ignored " segments; they gain traction, often by delivering the product or service at a lower price, resulting in the creation of a new market, and then are able to scale the product or service to a place where they are actually able to compete with the incumbents (Christensen, Raynor, & McDonald, 2015).

In a report prepared on Western Governors University (WGU) for the Christensen Institute, researcher Alana Dunagan states the following:

> Fundamentally, a successful Disruptive Innovation has three elements: an enabling technology [e.g., online learning] that makes a product more accessible to a wider population; a business model that targets non-consumers or low-end consumers [e.g., first-generation, working adult students]; and a coherent value network in which suppliers, partners, distributors, and customers are each better off when the Disruptive Innovation succeeds [e.g., average student age 37 years old, average time to degree 2.5 years, significantly reduced student costs, student satisfaction 97%]. (Dunagan, 2018, p. 10)

Another innovative aspect to the WGU model is the segmentation of the traditional faculty role into four separate functions: program mentors, course instructors, assessment and curriculum faculty, and evaluators. The program mentor role is especially unusual in that each student has a designated coach who reaches out each week or two to ensure that obstacles and challenges are resolved (Dunagan, 2018, pp. 5–6). Therefore, for higher education, an innovative mindset is one that transforms our thinking

254

and action to create novel solutions to broaden access to all learners (across their lives) and supports their success. In its third decade, WGU has graduated 100,000 students and has more than 100,00 enrolled who are able to begin every month, rather than the more restrictive fall/spring semester paradigm that is commonplace in traditional institutions. The focus is on achieving mastery of competencies rather than "seat time".

Other notable transformations in higher education that are in the news daily include Arizona State University (ASU) and Southern New Hampshire University (SNHU). The ASU transformation has resulted in increased enrollments by more than 40 percent and graduation rates by 20 percent, as well as significant increases in sponsored research. Their minority enrollment has been climbing over the past decade and now stands at 35 percent, and they have increased net revenue from online programs and have saved millions of dollars. This was all accomplished by, among other things, restructuring departments into transdisciplinary units, creating programmatically focused extension campuses, expanding online degree programs, and enhancing recruiting (Dumestre, 2018).

In 2003, SNHU had flat enrollments and a small student population (approximately 2,500). Their leadership team saw the potential for online learning and invested in this area to create their College of Online and Continuing Education (COCE), which now enrolls more than 80,000 students in over 200 degree programs (with on-campus enrollments steady at about 3,000 students) (Dumestre, 2018). SNHU has recently entered the competency-based education world through its new College for America, with approval from the U.S. Department of Education and their regional accrediting agency. At this point they offer programs through corporate and community partnerships, including McDonald's and Anthem, as SNHU President Paul LeBlanc believes "that this blend of academic and workforce education will help forge a new future for U.S. post-secondary education" (Dumestre, 2018, para. 28).

Another recent model for disruption that has been in the higher education news since it was first announced about two years ago is Purdue University's acquisition of Kaplan University (a for-profit online education provider focusing on working adult students) in an attempt to combine the strengths of two very different types of institutions (Lieberman, 2019). This move will impact Purdue's current online portfolio as they learn from "Kaplan's success in scaling its online offerings," an important component for success as "the online education market matures" (Lieberman, 2019, para. 12). This could clearly expand Purdue's scope and learner audience, for example, to the many adult working professionals who will need to upskill, as well as those interested in changing careers or those who never earned a higher education credential.

Clearly, the decisions made by all of these institutions disrupted the status quo and resulted in achieving their goals (e.g., increase enrollments, revenue, and graduation rates; attract new learner demographics; align with industry needs), which serve the respective universities, their learners, employers, and society. Other institutions will make different decisions, but these stories are among the most compelling in the higher education reinvention and transformation space because they found novel ways to expand access and success to leaners while aligning with the changing needs of learners, employers, and society.

EMPLOY SYSTEMS THINKING

Higher education alone cannot embrace disruption with an innovative mindset and address what we have presented in the preceding chapters. There are many actors and constituents who

256

impact and are impacted by our colleges and universities. In order to innovate, we need to ensure that all members of our "system" are represented in the thinking and processes in which we engage. Individual colleges and universities are a system in the most basic sense, as each has a "group of interacting, interrelated, or interdependent parts that form a complex and unified whole that has a specific purpose" (Kim, 1999, p. 2), including learners, faculty and staff, donors, governing boards, and private and corporate foundations, among others. So, clearly transformation requires that everyone at the institution is involved.

One could also argue that the higher education sector is a system that includes employers, federal and state governments that provide funding, parents, and so forth. In fact, we like thinking of higher education as a "nested complex adaptive system" (Brinkerhoff & Joyce, 2016, p. 11)—nested in the sense that we are a "part of," not "apart from," the larger context within which we operate. And we seem to exhibit the characteristics of a complex adaptive system, as colleges and universities are made up of many diverse and somewhat autonomous components that are interrelated and interdependent, linked through many interconnections, and yet behave as a unified whole. Additionally, universities are dynamic systems that can evolve, adapt, and adjust to environmental changes (Business Dictionary, n.d.).

As we explore how to think about postsecondary education through the lens of a system and systems thinking, it is worth noting that, for a long time, the predominant theory of organizations and related leadership strategies were based more on understanding the parts as a means to understanding the whole. Although this reductionist framework provided the basis for Frederick W. Taylor's scientific management theory and served us well during the linearity of work associated with industrialization and its related quest for efficiency, that is no longer the case. Increasingly, complexity theory offers useful insights and potentially impacts leadership in important ways (Schneider & Somers, 2006), particularly leadership within a large complex system like higher education that is transforming itself.

In a complex adaptive system, leadership and decision-making processes are more distributed. In an article discussing health-care reform, another industry with similar organizational attributes, the authors note that

> Most commentaries on the importance of systems thinking and complex adaptive systems on healthcare transformation insist that a change in "mindset" is necessary and that leadership has more to do with recognizing, connecting, mentoring, and developing good people, influencing and or/adapting to the boundary conditions and contexts, dynamically building relationships, and being vigilantly situationally aware and opportunistic in service of a shared vision and iterating, iterating, iterating. . . (Petrie & Swanson, 2018, p. 211)

Systems thinking recognizes those interacting, interrelated, or interdepending attributes and "the circular nature of the world we live in," typically involving

> moving from observing events or data, to identifying patterns of behavior overtime, to surfacing the underlying structures that drive those events and patterns. By understanding and changing structures that are not serving us well (including our mental models and perceptions), we can expand the choices available to use and create more satisfying, long-term solutions to chronic problems. (Goodman, 2018, para. 4)

By using a systems thinking perspective and the Baldrige Education Criteria for Performance Excellence (based on the Malcolm Baldrige National Quality Award [MBNQNA] that Congress launched in 1987 and expanded to include health care

258

and education in 1999), the University of Wisconsin-Stout (UW-Stout) demonstrated long-term progress in key priority areas, including increasing student enrollment, closing the achievement gap between majority and traditionally underrepresented minority students, and increasing student participation in experiential learning programs. The campus was the first educational institution ever awarded the Baldrige Award for Quality. According to the former provost and vice chancellor at UW-Stout, Julie Furst-Bowe

> [S]ystems thinking is based on the concept that all key processes in an organization are interrelated, and understanding these relationships is critical to obtaining desired results. The Baldrige criteria also require that senior leaders embrace systems thinking and promote that focus throughout the organization at all levels. The ultimate value in systems thinking in higher education is that it transcends institutional silos and provides campuses, such as UW-Stout, the ability to achieve institutional goals and sustain consistent performance improvement over time. (Furst-Bowe, 2011, p. 4)

As we identify the interacting, interrelated, or interdependent parts of our institutions, it is vital that we include not only internal entities and people (especially given the silos created by organizational structures) but also the entities and stakeholders that work with us to meet our institutional goals. For example, among the critical relationships colleges and universities have is that of the institution and its governing board. According to the Association of Governing Boards of Universities and Colleges (AGB), a key responsibility of boards is to sustain and advance the institution's mission, traditions, values, and reputation (Association of Governing Boards, n.d.-b). Given that a large part of their role is to provide oversight, and that the president and administration are responsible to the board, boards will be crucial in pushing their respective institutions out of their comfort zone, using evidence-based decision making to determine how to keep the institution both relevant to 21st century needs and financially viable. Clearly AGB, which was founded in 1921, appears to be aligned with current times, as their website describes a critical part of their work to "reinforce the value of higher education, innovate through the smart use of technology, and serve the needs of a shifting demographic," issues we have discussed repeatedly in previous chapters (Association of Governing Boards, n.d.-a, para. 1). Our boards need to be active participants in the re-envisioning effort since they, too, are an integral part of our ecosystem.

Accrediting bodies are also a vital part of the larger system. The U.S. Department of Education (n.d.-b) articulates four major functions of accreditation:

1. Assess the quality of academic programs at institutions of higher education.
2. Create a culture of continuous improvement of academic quality at colleges and universities and stimulate a general raising of standards among educational institutions.
3. Involve faculty and staff comprehensively in institutional evaluation and planning.
4. Establish criteria for professional certification and licensure and for upgrading courses offering such preparation.

Most academics and professional staff in higher education are familiar with accreditation, either programmatic (e.g., business, law, nursing) or institutional (e.g., regional accrediting agencies like Western Association of Schools and Colleges, national accrediting agencies like the Accrediting Council for Independent Colleges and Schools). Unfortunately, despite accreditation being a peer review system, many in academe see the process as cumbersome without adding much value. Despite this thinking, most academics also understand that accreditation is necessary for the institution to participate in federal assistance programs, including financial aid for students, which is why it is an important part of the larger system. If we are to embrace disruption with an innovative mindset, accrediting bodies must be flexible and both allow and push institutions to innovate new educational models and pathways to support creativity and innovation. Obviously, innovations need to be well thought out and accompanied by robust assessment (e.g., needs, process, outcomes). Supporting or encouraging pilot programs without worrying about losing accreditation could unleash unbounded creativity on the part of faculty and staff.

ENGAGE DESIGN THINKING

A systems thinking approach will ensure that we have all of the different perspectives that need to be represented as part of the whole; it is necessary but not sufficient. We need more than that to push higher education to innovate. Our modus operandi in higher education has typically been to implement incremental and piecemeal changes—for example, introduce new degree programs, add relevant courses, offer online experiences, and create cross-disciplinary courses. Given today's context, it may be more prudent to engage in a wipe-the-slate-clean approach to rethinking our goals and pathways to achieve them. One way to do this is to engage design thinking. The design school at Stanford University (known as the d.school) and the global design company IDEO have popularized the concept of design thinking as "a unified framework for innovation" (Szczpanska, 2017, para. 1), thus spreading its use far beyond design schools.

The d.school refers to the process as the human-centered design thinking cycle, identifying five iterative components or modes: empathize, define, ideate, prototype, and test (Figure 4.1).

261

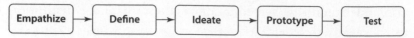

Figure 4.1. Stanford d.school human-centered design thinking cycle

Empathizing requires that one observe users to gauge what they need, engage them to better understand their beliefs and values, and immerse oneself in the user's experience by "walking in their shoes" for a while. For administrators, faculty, and staff in higher education, this means fully understanding the learner audience(s) on which they choose to focus, whether they are first-generation traditional-age college students, career switchers, or adult returning professionals wanting to upskill. Even if the decision is to "stick with" traditional-age learners, this new generation (and those coming after them) is very different from previous ones and requires observing, engaging, and immersing just as much as the "unfamiliar" learner audiences. Empathizing necessitates that we view the experience through the learner's lens rather than our own. Understanding the learner's journey, from their vantage point, broadens the view well beyond simply the points of intersection with the institution. Such a view creates a 360-degree perspective, unlocking insights into the many potential challenges learners may experience when they apply for admission, enroll, navigate the completion of courses, and ultimately acquire a credential. This empathetic view, or colloquially "walk a mile in a learner's shoes," opens new opportunities for the institution to modify course schedule grids to meet working student needs, or address food insecurity, childcare, or transportation needs that are part of learners' journey and that present impediments to their success.

The *define* mode takes those empathy findings and unpacks them "into needs and insights and scope a meaningful challenge" to "come up with an actionable problem statement" (d.school at Stanford University, n.d., para. 12). For higher education, this

262

problem statement should include such things as the need for both access and quality (i.e., not pitting one against the other), a holistic view of the diverse learners, and appropriate drivers of success (e.g., as opposed to rankings, SAT scores).

The define step allows you to then enter the *ideate* stage, where radical design alternatives are generated, "a process of 'going wide' in terms of concepts and outcomes—a mode of 'flaring' instead of 'focus' . . . to explore a wide solution space—both a large quantity and broad diversity of ideas" (d.school at Stanford University, n.d., para. 17). In this space, higher education might, for example, (a) reimagine alternatives to the credit hour standard, semester/quarter systems, and the nature of credentials, (b) expand experiential learning, (c) create stackable modules, (d) design competency-based opportunities, and (e) embrace prior learning assessments. These many ideas will eventually be pared down to a few that are *prototyped* in order to test functionality; the recommendation is to keep them "inexpensive and low resolution to learn quickly and explore possibilities" (d.school at Stanford University, n.d., para. 22). The ideate and prototype stages lead into the *testing* part of the process, which enables you to "gather feedback, refine solutions, and continue to learn about your users" (d.school at Stanford University, n.d., para. 27), and would require, for higher education, feedback from our many constituencies, including diverse learners, employers, various government entities, accrediting bodies, employers, and so forth (as the complementary systems thinking approach calls for). The design process has led to many outstanding products, processes, and services in such fields as health care, financial services, journalism, nonprofits, tech, retail, and transportation (Accidental Design Thinker, 2017; Stigliani, 2018), and could be useful for those in academe because, as Herbert Simon wrote, "Everyone designs who devises courses of action aimed at changing existing situations into preferred ones" (Simon, 1988, p. 67).

Redesigning higher education would benefit from using design thinking to keep us relevant.

CREATE SKUNK WORKS: AN ORGANIZATIONAL APPROACH TO INNOVATION

For many colleges and universities for whom the systems and design thinking approaches above sound overwhelming, we might again take our cues from outside academe and study industry's approach to innovation through such entities as Skunk Works. This name, adopted by Lockheed Aircraft Corporation in 1943 and inspired by the Li'l Abner comic strip, represented an organizational approach to innovation that was not constrained by bureaucracy, where a small group of professionals were given autonomy and flexibility to encourage creativity and radical change—in this case, in the aerospace industry (Rich, 1994). Their successes were innumerable (e.g., stealth fighter) and they are credited, among other things, with keeping the United States ahead of the curve technologically in a very dangerous world. They did this by taking on projects that others avoided because of their complexity and potential to fail, or that were too small to be of interest and value to their bottom line (Rich, 1994). Many successful companies today have adopted, and adapted, Skunk Works to further innovate, among them Google, Boeing, Amazon, Apple, Raytheon, Dupont, Ford, Nike, Nordstrom, IBM, Samsung, and Walmart (Nisen, 2013). And while not specifically calling it "Skunk Works," Christensen et al., (2015) indicate that they believe organizations "should create a separate division that operates under the protection of senior leadership to explore and exploit a new disruptive model" (p. 11).

The value of such an approach is that Skunk Works can innovate alongside current operations so that disruption is minimal until products, services, and approaches are proven to be valuable. The process utilized in Skunk Works typically mimics design thinking, resulting in prototypes that can be developed and evaluated quickly before large investments of resources are made (Rich, 1994). Creativity abounds in higher education; simply look at university research that has changed the world—artificial intelligence, the Internet of Things, the next generation of genomics, renewable energy, robotics, energy storage, advanced materials, 3-D printing, drug development. In fact, these categories, among others, were identified in a 2013 McKinsey Global Institute report as critical research areas that would have a transformative impact on the world and high potential as "disruptors" (Manyika et al., 2013). So, imagine if we unleashed this creative energy toward disrupting and transforming higher education!

Can we harness those curious and inventive minds toward creating an educational system that has the qualities it needs (flexibility, stackability, personalization, customization) to prepare graduates and post-traditional lifelong learners for a future that is unknown? Increasingly, postsecondary institutions are appointing chief innovation and chief strategy officers who are expected to identify new sources of revenue, new service delivery models (e.g., online, competency based), and/or cost efficiencies. Some have urged those interested in launching innovative practices to use a different approach than traditional planning models (Horn, 2018). The "business model concept" presented by Rita McGrath emphasizes a discovery-driven rather than the analytical approach typically used in strategic planning. This discovery approach emphasizes experimentation, prototyping, fast failures, and iteration with stakeholders. This approach might also be characterized as one that promotes an "outside-in rather than inside-out focus" (McGrath, 2010, p. 248), and embraces the Skunk Works mentality.

In 2015, the National Science Foundation (NSF) awarded $2 million to Purdue University to create "an independent engineering education 'Skunk Works' as part of a National Science Foundation effort to improve mechanical engineering education at universities in the United States" (Wasserman, 2015, para. 1). The faculty member who conceived of the project did so because

> [M]echanical engineering programs are typically stagnant due to various traditions that span decades. As an independent body, the "Skunk Works" can operate outside that tradition and red tape. It is designed to be a birthplace of new ideas that can be tested quickly to see what has legs and what doesn't. (Wasserman, 2015, para. 3)

Other colleges and universities have followed suit (many in engineering) with their own Skunk Works in order to seed innovation and creativity; these include University of Colorado-Denver, Northeastern University, University of Wisconsin-Madison, and Michigan State University. We can learn from these early adopters.

BREAK THE CYCLE THAT PERPETUATES SOCIOECONOMIC GAPS OF ACCESS AND SUCCESS

As we engage in processes to innovate so that we remain relevant, higher education needs to ensure that we are addressing the underlying forces that have led to some of the challenges we discussed in chapter 1. As we noted in the Introduction, our focus in this book has *not* been on analyzing the cultural forces behind those challenges. However, in redesigning higher education, we must recognize and address the systemic conditions that have created such things as the achievement gap—the convergence of many social, economic, and political issues have clearly led us to where we are today. As Dulin and Bildner (2018) caution, we always "run the risk of further entrenching a system where the less advantaged get training to be the "model work force of tomorrow," while the advantaged get a four-year residential experience that grooms them to be the "leaders of tomorrow" (para. 4). We have to ensure that those who have "never been particularly well served by our higher education system—the poor, low-income working adults and those from less educated families," are no longer disenfranchised (Dulin & Bildner, 2018, para. 4).

There is a lot of impressive work in this area. For example, the American Talent Initiative is a collaboration of colleges and universities with the highest graduation rates (i.e., at least 70 percent of students graduating within 6 years), working to expand access and opportunity for highly talented low- and moderate-income students (American Talent Initiative, n.d.). This group of colleges and universities includes Amherst; California Institute of Technology; Dartmouth; Emory; Georgia Institute of Technology; Harvard; Middlebury; Northwestern; Princeton; Stanford; Swarthmore; University of Chicago, University of California, Los Angeles; and Yale, among others. The National College Access Network also focuses on those underrepresented in postsecondary education and draws members from such diverse organizations as community-based nonprofits, public school districts, colleges and universities, youth mentoring programs, and state agencies, among others (National College Access Network, n.d.). Individual higher education institutions have also created programs designed to educate, motivate, and prepare students for success, such as the Pre-Collegiate Academic Outreach program at the University of Colorado-Denver (n.d.), Georgetown University's (n.d.) Institute for College Preparation, and Florida Gulf Coast University's (n.d.) Office of TRiO and Outreach Programs. The latter is an example of a Federal TRIO Program through the U.S. Department of Education, which focuses on "outreach and student services programs designed to identify and provide services for individuals from disadvantaged backgrounds" (U.S. Department of Education, n.d.-a, para. 1).

While there are some encouraging positive initiatives afoot, there continue to be a number of systemic issues that require attention and reform across all sectors and levels of education. For example, some critics assert that formulas used in the distribution of Federal Work-Study Program funds disadvantage students in lower-income brackets who would benefit the most. This allocation adjustment has long been ignored by policy makers who continue to leave the matter unaddressed, resulting in the largest percentage of federal work-study dollars going to private nonprofit schools, who tend to have fewer lower socioeconomic students than do other sectors (i.e., 2- and 4-year public institutions) (Baum, 2019). So, although higher education and its partners have made a lot of progress in this area, we still have a lot of work to do.

REDUCE ADMINISTRATIVE REDUNDANCIES

The systems thinking approach discussed earlier in the chapter should enable institutions to broadly explore the interacting components of our system as we engage the design thinking process to meet current and future needs and break the cycle that produces socioeconomic gaps. Incorporating these approaches will potentially unveil opportunities where we might achieve economies of scale and manage costs associated with necessary administrative functions.

Economists often talk about economies of scale, defined as

> the cost advantage experienced by a firm when it increases its level of output. The advantage arises due to the inverse relationship between per-unit fixed cost and the quantity

produced. The greater the quantity of output produced, the lower the per-unit fixed cost. Economies of scale also result in a fall in average variable costs (average non-fixed costs) with an increase in output. This is brought about by operational efficiencies and synergies as a result of an increase in the scale of production. (Corporate Finance Institute, n.d., para. 1.)

In a 2019 article, Grant Thornton clarified some of the benefits and processes associated with a "synthetic merger." Basically, each institution maintains a separate identity from a public-facing perspective (e.g., brand name, faculty, students, and endowment), whereas the behind-the-scenes operations are combined to the greatest extent possible, leveraging best practices and acquiring economies of scale by reducing administrative overhead (i.e., human resources, IT, business and billing functions). A corporate example of a synthetic merger is the merger between Air France and KLM airlines, where both have maintained a separate public identity but are fully integrated in their operations (Grant Thornton, 2019). Other examples include some states that have begun regionalizing 911 operations in order to gain economies of scale, resulting in better service by combining resources and gaining more advanced technology, more effective training, and improved response time (Schoenberg, 2016). The health-care industry has also ventured into the space of mergers and acquisitions to achieve economies of scale, which inevitably enable them to eliminate redundant services, resulting in reduced costs and improved efficiency for patients (LaPointe, 2017). These include Advocate Health Care and Aurora Health Care, as well as Catholic Health Initiatives and Dignity Health (LaPointe, 2018). The same is true when America's largest supermarket chain, Kroger, merged with North Carolina–based grocer Harris Teeter in 2014 and, among other things, leveraged Harris Teeter's technology to accelerate Kroger's own digital position in anticipation of Amazon either establishing a grocery or acquiring a grocery business (Cain, 2019), which eventually Amazon did through its acquisition of Whole Foods.

Thinking about economies of scale in higher education begs such questions as whether every university in a state system needs its own accounts payable, human resources, purchasing, and similar departments, or whether small colleges and universities within close proximity could share some of these back-end services. A good example of this is the Common Management System of the California State University System, where all 23 campuses share their administrative systems (e.g., human resources, financial, student information), replacing and consolidating individual campus-based legacy systems into a shared common platform. Its advocates hailed it for improving functionality, reducing redundancy, and saving scarce budget dollars (California State University, n.d.; Meyer, 2012). This could also be done across institutions, not only within a university system. Chapter 3 explored the many benefits of collaboration among higher education institutions, so we might imagine consortiums to consolidate administrative functions to create a win-win situation for all.

LESSEN NOISE TO ENHANCE MOBILITY

Another major challenge that requires collaborations and partnerships across higher education is that of enhancing mobility for learners across their lifetimes. In chapter 3, we talked about the importance of providing a diverse set of on-ramps and pathways to and through continual learning, beginning in undergraduate education and extending throughout the learner's life. To accomplish this, higher education must collaborate across institutions on some of the fundamental barriers that inhibit mobility—for example, differing course numbering systems, nomenclature, and the credit hour standard. As a sector, we need the following:

·   Comprehensive learner records,
·   Financial aid that aligns with the movement of learners across their lifetimes (e.g., short-term Pell Grants),
·   Accreditation that supports the new realities of learner demographics, employer needs, technological innovation, and the global economy, and
·   Credentials that reflect competencies and a more inclusive approach to accepting prior learning and the variety of ways and places that people acquire knowledge and skills.

Without these changes, such things as the rebundling of modularized educational experiences across venues and institutions, and continual learning across one's lifetime, cannot be optimized.

Some of the work to address the barriers has started, but it is not progressing at the pace necessary if we are to meet the many challenges of producing the outcomes required to sustain workforce and societal needs. For example, there are many advocating for changes in Pell Grants, including such alterations as raising the minimum value, allowing use for short-term educational programs, and supporting year-round grants. Advocates include such prominent organizations as the National Association of Student Financial Aid Administrators, the Institute for Higher Education Policy, National College Access Network, Business Roundtable, American Association of Community Colleges, the American Council on Education, and many members of Congress. Despite this broad-based interest and advocacy, the many discussions have not yet led to meaningful action.

As described in chapter 3, there are also groups exploring, among other things, the idea of a comprehensive learner record that captures what has been learned, not what "seat time" has occurred in what course. Naturally, the challenge is to develop technical and normative standards that can be widely embraced (Mintz, 2017). The IMS Global Learning Consortium is one such leader in trying to advance adoption and scalability of educational technology. This nonprofit, member-driven group consists of companies (e.g., IBM, Google, Microsoft, Pearson, Parchment Inc., National Student Clearinghouse, Canvas, Blackboard, Ellucian, Credly); public school systems (e.g., Seattle Public School, Palm Beach County, New York City Department of Education, Chicago Public Schools); universities (e.g., University of California; University of Notre Dame; University of Michigan; University of Toronto; Penn State; Indiana University; University of Maryland, Baltimore County); and the Bill & Melinda Gates Foundation. IMS Global has some 518 members across 22 countries and is committed to "the adoption of innovative solutions that support competency-based education and the transferability of learner micro-credentials within and across institutions, nontraditional learning opportunities and employment centers" (IMS Global Learning Consortium, n.d., para 5). As mentioned previously, Lumina-funded projects with the American Association of Collegiate Registrars and Admissions, the National Association of Student Personnel Administrators, and the National Institute for Learning Outcomes Assessment are all providing leadership and development in the comprehensive learner record initiatives. So, movement here is well under way.

NURTURE TRANSFORMATIONAL LEADERSHIP

Finally, engaging in the thinking and processes we have described requires special leadership. In the introduction to its eighth edition of the most comprehensive survey of college presidents, the American Council on Education (ACE) and the

272

TIAA Institute cite the unprecedented complexity that college presidents face today and encouragingly state that innovative leaders have begun to emerge (Soares, 2018). These people, they tell us,

> are able to make decisions based on a long-term vision shaped by the distinctive history and identity of the campus they lead. They have a tolerance for taking strategic risks associated with potential policy shifts and thrive on turning challenges or moments of campus crisis into opportunities or accelerants for change. Innovative leaders also strive to create continuity on their campuses and sustain progress. Finally, these leaders are able to establish and leverage both internal and external networks to help them achieve their goals. (Soares, 2018, p. 1)

Our question is whether those attributes are enough given the multitude of complex challenges facing higher education. To stay relevant, should the vision continue to be shaped by the history and identity of the campus, *or* is a radical change warranted? Is continuity what is called for, *or* is disruption what is needed?

If institutions decide they want an innovative leader willing to embrace disruption (who pulls together a senior team with the same mindset), what attributes would they look for in a president, provost, and other senior administrators? One fitting definition of an innovative leader is a creative visionary who has big ideas and who can motivate people to turn those ideas into reality (Baumgartner, n.d.). Another reminds us that innovation is "about much more than inventing. It's about figuring out how and where you can add unique value. It's about how fast you can unlearn, relearn and master new skills. It's about how you engage others at a deeper, more humanistic and passionate level" (Tucker, 2017, para. 3).

273

Our favorite set of leadership skills (among many in the literature) comes from Robert Tucker (2017) and includes continually embracing the opportunity mode of thinking, assaulting assumptions, developing empathy for the end customer, proactively thinking ahead of the curve, continuously fortifying your idea factory, and building buy-in. Tucker's set calls out the need to free oneself of assumptions because "innovation begins where assumptions end," and "we can either assault our assumptions, or somebody else will do it for us and reap the benefit" (Tucker, 2017, para. 9). This, more than anything else, leads to outside-the-box, entrepreneurial thinking which results in innovation, and the right type of leadership is one that can build a culture of innovation. Building a culture of innovation requires (a) a commitment to creating an organizational culture that develops happy and motivated employees who have opportunities for collaborations and conversations at all levels of the organization, (b) a customer/student-centric focus that is motivated by doing something important, (c) leadership at all levels that is committed to innovation, and (d) a sense of urgency. Without meeting these criteria, the capacity to sustain organizational innovation is not likely to occur (Chodary, 2014). Given the third-party entities that are stepping in to fill many of the voids we discussed in chapters 1 and 3, it seems imperative that leaders in higher education challenge their own and higher education's assumptions and nurture innovative organizational cultures.

One recent headline and accompanying story in the *Chronicle of Higher Education* perhaps sums up what it takes to be a leader in higher education today. The headline: "U. of Tulsa Has a Billion-Dollar Endowment for Just 4,000 Students. Why Is It Cutting Programs?" (Supiano, 2019). The current provost and executive vice president for academic affairs, Janet Levit, is leading a plan to reimagine the university, which involves cutting programs and offerings (including at the graduate level) and restructuring, and

274

moving from departments to interdisciplinary divisions in parts of the university, among other changes. The goal is to create "a high-touch undergraduate institution that provides all students with a firm grounding in critical and creative thinking, and that is STEM-heavy with a professional, practical focus" (Supiano, 2019, para. 4). Although there are obviously internal supporters who share this vision, there are also dissenters, not unexpectedly. This university has made the decision of where to focus their energy and resources and is not trying to be "all things to all people." Not every leader at every institution will make the same decisions as the University of Tulsa, and that is good news. Maintaining diversity among institutions (which has traditionally been a hallmark of U.S. higher education) will serve all learners well if we ensure access to and plan for success of all.

The story of Sweet Briar College in Virginia is also a tale of innovative leadership at work. A few years ago (2015), the college was on the brink of closure, with many questioning the continued relevance of a women's college. It is now identified as one of the most innovative campuses by U.S. News and World Report (n.d.). The college made several bold decisions, including (a) implementing a complete overhaul of their general education approach by developing an interdisciplinary "Leadership Core"—which includes courses such as Design Thinking, Sustainable Systems, and Contemporary Ethical Questions—substantially reducing the cost of attendance by 32 percent, (b) implementing a different academic calendar that offered greater flexibility for short courses, internships, and research, (c) expanding support for experiential learning, (d) and replacing 20 traditional academic departments with three collaborative interdisciplinary centers of excellence (e.g., engineering, science, and technology in society; human and environmental sustainability; and creativity, design, and the arts) (Moody, 2017). Showing signs of renewed health, the college reported a 42 percent increase in new student enrollment for the 2018–2019 academic year (McCambridge, 2018). This type of dramatic change would not have been possible without clear and dynamic leadership of both the new board and president of the college.

Finally, when we think about the leadership necessary to create and implement innovative changes in higher education, we believe that leadership not only is the responsibility of the president and senior administrative team but is also shared throughout the organization. It is deans, chairs, division heads, and so forth who can unleash creativity in their colleagues and staff by creating a culture that is open to radical ideas from everyone. As Scott Cowen, former president of Tulane University and author of *Winnebagos on Wednesdays: How Visionary Leadership Can Transform Higher Education,* states while discussing presidential leadership, "The ability to find the balance between preservation and innovation, between inside and outside perspective, is what we should look for in our leaders" and the capacity to ask "what-if and why-not" (Cowen, 2018, p. 200).

CONCLUSION

As institutions engage in a soul-searching process to determine who and what they will be in the future, we should remain optimistic about our place in the education of learners. For those who decide to broaden or change their missions, colleges and universities have the requisite talent and creativity of our faculty and staff to create and implement innovative new pathways to, and new models of, education and the business processes that support it.

Alternatives are cropping up everywhere. For many years, the college degree and transcript signified job preparation, but that is no longer necessarily true according to many employers and graduates themselves. Many employers tell us that the degree simply shows that the graduate persisted through 4, 5, or 6 years to meet their goal; it does not indicate or guarantee the knowledge, skills, and competencies that they have gained. In his book *A New U: Faster + Cheaper Alternatives to College* (2018), Ryan Craig identifies 65 pages' worth of alternatives to college, including paid apprenticeships, no-fee boot camps, tuition-paid boot camps, income-share programs, and online education in fields such as medical sales, medical laboratory science, digital marketing, data science, web development, cybersecurity, software development, entrepreneurship, tech sales, product management, hospitality, retail pharmacy and management, financial services, law enforcement, health science, financial operations, insurance underwriting and claims, manufacturing, and skilled trades (Craig, 2018). As a result of these alternatives, some employers are already varying their approach to finding talent, using these programs because they focus on skills employers do not see in college graduates. The advantage to employees is that these alternatives are typically taught by practitioners in actual or simulated work environments, and they enable learners to demonstrate competencies. The challenge with all of these alternatives is that many are morphing into college replacement programs, and that will not serve higher education well.

Yet, like others, we still view higher education as increasingly relevant in shaping our world and addressing its challenges, if we think beyond the way we have always done business. One of the five principles to protect America's leadership in innovation, according to the Business Roundtable (2019), is to "have the best education system and the most skilled workforce globally," and that education system should "fully unlock the potential of its human capital" (p. 4).

Former Secretary of Labor Robert Reich summed it up when he stated: "It's an absurd conceit of contemporary America that the only route to a middle-class life must be through a four-year university degree" (Craig, 2018, p. xiv). Let us put aside that

277

conceit and focus on meeting the needs of all learners, employers, the nation, and the world. Pursuing an agenda that embraces a holistic, learner-centric, flexible approach, and demonstrating a willingness to think and act boldly, we are confident that we can navigate the complexities of our current situation and ensure our relevance in the future.

REFERENCES

Accidental Design Thinker. (2017, September 16). *40 design thinking success stories*. Retrieved from https://theaccidentaldesignthinker. com/2017/09/16/40-design-thinking-success-stories/

American Talent Initiative. (n.d.). *What we do*. Retrieved from https:// americantalentinitiative.org

Anand, N. A., & Barsoux, J. (November-December 2017). What everyone gets wrong about change management. *Harvard Business Review 95*(6), 79–85. Retrieved from https://hbr.org/2017/11/what-everyone-gets-wrong-about-change-management

Association of Governing Boards. (n.d.-a). *AGB board of directors' statement on board accountability*. Retrieved from https://agb.org/sites/default/ files/agb-statements/statement_2007_accountability_0.pdf

Association of Governing Boards. (n.d.-b). *Enabling excellence: About us*. Retrieved from https://agb.org/about-us/

Baum, S. (2019, March 21). *Rethinking federal work-study: Incremental reform is not enough*. Retrieved from Urban Policy: https://www.urban. org/research/publication/rethinking-federal-work-study-incremental -reform-not-enough

Baumgartner, J. (n.d.). *What is innovative leadership?* Retrieved from Inno-vationManagement: http://www.innovationmanagement.se/imtool-articles/what-is-innovative-leadership/

Bower, J., & Christensen, C. M. (January/February, 1995). *Disruptive tech-nologies: Catching the wave*. Harvard Business Review. Retrieved from https://hbr.org/1995/01/disruptive-technologies-catching-the-wave

Brinkerhoff, D., & Joyce, P. (2016, May 2). *Systems thinking and higher education: Innovation ecosystem assessment and application in the Philippines.* Retrieved from http://www.aplu.org/projects-and-initiatives/international-programs/knowledge-center-for-advancing-development-through-higher-education/knowledge-center-library/systems-thinking-and-higher-education-presentations/file

Buchanan, R. (1992). Wicked problems in design thinking. *Design Issues VIII*(2), 5–21.

Business Dictionary. (n.d.). *Complex adaptive system (CAS).* Retrieved from http://www.businessdictionary.com/definition/complex-adaptive-system-CAS.html

Business Roundtable. (2019). *Innovation nation: An American innovation agenda for 2020.* Washington, DC: Author.

Cain, A. (2019, January 21). *The CEO of Kroger, America's largest supermarket chain, explains why the company's merger with the country's 6th-favorite grocer puts them in the perfect position to take on Amazon and Whole Foods.* Retrieved from Business Insider: https://www.businessinsider.com/kroger-ceo-harris-teeter-amazon-whole-foods-2019-1

California State University. (n.d.). *Common Management System (CMS).* Retrieved from http://www.calstatela.edu/cms

Chodary, A. (2014). Four critical traits of innovative organizations. *Journal of Organizational Culture, Communications and Conflict 18*(2), 45–58.

Christensen, C. M., Raynor, M., & McDonald, R. (2015). What is disruptive innovation? Twenty years after the introduction of the theory, we revisit what it does—and doesn't—explain. *Harvard Business Review December,* 2–11.

Corporate Finance Institute. (n.d.). *What are economies of scale?* Retrieved from https://corporatefinanceinstitute.com/resources/knowledge/economics/economies-of-scale/

Cowen, S. (2018). *Winnebagos on Wednesdays: How visionary leadership can transform higher education.* Princeton, NJ: Princeton University Press.

Craig, R. (2018). *A new U: Faster + cheaper alternatives to college.* Dallas, TX: BenBella Books, Inc.

d.school at Stanford University. (n.d.). *Design thinking bootleg.* Retrieved from Hasso Plattner Institute of Design at Stanford: https://static1.

squarespace.com/static/57c6b79629687fde090a0fdd/t/5b19b2f2a
a4a99e99b26b6bb/1528410876119/dschool_bootleg_deck_2018_
final_sm+%282%29.pdf

Dulin, A., &. E. Bildner (2018, October 3). Fit in, stand out or do nothing. *Inside Higher Ed*. Retrieved from https://www.insidehighered.com/digital-learning/views/2018/10/03/facing-disruption-colleges-can-fit-stand-out-or-do-nothing-opinion

Dumestre, M. (2018, September 18). *Creative destruction: The new economic reality in higher education*. Retrieved from Academic Impressions: https://www.academicimpressions.com/blog/how-is-higher-education-changing/

Dunagan, A. (2018, September 5). *Aligning the business model of college with student needs: How WGU is disrupting higher education*. Retrieved from Christensen Institute: https://www.christenseninstitute.org/wp-content/uploads/2018/08/WGU-Final.pdf

Florida Gulf Coast University. (n.d.). *Office of TRiO and Outreach Programs*. Retrieved from https://www2.fgcu.edu/studentservices/SSSAOP/

Furst-Bowe, J. (2011). Systems thinking: Critical to quality improvement in higher education. *Quality Approaches in Higher Education 2*(2), 2–4.

Georgetown University. (n.d.). *Institute for College Preparation*. Retrieved from https://icp.georgetown.edu

Goodman, M. (2018). *Systems thinking: What, why, when, where, and how?* Retrieved from Systems Thinker: https://thesystemsthinker.com/systems-thinking-what-why-when-where-and-how/

Graham-Leviss, K. (2016). *The five skills that innovative leaders have in common*. Retrieved from https://hbr.org/2016/12/the-5-skills-that-innovative-leaders-have-in-common&ab=Article-Links-End_of_Page_Recirculation

Grant Thornton. (2019, February 19). *Synthetic merger: A fine elective for higher ed*. Retrieved from https://www.grantthornton.com/library/articles/nfp/2019/synthetic-merger-higher-ed.aspx

Horn, M. (2018, April 3). *How universities should manage innovation*. Retrieved from Forbes: https://www.forbes.com/sites/michaelhorn/2018/04/03/how-universities-should-manage-innovation/#176ce0927c4b

280

IMS Global Learning Consortium. (n.d.). *Advancing digital credentials and competency-based learning*. Retrieved from http://www.imsglobal.org/initiative/advancing-digital-credentials-and-competency-based-learning

Keynes, J. M. (1936). *The general theory of employment, interest and money*. New York, NY: Harcourt, Brace and Company.

Kim, D. (1999). *Introduction to systems thinking*. Encino, CA: Pegasus Communications, Inc.

Kotter, J. (December, 2001). What leaders really do. Retrieved from Harvard Business Review: https://hbr.org/2001/12/what-leaders-really-do

LaPointe, J. (2017, August 31). *Key strategies for health systems to achieve economies of scale*. Retrieved from Revcycle Intelligence: https://revcycleintelligence.com/news/key-strategies-for-health-systems-to-achieve-economies-of-scale

LaPointe, J. (2018, July 20). *How hospital merger and acquisition activity is changing healthcare*. Retrieved from Revcycle Intelligence: https://revcycleintelligence.com/features/how-hospital-merger-and-acquisition-activity-is-changing-healthcare

Lieberman, M. (2019, January 9). *Purdue's online strategy, beyond "global."* Retrieved from Inside Higher Education: https://www.insidehighered.com/digital-learning/article/2019/01/09/purdue-prepares-online-expansion-support-newly-acquired-profit

Manyika, J., Chui, M., Bughin, J., Dobbs, R., Bisson, P., & Marrs, A. C. (2013). *Disruptive technologies: Advances that will transform life, business, and the global economy*. San Francisco, CA: McKinsey Global Institute.

McCambridge, R. (2018, September 11). *Back from the brink: Sweet Briar called one of the nation's most innovative schools*. Retrieved from NPQ Nonprofit: https://nonprofitquarterly.org/2018/09/11/back-from-the-brink-sweet-briar-called-one-of-nations-most-innovative-schools/

McGrath, R. G. (2010). Business models: A discovery driven approach. *Long Range Planning 43*(2–3), 247–261.

Meyer, L. (2012, March 22). *California State University standardizes administration systems across all 23 campuses*. Retrieved from Campus Technology: https://campustechnology.com/articles/2012/03/22/california-state-university-standardizes-administration-systems-across-all-23-campuses.aspx?=CTCLV

Mintz, S. (2017, January 12). *Reimagining the college transcript.* Retrieved from Inside Higher Education: https://www.insidehighered.com/blogs/higher-ed-gamma/reimagining-college-transcript

Moody, J. (2017, September 6). Update: *Sweet Briar College introduces sweeping changes.* Retrieved from News & Advance: https://www.newsadvance.com/news/local/update-sweet-briar-college-introduces-sweeping-changes/article_31d672ec-9308-11e7-9a0e-bf98c76ff9fe.html

National College Access Network. (n.d.). *About.* Retrieved from http://www.collegeaccess.org

Nisen, M. (2013, February 19). *17 of the most mysterious corporate labs.* Retrieved from Business Insider: https://www.businessinsider.com/coolest-skunk-works-2013-2

Petrie, D. A., & Swanson, R. C. (2018). The mental demands of leadership in complex adaptive systems. *Healthcare Management Forum* *31*(5), 206–213.

Rich, B. (1994). *Skunk Works.* New York, NY: Little, Brown and Company.

Schneider, M., & Somers, M. (2006). Organizations as complex adaptive systems: Implications of complexity theory for leadership research. *Leadership Quarterly 17*(4), 351–365.

Schoenberg, S. (2016, September 2). *Despite cost benefits, cities and towns slow to regionalize 911 dispatch centers.* Retrieved from MASS Live: https://www.masslive.com/politics/2016/09/despite_cost_benefits_cities_a.html

Simon, H. (1988). The science of design: Creating the artificial. *Design Issues 4*(1/2), 67–82.

Soares, L. G. (2018). *Innovative leadership: Insights from the American College President Study 2017.* Washington, DC: American Council on Education.

Stigliani, I. (2018, February 14). *Design thinking—The key to successful innovation?.* Retrieved from Forbes: https://www.forbes.com/sites/imperialinsights/2018/02/14/design-thinking-the-key-to-successful-innovation/#27355c63301e

Supiano, B. (2019, April 15). *U. of Tulsa has a billion-dollar endowment for just 4,000 students. Why is it cutting programs?.* Retrieved from the Chronicle of Higher Education: https://www.chronicle.com/article/U-of-Tulsa-Has-a/246117

Szczpanska, J. (2017, January 3). *Design thinking origin story plus some of the people who made it all happen.* Retrieved from https://medium.com/@szczpanks/design-thinking-where-it-came-from-and-the-type-of-people-who-made-it-all-happen-dc3a05411e53

Tucker, R. (2017). Six innovation leadership skills everybody needs to master. Retrieved from Forbes: https://www.forbes.com/sites/robertbtucker/2017/02/09/six-innovation-leadership-skills-everybody-needs-to-master/#40f24a555d46

University of Colorado-Denver. (n.d.). *Pre-Collegiate academic outreach.* Retrieved from http://www.ucdenver.edu/academics/degrees/pre-collegiate/Pages/default.aspx

U.S. Department of Education. (n.d.-a). *Federal TRIO programs.* Retrieved from Office of Postsecondary Education: http://www2.ed.gov/about/offices/list/ope/trio/index.html

U.S. Department of Education. (n.d.-b). *Overview of accreditation in the United States.* Retrieved from https://www2.ed.gov/admins/finaid/accred/accreditation.html

U.S. News & World Report. (n.d.). *Most Innovative Schools.* Retrieved from https://www.usnews.com/best-colleges/rankings/national-liberal-arts-colleges/innovative?_page=3

Wasserman, S. (2015, June 18). *NSF funds $2 million Skunk Works to improve STEM education.* Retrieved from engineering.com: https://www.engineering.com/Education/EducationArticles/ArticleID/10282/NSF-Funds-2-Million-Skunk-Works-to-Improve-STEM-Education.aspx

INDEX

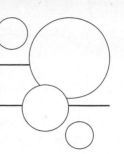

290

General Education Diploma
(GED), 170
Generational diversity, in
workplace, 48
Geographic issues, access
and, 17–18
George Washington
University, 185
Georgetown University,
12, 221, 267
Georgia Institute of
Technology, 121
Gig economy, rise of, 47
Gillespie, Ron, 130
Global Attainment and Inclu-
sion Network (GAIN), 221
Global development chal-
lenges, 94–95
Global health, 94
Global mindset, 134–135
Globalization: competition
and, 41; cultural agility
and, 41; employment and,
40–43; language and, 42;
multicultural workplace
and, 109–110; politics
pushing back on, 43; study
abroad and, 42
Go Pro Early apprenticeship
program, 209
Goal-directed practice, with
targeted feedback for learning, 165–166
Google, 206
Governance structures,
shared, 230–231
Graduation rates: data collection methods for, 16–17; of

parents impacting students,
14–15; PLAs and, 175–176;
public concern with, 14–18;
race and, 15; socioeconomic
status and, 14
Grand challenges, 94–95
Grand Challenges Scholars
Programs (GCSP), 97
Guardian Workplace Ben-
efits study, 47
Guest, David, 153
Guild Education, 183
Gun violence, Gen Z
stress from, 58

H

Hamilton Project, Brookings
Institution, 25
Hamilton Southeastern (HSE)
Schools, 197
Happiness, factors of, 91. *See
also* Well-being
Harper College, 209
Hayward Promise Neighbor-
hood (HPN), 218
HBCUs (Historically Black
Colleges and Univer-
sities), 161
HCC (Holyoke Community
College), 211
Health, global, 94
Health-care industry: AI in,
120; broader skills for,
155–156; employment
growth in, 29; synthetic
mergers in, 269; systems
thinking and, 258
Her, 116